Producing Guanxi

Andrew B. Kipnis

Producing Guanxi

Sentiment, Self, and Subculture in
a North China Village

Duke University Press ✸ *Durham*
and London 1997

© 1997 Duke University Press

All rights reserved

Printed in the United States of America

on acid-free paper ♾

Typeset in Minion

by Tseng Information Systems, Inc.

Library of Congress

Cataloging-in-Publication Data appear

on the last printed page of this book.

To my families in China and America

Contents

List of Maps and Figures

Maps

Figures

Acknowledgments

In a work that examines the production of selves within human relationships, it seems especially important to acknowledge the relationships that shaped the author. As in any ethnography, my greatest debt is to the people who showed me their lives. In so doing, the residents of Fengjia not only gave me information but also influenced my modes of thinking and seeing and, thus, the self that wrote this book. For offering their friendship and ideas, entertaining me, and looking after my physical comfort, I thank all of the Fengs, Zhangs, Lins, Zhaos, and Jias whom I met.

The leaders and staff of the Zouping County Office of Foreign Affairs handled all of the arrangements while I was in Zouping County and graciously shared their knowledge and warmth. I especially thank my old friends Shi Changxiang, Han Zhenguang, and Lao Li.

This book began as a dissertation at the University of North Carolina anthropology department. The intellectual climate there was open and diverse, and many faculty members and graduate students made my stay there enjoyable and productive. Dottie Holland and Judy Farquhar each read my dissertation more times than I care to remember. Dottie additionally saw me through two earlier projects, while Judy taught me about research in and on China. James Peacock, Jane Bachnik, and Bob Daniels introduced me to the arts of ethnography and sat on my dissertation committee. Sandy Seaton eased my learning of Mandarin while including me in his club of beer-drinking sinologues. Fellow graduate students Carolyn Bloomer, Chang-Hui Ch'i, Patsy Evans, Allison Green, Rebecca Henry, Jia Huangguang, Bill Lachicotte, and Anne Larme provided comradery and inspiration during my writing of the dissertation. The university funded my fall 1989 research trip to China.

The Johns Hopkins/Nanjing University Center for Chinese and American Studies funded my stay in Nanjing for two academic years. Friends and teachers I met there—including John Berninghausen,

George Brown, Chen Erjun, Louisa Coan, Dick Gaulton, Bruce Jacobs, Steve Judd, Liu Linyuan, Beth Notar, Eric Politzer, Doug Reed, Ren Donglai, Ruan Bingsen, Ray Seidleman, Mark Wallace, Zhao Weina, and Zhang Jialin—created a stimulating intellectual environment.

The Committee on Scholarly Communication with the People's Republic of China funded most of my research in Fengjia, as well as bringing me together with other Zouping Project members for conferences at Wingspread and in Los Angeles. Project members Guy Alitto, Bill Chang, Bob Geyer, Gail Henderson, Huang Shu-min, Stew Odend'hal, Jean Oi, Mike Oksenberg, Lynn Payne, Les Ross, Terry Sicular, Kathlin Smith, and Andrew Walder provided practical assistance and a vigorous scholarly atmosphere throughout.

I got a good start on revising my dissertation during a year-long postdoctoral fellowship at the East-West Center in Hawaii. Geoff White and David Wu maintained a hospitable working environment there despite the turmoil going on around them. During the revision process George Brown, Susan Brownell, Richard Gunde, James Hevia, Andrew Wank, Geoff White, Scott Wilson, Mayfair Yang, Michelle Yik, and Angela Zito all gave useful suggestions. Guy Alitto and Kim Faulk shared aspects of their own unpublished research in Zouping County with me. Northern Kentucky University provided a summer fellowship and release time during which my revisions were completed. My colleagues James Hopgood, MaryCarol Hopkins, Tim Murphy, Sharlotte Neely, David Potter, Steve Richards, and Barbara Thiel have been a constant source of support. Beth Merten helped with the figures and maps.

At Duke University Press, Ken Wissoker guided me through a long review process while three anonymous reviewers gave careful readings. The book evolved considerably through this period and is much better for it. I also thank Pam Morrison and Katherine Malin for their careful copyediting. Three chapters draw on materials published earlier. I thank the University of Chicago Press for the reuse of materials from *Body, Subject and Power in China* (Kipnis 1994 © 1994 by The University of Chicago. All rights reserved.), Cambridge University Press for materials that appeared in *Comparative Studies in Society and History* (Kipnis 1995b © 1995 Society for Comparative Study of Society and History), and Sage Periodicals Press for materials that appeared in *Modern China* (Kipnis 1996 © 1996 Sage Publications, Inc.).

My families on both sides of the Pacific supported me in every way possible. My parents, David and Dorothy Kipnis, gave me the confidence to complete this project and made specific editorial suggestions.

My wife, Ren Kejia, nurtured me for the seven years during which I wrote this book and gave me critical advice on the translation of many Chinese terms. My parents-in-law, Ren Jianping and Da Qingling, housed and welcomed me for long stays in their already crowded Nanjing apartment, and watched after my son while I completed my research. To all of my families, I dedicate this book.

Introduction

During my fourth month of fieldwork in Fengjia, a rural village in the People's Republic of China (PRC), I learned of a Cultural Revolution (1966–68) prohibition on interclass[1] weeping at funerals. Though I knew that policy at that time had emphasized glorifying the "red" classes and struggling against the rich peasants and landlords, I could make little sense of this prohibition. If, for example, the deceased person were a "poor peasant," wouldn't it be most "revolutionary" if everyone, regardless of class, honored the deceased by weeping at the funeral? I later learned that I had a mistaken view of weeping at funerals. Weeping was not simply a matter of honoring the deceased; it also claimed a relationship to the deceased and his or her family. Thus, the ban on interclass weeping did not prevent bad classes from honoring "red" ones, but rather discouraged the formation of interclass relationships, a reasonable objective given the politics of that time.

The above prohibition is just one example of the place of relationship (*guanxi*) formation in everyday village life, and the role of embodying human feelings (*ganqing*) in those relationships.[2] The first time I went to Fengjia village I was both frustrated and fascinated by the amount of time spent in introductions, banquets, drinking tea, lighting cigarettes, and otherwise participating in the small rituals that produce *ganqing* and *guanxi*. As I spent more time in the village I realized that these practices were not limited to the official entertainment of foreign researchers. Living at the Fengjia guest house, I could often observe village leaders entertaining officials from other villages and counties. More importantly, every household I visited was set up to receive guests in a similar manner. In addition, the villagers themselves recognized the centrality of these practices, describing the people of the area as particularly hospitable (*haoke*). After less than a month in Fengjia I concluded that the production and reproduction of human relationships — by means of "guesting" and "hosting," attending and giving banquets,

PEOPLE'S REPUBLIC OF CHINA

Map 1   People's Republic of China

Map 2   Shandong Province

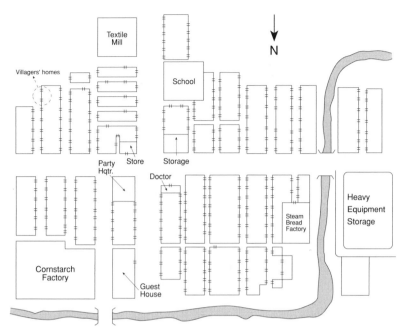

Map 3   Fengjia in 1989
Source: Adapted from map originally drawn by Stewart Odend'hal.

giving and receiving gifts, and a variety of other methods—was a primary activity for most villagers. I decided to make it the focus of my study.

Fengjia sits on a plain of fertile farmland less than twenty miles south of the Yellow River, in Zouping County, Shandong Province, between the cities of Jinan and Zibo (see maps 1 and 2). In 1989 more than 60 percent of the village's population of approximately 1,150 belonged to the four branches of the Feng family. Zhangs, Lins, Jias, and a few other families comprised the rest of the population. Physically the village consisted of approximately four square blocks of one-story, brick, courtyard-style houses with a handful of larger structures, including the party headquarters, a cornstarch factory, a textile mill, an elementary school, and a guest house (see map 3). Surrounding the buildings were flat fields of either cotton, a rotation of winter wheat and summer corn, or, in a few places, vegetable gardens and orchards. Two paved and two dirt roads connected Fengjia to the towns and villages to the north, south, east, and west. Most Fengjia households had income both

Figure 1   Women working in wheat field.

from farming corn, wheat, and cotton and from working at one of the factories or some other sideline (figures 1 and 2).

Zouping County itself is familiar to historians as the site of Liang Shuming's Rural Reconstruction Institute (see Alitto 1979:chapter 11). During the early 1930s, with the backing of the provincial government, Liang and others founded the institute to train rural reconstruction cadres and to research and experiment with "plans, programs and policies" (Alitto 1979:242) for rural development. A hospital, library, social survey department, and normal school were affiliated with the institute. When I was in Fengjia, the legacy of the institute's efforts in the area of education were still apparent. Several older Fengjia men had studied at the institute and a few knew Liang as a teacher. Education levels in the village were high for rural China, with Fengjia children testing into college at a rate double the provincial average for rural *and* urban children (see chapter 9). The old normal school had been reincarnated as Zouping's excellent, no. 1 high school, and the brightest of Fengjia's teenagers went to school there.

As has been noted by so many others, family relationships both agnatic and affinal occupy a central place in the lives of Chinese rural people (Cohen 1976; Fei 1939, 1986; Freedman 1966; Gallin 1966; Pasternak 1972; R. Watson 1985; A. Wolf 1985; Wolf and Huang 1980; M. Wolf 1968, 1970, 1972; Martin Yang 1945). Fengjia residents were certainly no exception. The management of family relationships was a premier topic both in everyday conversation and in most of the popular media con-

Figure 2   Women working in textile mill.

sumed in the village. Local opera dealt almost exclusively with the managing of family relationships, while, at least in 1989, *Required Reading for Parents* (*Fumu Bi Du*) was the only widely read magazine. However, though villagers invested much effort in the production of family relationships, they also constructed extrafamily relationships with friends and fellow villagers. Moreover, the techniques used to manage these relationships were the same as those used in family relationships. Steven Sangren notes that

> Chinese establish corporate groups very similar in form and function to lineages on bases other than kinship. Consequently analysis of Chinese lineage corporations is best framed in the wider context of all formally constituted groups. (1984:391)

Though lineage relations per se did not occupy a central place in Fengjia, Sangren's insight still resonates. I will write of family and extrafamily relations together.

Guanxi and Culture, *Guanxi* as Practice

In his study of the relationship of moral discourse to social life in rural China, Richard Madsen divides the preexisting literature into two types:

Important books had been written by Western intellectual historians like Stuart Schram and Frederic Wakeman on traditional and modern themes in Maoist ideology, and careful studies were being conducted by a host of political scientists and sociologists on contemporary Chinese social structure. But while the intellectual historians were carefully analyzing ideas, the social scientists were generally discounting the importance of those ideas and explaining actual Chinese political behavior in terms of the pursuit of economic and political interests. (1984:ix)

Though the works of Madsen, Mayfair Yang (1994), and a few others are exceptions, a similar statement could be made regarding the use of the concept of culture in sinological studies of *ganqing* and *guanxi*.

On one side are those philosophers and cultural historians who see *guanxi* and *ganqing* as a sort of Confucian cultural essence. Ambrose Yeo-chi King (1991), for example, recently contributed an analysis of *guanxi* as Confucian social theory to a volume entitled *The Living Tree: The Changing Meaning of Being Chinese Today*. He concluded: "As a socio-cultural concept *kuan-hsi* [*guanxi*] is deeply embedded in Confucian social theory and has its own logic in forming and in constituting the social structure of Chinese society" (1991:79). As the volume title indicates, King portrayed *guanxi* as a Confucian logic in order to locate a common cultural essence among people of Chinese origin in the People's Republic, Taiwan, Hong Kong, Singapore, and throughout the diaspora.

On the other side are those economists, political scientists, and sociologists who concentrate on the contemporary political economy of communist China. Against those who would portray *guanxi* and *ganqing* as Confucian culture, they insist that such practices are practical adaptations to communist socioeconomic structures. Writers like Andrew Walder and Jean Oi describe *guanxi* and *ganqing* as types of "clientelist" relationships that have parallels in other communist and even noncommunist nations. Oi concludes:

The existence of the clientelistic politics and evasion that I describe at the lowest tier of the rural bureaucracy may invoke similar accounts of official malfeasance and the importance of personal ties in imperial China. Parallels exist, but one should not conclude that the root of either corruption or patronage is cultural. This behavior is neither inherently Chinese nor traditional. (1989:228)

I am sympathetic to the gist of Oi's statement. In forming *guanxi* and *ganqing*, Chinese people are reacting to social pressures that have parallels elsewhere in the world. Certainly, it would be a mistake to view Confucian "culture" or "tradition" as a sort of unmoved mover in a Newtonian logic of social causality. Moreover, like Oi, I argue that practices of *guanxi* production in modern rural China must be understood in the context of more than forty years of Chinese Communist Party (CCP) policy. However, there is another sense in which I would insist that the practices of *guanxi* production are cultural. As communicative actions, practices like gift giving or weeping at funerals presume a shared nexus of comprehensibility — that is, common cultural assumptions.[3]

Though this study is indebted to the insights of both those who have interpreted Confucian texts and those who have analyzed communist social structures, its theoretical starting point differs from each. Like King, I am interested in the cultural significance of *guanxi* and *ganqing*. However, I view this significance as a modern phenomenon rather than a manifestation of an ancient textual tradition. Like Oi, I ground my analysis in the practical actions of modern rural people living in a socialist state. However, I insist that these practices have a cultural specificity that requires interpretation.

The phrase "the production and reproduction of human relationships" suggests my primary theoretical emphasis. By saying that relationships are *produced,* I wish to emphasize that their existence is dependent upon the continuing work of human actors. Human relationships are the by-products of neither biological generation, a Confucian worldview, nor any sort of abstract "social structure" that works outside of or above human subjects; they are the results of purposeful human efforts, of a type of practice. In practices, actors skillfully adopt strategies and draw on cultural resources in the pursuit of contemporary ends. They simultaneously utilize past cultural logics and generate new ones. Viewing social action as *practice* implies that villagers exercise their own judgment rather than blindly act out the dictates of tradition. Practices are not merely "remnants" of tradition, but rather are activated or vitalized in present village life.

As with all attempts to transcend the difficulties of "objectivism" and "subjectivism," or "structuralism" and "economism" with a theory of practice, I am greatly indebted to the works of Pierre Bourdieu (1977, 1990). I take as my starting point Bourdieu's vision of practice as simultaneously acting in the present and relying on shared understandings from the past, as skillfully manipulating time rather than mechanically acting out atemporal rules. My emphases, however, are more processual and cultural, less structural and political than his. Instead of delineating an internalized, unreflexive "habitus," I focus on the constant, reflexive manipulation of social options. I take inspiration from de Certeau (1984), who examines the continual modification of what is borrowed from the past and presented from above in the "making do" that constitutes a "practice of everyday life."[4]

In presenting social actions like gift giving and weeping at funerals as practices that produce *guanxi* and *ganqing*, I suggest a means/ends relationship between these practices and *guanxi*. Here I will caution that this relationship is not always simple, linear, final, or explicit. First, an instrumental logic that separates the actor from object worked upon is inappropriate for describing *ganqing*-producing practices. In a very real sense, when Fengjia villagers re-create their networks of relationships, they also re-create themselves. If one considers the self to be socially determined (a logic, I will argue below, that is implicit in certain practical conceptions of *ganqing* and *guanxi*), then one's relationships in fact constitute one's self.

Moreover, Fengjia residents see the formation of relationships simultaneously as means and ends. A wide range of friendly and family relationships in itself is seen as a desired state. The opposite, solitary state (that of a "loner") is seen as disastrous. This valuing of relationships for themselves is reflected in general evaluative comments on the state of an individual's or family's network of relationships and in claims about fellow villagers' skill at creating and maintaining relationships. Statements like "He is good at creating networks of relationships" (*Tade guanxi gaode henhao*) or "Their relationships are not so good" (*Tamen de guanxi buzenmayang*) are far from rare. Thus, excessive instrumentalism in the form of questions like "What does she want out of that relationship?" is both overly cynical and ethnocentric. Such a question both evokes an image of a completely separate actor (Fengjia woman) and object acted upon (relationship) and implies that relationships are never ends in themselves.

On the other hand, relationships have a decisive influence on much of social life. If a couple's friends and relatives are all poor, and they are expected to help friends and relatives, then they are also likely to remain or become poor. If one's friends and relatives are all intellectuals, and one continually discusses highbrow issues with them, then one becomes more intellectual oneself. As noted above, relationships are constitutive of one's self. In addition, they are constitutive of families, villages, and perhaps any other social group one could name. It would be naive to think that villagers are not conscious of these considerations when forming relationships and, thus, wrong to say that the formation of relationships in itself is always the sole and final end of the practices this book discusses.

That processes of self formation are immanent in practices of *guanxi* production makes practice theory an especially appropriate starting point for an examination of *guanxi*. As Bourdieu emphasizes, both objectivism, which lays out rules of human behavior independent of individual consciousness, and subjectivism, which presupposes an individual will that transcends social and historical inertia, omit processes of self formation from social analysis. To understand self formation in *guanxi* production, one must begin with the self that is made as it makes, that is conditioned by its history as it forges its future, that is neither the slave of structural rules nor the king of rational calculation—in brief, precisely the self that Bourdieu attempts to show us in *The Logic of Practice* (1990).

Subjectification

What is a person, an actor, a subject? Where does agency reside? Though scholars have debated these questions for centuries, many of the social sciences—especially economics, political science, and psychology—take the rational, unitary, and noncontradictory Cartesian subject as their starting point. In contrast, cultural anthropologists have long argued that this view is itself a cultural artifact (see Holland and Kipnis 1994 for a review), while Michel Foucault (1975, 1978, 1979) has described and historicized the microprocesses in which this sort of subjectivity developed. Since the publication of Foucault's genealogies, social theorists of many predilections have questioned mainstream social science's deployment of the rational unitary subject (e.g., Henriques et al. 1984). The shaping of subjectivities has received as much attention as the choices that subjects make; the inherent inconsistencies and politics of the processes of this shaping have been highlighted as much as their linearity and rationality. Dorinne Kondo's *Crafting Selves* (1990) exemplifies the power of such an approach in another East Asian context.

Since the creation of *guanxi* involved villagers in the social recreation of themselves, discussions of *guanxi* production illuminate and are illuminated by this theorizing of the subject. Through the production of *ganqing*, Fengjia villagers constituted shifting, multiple actors whose agency was contradicted by the histories of their past construction; they dialectically re-created themselves as their subjectivities emerged within processes of *guanxi* formation. However, though shifting and contradicted, these subjects should not be seen as so many images on an MTV screen, as ephemeral and infinitely malleable. The production of *guanxi* involved commitments, and villagers were keenly aware of how new or changing commitments might contradict already existing ones. Villagers and their commitments did change. However, this change occurred over periods of months and years and, thus, cannot be imagined outside of lived time.

In brief, I resist both the pregiven and unitary subject conceptualizations of mainstream social science and the decentered, agentless ones of much post-structuralist theory. By rejecting these two types of conceptualizations, I follow an already well articulated position in Western social theory (Holloway 1984; Smith 1988; Mahoney and Yngvesson 1992). However, paying attention to the cultural specificity of *guanxi* production allows the expansion and development of this position. Here, Sun Lung-kee's (1987) discussion of *ganqing*'s power to constitute the individual and the social both illuminates social process in Fengjia and illustrates the relevance of these processes to recent theorizations of the subject.[5]

For Sun, the *xin* or heart/mind and locus of individual motivation is always defined socially through *ganqing*. Through this theorization, Sun directly links practices of *ganqing* production to subject formation. In addition to constituting individual heart/minds, *ganqing* also define the boundaries (ever shifting) of the group of people whose "magnetic fields of human feeling" (*renqingde cilichang*) constitute individual heart/minds. In short, *ganqing* simultaneously define the individual and the social. Through the managing of *ganqing*, villagers create and are created as subjects.

Deceptively simple, the theoretical value of Sun's formulation lies in his firm grounding of subject formation processes in interpersonal relations. Feminist Lacanians have provided some of the most sophisticated theorization of the subject to date (Mitchell and Rose 1982; Henriques et al. 1984; Holloway 1984). Yet, as Maureen Mahoney and Barbara Yngvesson (1992) argue, these theorists rely too heavily on the positioning of subjects by and in language. Subjects exist not only in discourse, but also in all kinds of ongoing social interaction. Though language perhaps mediates all human action, it does not subsume all agency and subjectivity.[6] Mahoney and Yngvesson use this insight to argue, against Lacan's theorization of child development, that infants participate in social interaction, and hence exist as active subjects, long before they can talk. Extending their argument, by way of Sun, to subject construction in Fengjia, I argue that villagers not only occupy (interpellate?) subject positions through speech but also shape subjectivities in all processes of social exchange, including gift giving, ritual, and emotional interaction. By locating the social dimension of subject construction in *ganqing* rather than language, Sun provides a theoretical standpoint from which subjectivity is not reduced to simply a desire to occupy subject positions in language.

Margot Lyon argues that "social relationships are necessarily bodily" (1995:254). When we manipulate the desires and subjectivities of others or allow or resist others' manipulations of ourselves, we do more than rework words. Feelings—in all of their physical, bodily, and social richness—as much as language, are where subjectivity lies. To reduce the former to the latter is an ideational simplification of the highest order.

Methodology and Research Situation

The research for this study took place within the context of a large project funded and negotiated by the Committee on Scholarly Communication with the People's Republic of China (CSCPRC). In 1985 a CSCPRC team led by political scientist Michel Oksenberg began negotiations with the Chinese and Shandong Academies of Social Science to designate a rural research site for American scholars. Eventually the negotiators settled on Zouping County (map 2), in part reflecting the interests of one of the senior American researchers, historian Guy Alitto, in Liang Shuming's Rural Reconstruction Institute.[7] Because the county was not officially "open" to foreign visitors, researchers had to obtain special permits before entering the county and remain in close contact with representatives from the county's Foreign Affairs Office (FAO) while they were there. Within the county, researchers could live at one of two places: the guest house in the county seat or a guest house constructed partially with CSCPRC funds in the village of Fengjia. Though several other villages within the county were open to the researchers for day visits, researchers were not supposed to spend the night there. Since I was interested in conducting long-term ethnographic research in a rural village, I chose to live in the Fengjia guest house.[8]

Initially eleven scholars—an historian, two economists, two sociologists, two anthropologists, two political scientists, a veterinary scientist, and an environmental specialist—were selected to do research for a five-year period that began in the summer of 1987. I first went to the village

Figure 3   Calligraphy reading "Prosper Collectively."

in the summer of 1988 as a research assistant to one of the anthropologists, Judith Farquhar. Later I developed my own project.

Compared to neighboring villages, Fengjia in 1988–90 was slightly wealthier and considerably more collectivized. A large piece of calligraphy of which there were copies displayed prominently in both the office of the party committee and the home of the party secretary said "Prosper Collectively" (*jiti zhi fu;* see figure 3). Though land was allocated to individual families, in accordance with the responsibility system (*zerenzhi*) implemented in 1978,[9] plowing, seeding, and some irrigation and harvesting were still done collectively. The result was a relatively equal distribution of wealth. Moreover, village regulations standardized and subsidized house building, preventing the relatively well-off from ostentatiously displaying their wealth by building extraordinarily large homes. Consequently, in 1988 every family in the village owned a one-story brick house (figure 4). Politically, the village had been comparatively stable (considering the rampages most of the countryside had gone through), with Party Secretary Feng retaining power as village head for more than twenty years. In addition, the village had a reputation for obeying party mandates. Though not a subsidized "model" village,[10] Fengjia's lack of any extremely impoverished families, its political stability, and its willingness to follow party leadership were certainly factors in the selection of this village as a research site for foreign social

Figure 4   Village housing.

scientists. In addition to CSCPRC scholars, researchers from other foreign countries and from Chinese government research institutes in Beijing have visited Fengjia.

Compared to other villages in Zouping County and the Huimin prefecture, Fengjia occupied an economically and geographically intermediate but rather unique position. Many of the villages in the southeastern part of Zouping County were considerably more industrialized than Fengjia. They had better access to the urban center of Zibo and to the railway line that runs from Jinan to Qingdao. According to officials from the FAO, many of these villages both ran collectively organized factories and encouraged individual families to participate in the nonagricultural private sector. Such families either started their own businesses or sent members to Zibo and other neighboring urban areas to work in privately owned enterprises. Between 1988 and 1990 most Fengjia residents stayed in Fengjia to farm and work at the village factories. Few households started their own businesses and most continued to derive more than half their income from agriculture.[11] Most of the villages to the north of Fengjia, especially those outside of Zouping County, were, like Fengjia, primarily agricultural. However, these villages were generally poorer than Fengjia. Fengjia was fairly unique in being both primarily agricultural and relatively prosperous.

How has the particularity of Fengjia influenced my research? The CCP leadership certainly did not encourage the practices of relationship reproduction that I studied there. One can only assume that if such practices are tolerated in a village that is open to foreign researchers then they are tolerated in most places. At least one other study, Yunxiang Yan's (1993) dissertation about a Heilongjiang village, describes gift-giving practices very similar to the ones I record here. One could speculate that the voice of official discourse speaks more softly in other villages. However, given that the CCP articulates its propaganda as much through mass media as through the mouths of village-level party leaders, one could hardly expect it to be mute. Certainly, personal relationships in a village less collectivized and less egalitarian than Fengjia would have a different tone. Where services such as irrigation are organized by individual families and friends instead of by the village and where vast differences in wealth develop among neighboring families, one can only expect that economic considerations would play more of a role in decisions about the production and reproduction of relationships.[12] Where villagers participate in an extravillage private economy or join the "labor tide" and seasonally migrate to wealthier areas in search of work, one might expect an expanded scope of extravillage ties.

Further discussion of how a change of site might have affected this research could only degenerate into pure speculation. More worthwhile is a closer consideration of the research situation in Fengjia. While in the village, I lived in the guest house[13] at the north end of the village (see map 3). The guest house had a staff of two Fengjia men, a cook in his fifties and a general attendant around twenty years old. Cook Feng lived alone with his wife in one of the only smaller sized houses in the village. His son had graduated from a school of Chinese medicine and was now a doctor in the county seat, where Cook Feng planned on retiring. He enjoyed calligraphy and covered the walls of his home with his work. He also loved socializing (cooking at the banquets of his friends and neighbors for the fun of it) and was a well-known matchmaker, responsible for some twenty-odd couples in the village, including the match of the general attendant, Feng Bo. Feng Bo underwent many changes during the course of my research, growing from a rather taciturn teenager to a confident husband and father. He lived with his parents and, until she married, his younger sister. When not working at the guest house, he helped farm his household's land and by 1995 was dreaming of starting a photography business. Upon observing some facet of village life that confused me, I would often return to the guest house and ask Cook Feng or Feng Bo for an explanation.

Also living at the guest house whenever foreigners were present was a representative from the county FAO, along with whatever other researchers or village guests happened to be in town. The FAO representative was himself a friend of many Fengjia villagers. He did not directly concern himself with the substance of my research. Since I was not supposed to leave the village unaccompanied (as mentioned above, except for designated villages, the county was closed to foreigners), he was responsible for making arrangements for my coming and going. Within the village, however, I usually visited people's houses unaccompanied. Occasionally the FAO representative would follow me on my rounds of the village. On these occasions I would try to avoid what I thought might be "sensitive" topics. However, sometimes the very topics I thought were sensitive came up in discussions initiated by the representative himself. Overall, the presence of the FAO representative had little effect on my particular topic of research. Given that all ethnographic research in China is officially approved and to some extent "surveilled," I was relatively pleased with my "freedom" within the village.

In all, I made eight trips to Fengjia: two months in the summer of 1988, a month and a half in the winter of 1989, two weeks in April of 1989, two weeks in June of 1989, a month and a half in November and December of 1989, two weeks in June of 1990, and two brief checks in the summers of 1992 and 1995. I undertook my most wide-ranging research during my first trip. Updating the census of the village, copied the previous year by anthropologist Huang Shu-min, I visited all of the households in the village and surveyed the variety of living arrangements. Assisting on a medical anthropology project, I visited the families of sick villagers and got a feel for the types of afflictions from which Fengjia residents suffered. I also began studying local dialect with Teacher Feng Rugong. Teacher Feng lived with his wife, son, daughter-in-law, and two grandchildren just down the street from the guest house. Having graduated from the high school during the 1930s, Feng Rugong had been a teacher in many Zouping County schools before retiring to the village of his birth. When I was in Fengjia, he drew a modest pension and spent his time raising his grandchildren, maintaining his health through long morning walks and tai chi exercises, and socializing with friends. Thoughtful, careful with his appearance, and well mannered, Teacher Feng perhaps embodied the attitudes Liang Shuming hoped to inculcate. He unselfishly contributed much time to my project.

That first summer many other researchers visited the village, and I benefited from their observations on the village's and county's ecology, health care, political economy, and history. On later trips I was usually the only foreigner in the village and concentrated on observing and asking about practices of relationship reproduction. From mid-November to mid-February was the village's agricultural slack season—a time when farmers had the most free time to speak with researchers and when most weddings took place. The research I undertook during this period was the most productive. I took the April trip to observe practices associated with the *Qingming* holiday.[14] The June trip of 1989 was taken to observe the practices of visitation that occur after the wheat harvest. However, the massacre in Tiananmen Square and subsequent rupture of research relations between the CSCPRC and the PRC prematurely ended my June 1989 trip. Furthermore, though I had originally planned to spend most of the fall of 1989 in the village, I was not able to return until November.[15]

Being in the village during the Tiananmen Massacre was interesting though stressful. Village leaders, though not necessarily supportive of the students, were definitely concerned about what a change in the leadership at the top of the party might mean for their village. On June 6, Party Secretary Feng declared a youth curfew in the village. He said that if young people got together at night, they might say things that they should not, and that in general people should unify their thought around the party line and concentrate on the upcoming harvest rather than political events. Both during my June 1989 visit and afterwards, Fengjia residents asked me about the student protests in the city of Nanjing (where I had been in May of 1989) and expressed their opinions about the movement and subsequent crackdown. Though perhaps lacking the vigor of discussions in large cities, their concern about and discussion of national events reminded me of the influence of state politics on village life. In my subsequent visits, I began to focus on the historical connections of village practices to state politics and especially on the evolution of relationship-producing practices after the end of the Great Proletarian Cultural Revolution (GPCR) decade of 1966–76.

In the periods between my trips to the village, I returned to Nanjing, where I lived at the Johns Hopkins/Nanjing University Center for Chinese and American Studies. There I studied Chinese language, politics, and history and reviewed local newspapers and other sources not easily available outside of the PRC. In all, I spent nearly two years in Nanjing, and eventually married another university student there. Though the cultural and social distance between urban and rural China at times seemed to exceed that between the United States and China, my fieldwork benefited from my exposure to Mandarin dialect in Nanjing, my conversations with urban Chinese friends and family, and the opportunity to reassess research strategies with other intellectuals.

Linguistic difficulties, though a central methodological concern for interpretive anthropology, are rarely directly addressed in ethnographies. The dialect of Mandarin spoken in Fengjia village was difficult to understand even for native speakers of Mandarin upon first entering the village. However, it did not differ from Mandarin as much as, for example, Shanghainese or Cantonese. I saw native speakers of Mandarin enter the village and adjust to the local dialect within a month. Fengjia residents, on the other hand, could understand standard Mandarin, and in many cases could speak it themselves, with varying degrees of accent. During all of my visits I studied local dialect with Teacher Feng three or four times a week. I asked him to translate into Mandarin words I did not understand, and I developed specific vocabularies and question/answer frames for topics in which I was particularly interested. I tested them by speaking to individuals whose Mandarin was particularly poor. If I could hold a coherent conversation on a given topic entirely in local dialect, I felt that I had begun to understand it. In writing, I have continued paying close attention to problems of translation. Because Fengjia residents speak of and use speech in practices that are different from our own, the "corresponding" English words that one finds in a dictionary are often inappropriate translations. Differences such as those between *guanxi* in Chinese and "personal relationship" in English, or *jingyi* in Chinese and "respect" in English are elaborated throughout this study.

Ability to speak standard Mandarin was also one of the factors that influenced my relationships with individual Fengjia residents. Initially my closest contacts were highly educated old men. Party Secretary Feng had arranged in advance for these men to talk to researchers. They had more free time, spoke clearer Mandarin, and were more academically oriented than most residents. Secretary Feng also required those who held leadership positions in the village to talk to us. As far as I could tell, in arranging these informants Secretary Feng was not trying to limit or control the researchers; rather, he was offering us the people whom he felt understood the most about the working and history of the village. However, though I certainly relied on these people, I did not want to limit myself to educated old men and village leaders.

Weddings provided me with another opportunity to cultivate contacts. If I hadn't already met them, Secretary Feng would arrange to introduce me to families who were planning marriages while I was in the village. Some of these families were quite pleased to have me attend their sons' weddings and were more than happy to answer my questions. However, I still found it easier to build relationships with the more educated families, as they both tended to speak more standard Mandarin and appreciated my own educational aspirations.

It was through the first summer's visiting of sick villagers that I established my best relationship with a relatively uneducated family. An old man had suffered a stroke. He had a large family, and scores of his relatives came to visit. I went to their house several times, on one occasion bringing a gift of preserved fruit. The man's wife saw my visiting and bringing a gift as quite respectful. Furthermore, the man's fifth son had studied Mandarin during an eight-year army assignment in Beijing and loved to talk; he was also head of the village's militia. Proud of his martial abilities, he often told me of his run-ins with thieves and vandals in Fengjia's fields, gardens, and orchards. By contrasting the attitudes and dispositions of this family's members with those of more educated families, I learned how educational attitudes and aptitudes influenced the cultural politics of the village.

I also attempted to compensate for my relatively limited conversational contacts with women. Though I would often speak to several members of the same family at once, including women who were by no means mute, most of my central questions were responded to by men. However, in two of the extended families in which I attended weddings, there were women who were fairly comfortable talking to me. Mrs. Zhang had come to the village with her teenaged daughter when she remarried a local water bureau cadre who resided in Fengjia. Gentle and soft spoken, she filled her house with Buddhist statuettes and images. She often spent her time helping out with her husband's (now also her) numerous grandchildren. The other was a young mother married to an accountant in the cornstarch factory. Cheerful, hard working, and the pride of even her mother-in-law, she could farm, tailor clothes, and do housework at the same time that she responded to my questions. I diligently pursued both of these women and they were kind enough to spend a fair amount of time speaking with me. In both of their families I heard explicit articulations on the importance of sexual equality.

In addition to asking questions, I also indulged in "participant observation." My participation consisted of forming my own relationships with villagers: giving and receiving gifts, attending and hosting banquets, being received as a guest and acting as host, and otherwise participating in practices of relationship production. My observations consisted of attending weddings, funerals, and other assorted rituals; noting the arrangement of houses and utilization of space; and watching interaction between guests and hosts and among family members in a variety of contexts. Because my position as a researcher in an officially approved project allowed me entrance into virtually all the households of the village, the range of households in which I observed practices of relationship reproduction was wider than those upon which I relied for answers to questions.

Some may insist that because this study is based on government-arranged research, it is necessarily an idealization of village life. I would counter that the variety of voices that I heard in Fengjia convinced me that villagers were not merely regurgitating a predigested party line or putting on an act for my benefit. Certainly I avoided some topics. Moreover, given the official nature and size and scope of the project, it would be impossible for me to conceal the identity of individual villagers. I have also avoided detailed descriptions of the social backgrounds of some of the individuals I quote. However, I believe it possible to say much of interest without pursuing secrets or sources of shame.

The notion that valid ethnography demands that the ethnographer be "free" to pursue *the* truth about social life without supervision or oversight suffers from unreflected notions of "truth" and social life. Social life is something that is practiced, constructed, and reconstructed by fellow humans; it is not an unchanging specimen, to be discovered and dissected by the researcher. That my project was negotiated with village and county leaders, that limits were placed and fees were charged, was reasonable and workable if not always ideal. In the end, the angle on social life that I chose to investigate was both one that impressed me as central to what people were doing and one that I thought was politically and ethically feasible.

The strength of ethnography, of doing long-term research with a limited number of people in a single place, is that it offers the researcher the opportunity to develop a sense of locally significant *questions* and the strategies for answering them within the context of the field experience. Conceivably a researcher could develop significant questions from the secondary literature on a given place and design a wide-ranging survey that would result in data from a larger range of informants. However, in most research situations the secondary literature is partial at best and insufficient for a survey. This was certainly true for Fengjia. I did not go into Fengjia planning to study practices of relationship reproduction,

and I did not see the importance of placing the evolution of these practices within the context of changing national policy until after Tiananmen 1989. My development of research questions and strategies for answering them make sense only in the context of the research situation
described above.

Organization of the Book

The division of this book into two parts reflects my attempt to write
about cultural specificity without essentializing it. Part I examines specific practices of *guanxi* production in Fengjia. Though the subject matter is quite narrow — gift-giving practices in one village over a two-year
period, for example (chapter 3) — the vantage is quite distant. I try to
understand the cultural logics that villagers presume or assert in undertaking these practices and to contrast these logics with those of other
places. Though necessary for the task of cultural translation, this exploration of cultural difference reifies. The search for intersubjectivity
mutes polyvocality; the cultural contrasts suggest an essentialized Confucian Other.

Part II attempts to de-essentialize this portrait. It contextualizes
Fengjia's practices of *guanxi* production within a history of the People's
Republic of China and describes contrasting and conflicting versions of
ganqing and *guanxi* in different Chinese contexts. In the end, it returns
to Fengjia with an exploration of how differences generated in national
policies intertwine with, and inject polyvocality into, local practices of
guanxi production. The subject matter is broader, but the vantage is
nearer. Rather than general cultural contrasts, which obscure local difference, part II explores the modernity and multiplicity of practices of
guanxi production in the PRC.

I Practices of *Guanxi* Production

Introduction

How does one describe the cultural specificity of the production of *guanxi* in Fengjia? Marcel Mauss's conception of a "'total' social phenomenon . . . at once legal, economic, religious, aesthetic, morphological and so on" (1967:76) is a compelling starting point. In at least two senses, *guanxi* "totalize" phenomena often assumed to be separate. First, as suggested by Mauss's concept of "total prestation" and Sun's theorization of *ganqing*, *guanxi* simultaneously produce individuals and the social. Second, the production of *guanxi* simultaneously creates human feeling and material obligation.

To emphasize the material obligations involved in *guanxi*, some sinologists translate the term as "particularistic tie" (e.g., Jacobs 1979; Walder 1986). By occasionally using *guanxi* to refer to the more material aspects of social reciprocity in Fengjia and *ganqing* to refer to the human feelings involved, I in one sense follow this translation. However, I also mean to critique it. *Guanxi* involve human feelings and *ganqing* involves material obligation. The terms are often interchangeable, and my usage reflects this mutuality.[1] The more *ganqing* there is, the closer the *guanxi*. The closer the *guanxi*, the more it can be relied upon to bring economic, political, and social benefits. Such benefits in turn produce stronger *ganqing*. At most, *ganqing* and material obligation are analytically separable as moments of (what Mauss recognized as) a single process. In practice, Fengjia residents did not usually undertake one to gain the other, a notion difficult to convey in English sentences.

Several pitfalls should be avoided here. An economism that privileges material motives in *guanxi* must be shunned.[2] Likewise, the view that *guanxi* is a sort of dialectical operation that bridges a Cartesian divide between material and spiritual relations is inappropriate. Economic relationships are severed from neither emotional relationships nor the production of self, so there is no divide to bridge. In *guanxi*, feeling and instrumentality are a totality. Additionally, one should not romanticize *guanxi*. First, just as one may abuse, cheat in, and lie about either affairs of the heart or economic transactions, so may one abuse, cheat in, and lie about *guanxi*. Secondly, the unity of economy and *gan-qing* implies that matters of the heart involve economic calculation as much as it implies that exchange has a moral dimension. As Jonathan Parry (1986) points out (cf. Bloch 1989:168–169), Mauss is often misread as opposing morally governed gift exchange to amoral commodity exchange. A more nuanced reading sees the gift as transcending the Western bourgeois opposition of amoral commodity exchange and moral kinship. Likewise, in Fengjia, *guanxi* can be seen as unifying what Western bourgeois relationships separate: material exchange and affectionate feelings.

However, though *quanxi* may be more total (in a Maussian sense) than Western social relationships, they do not constitute a generic form of social totality. As Bloch (1989) points out, Mauss uses his notion of total social phenomena to discuss "the forms and functions of exchange" in all "archaic" (i.e., noncapitalist) societies. What Mauss saw as a similar totality in the nonbourgeois exchange of so many times and places, I prefer to see as a series of contrasts to the unique singularity of modern, Western, bourgeois exchange. There are many, historically situated ways for social practices to be "total," and the production of *guanxi* is just one of these. If one follows writers like Mauss and Polanyi (1957), the Western bourgeois revolution was precisely one of prying economic relationships out of their embeddedness in social life. Consequently, Western states that have experienced bourgeois revolutions have seen the emergence of two separate spheres of human relations: one venal and "self-interested," governed by contracts and the rules of the market; the other pure and altruistic, governed by emotional spontaneity and above economic considerations. Thus, to say that *guanxi* are a "total social phenomenon" in a sense says more about ourselves than about the Chinese. Our history is one of the bourgeois reification of economic activity. Chinese history is not.[3]

The six chapters of part I present specific practices of *guanxi* production in Fengjia village from 1988 to 1990. Some might sum up these activities with the term "village reciprocity" and leave it at that. However, a generic "village reciprocity" is no more revealing than a generic "total social phenomenon." Both are empty labels that derive their significance primarily from the contrast they evoke with the West, where they are supposedly absent. To go beyond such contrasts, toward an understanding of local forms of intersubjectivity and local processes of inclusion, exclusion, and power, one must examine the details of actual practice.

1 Everyday *Guanxi* Production

In 1988–90 Fengjia, every time one asked for or granted a favor, expressed sympathy, or called on a friend—that is, every time one invoked *guanxi* to achieve something in the world—one metonymically[1] re-created that *guanxi*. Thus, in addition to the elaborate organization of *guanxi* production on ritual occasions, Fengjia residents (re)produced *guanxi* in their daily lives. Indeed, many of the techniques of ritual *guanxi* production—labor exchange, the use of kinship names, the embodiment of *ganqing*—came from everyday activity. After a brief introduction to a local typology of interpersonal relationships, this chapter examines the everyday techniques of *guanxi* production.

Types of *Guanxi*

In 1988–90 Fengjia, most residents recognized four basic categories of friendly relationships: family members (*benjiaren*), relatives (*qinqi*), fellow villagers (*xiangqin*) and friends (*pengyou*). These categories overlapped, and the same person (even within the same relationship) could be seen as a member of several categories, depending on the circumstances. Family members certainly included all those who lived together as one economic unit. Following village administrative categories, I refer to such units as households (*hu*). Depending on context, members of agnatically related households might also be considered family members. However, such agnates could also count as fellow villagers (*xiangqin*). The flexibility of the term "family member" and the importance of the category "fellow villager," which included households of different surnames, reflected the near absence of formal lineage organization in 1988–90 Fengjia.[2]

Affines were usually referred to as "relatives" (*qinqi*), a term embracing three major categories: mother's sister's family (*yiyi jia*), father's sister's family (*gugu jia*), and mother's mother's family (*laolao*

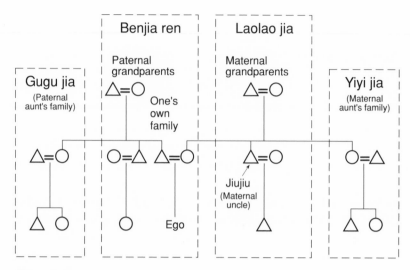

Figure 5   Kinship relations in Fengjia.

jia). Since village kinship was reckoned patrilineally, the last category (*laolao jia*) additionally included all of the mother's brother's (*jiujiu*) families. Because of a tendency toward village exogamy, these relatives usually lived in different villages. However, where they had married within the village, they also counted as fellow villagers.

Villagers had friends living in and outside of Fengjia. However, a friend from within the village was usually categorized as a fellow villager. One exception (and an example of the situation specificity of relationships) was at wedding ceremonies, where those who gave "congratulatory gifts" were considered "friends" whether they came from inside or outside the village.

Two caveats further complicate this terminology. First is the messy fact that in patrilocal marriages women "change" families. The completeness of this transfer, I will argue, was a constantly negotiated social problem. As a consequence, married women at times referred to their natal relatives as "family members" instead of "relatives." Second, relationships were constituted between households as well as between their individual members. Because the general unit of economic accounting was the household, and because *guanxi* always involved material obligation, the *guanxi* of individuals always involved the other members of their households. Though household members might differ over which *guanxi* were most important, gifts were usually seen as coming from households as units.

Embodying *Ganqing*

To convey *ganqing*, it must have a discernible form. Gift giving, toasting, and serving food at banquets, and ritualized decorum like bows and *ketou* (kowtow) are all methods of materializing *ganqing*. Here, I would like briefly to describe the generation of *ganqing* through its direct embodiment in specific human emotions. This embodiment should not be understood as the external representation of an underlying pregiven reality. Rather, it is a claim about what one wants a relationship to be in the future that participates in the reconstitution of future reality. The sentimentality of the present shapes the future rather than representing a static past.[3]

The embodiment of *ganqing* was important to both ritual and everyday practices of *guanxi* production. In ritual, such embodiment was orchestrated or at least expected. At funerals there were specific times for women to wail and for *xiaozhe* (direct patrilineal descendants of the deceased) to weep. The GPCR ban on interclass weeping at funerals was clearly aimed at prohibiting the interclass *guanxi* production that results from such embodiments of *ganqing*. At weddings the bride was expected to act embarrassed, the groom's father happy, and the groom ambivalent. At a "dowry party" (*song hezi*)[4] the bride's parents should be sad (because their daughter is about to leave home). That these *ganqing* were expected in no sense made them less "authentic." When witnessing such displays, I was always moved by the embodiment of powerful *ganqing*. However, such orchestration does imply a notion of emotional authenticity different from that typically recognized in American pop psychology. Few in Fengjia would acknowledge a "true" emotional life, where "spontaneous" feelings well up from an utterly individual heart regardless of the surrounding social circumstances.

Though not orchestrated, embodied *ganqing* played an important role in everyday *guanxi* production as well. On the few occasions when I was sick in the village, I received a stream of visitors. Though I only wanted to rest by myself, read English novels, and generally pretend I wasn't in Fengjia, I had to deal with well-meaning friends. On one such occasion I must have let my irritation show; one man said, "You should be happy to have so many people embody concern [*guanxin*]." "Why?" I asked. "Because if they didn't embody concern, they wouldn't be your friends any more."

On another day there was a fire in the cornstarch factory. People throughout the village grabbed buckets and ran over to the factory. There were two faucets near the fire where buckets could be filled. After filling their buckets, these helpers ran them over to men standing on ladders who passed them to others on the roof who doused the fire. There were more people filling buckets than the faucets could accommodate; lines formed behind the faucets; people began pushing and butting. Eventually, the fire was put out without much damage. Afterwards, I asked Teacher Feng why people would butt in line in such a situation. He explained "when a lot of collective equipment is endangered, everyone wants to communicate concern." Embodying concern generates a collective *ganqing* and helped Fengjia residents manage both their individual *guanxi* and their *guanxi* with the village as a whole.

Of course, individuals also embodied *ganqing* on more mundane occasions. Once a man selling watermelons bicycled into the village loudly hawking his produce. A woman immediately walked out from her courtyard and yelled at him, angrily proclaiming that he had cheated another resident on his last trip. No one bought anything and the hawker went on to the next village. The anger of the woman embodied a *ganqing* in sympathy with her previously cheated fellow villager that seemingly swayed all those who might otherwise have bought some watermelon. I would not reduce all emotional activity in Fengjia to the single dimension of *guanxi* production, but I believe that in many contexts the embodiment of emotion is interpreted in precisely this fashion.

Visiting, Exchanging Favors, Helping Out

Visiting, whether to lend a hand or to socialize, was another important practice of *guanxi* production. In hot weather, those with free time set up stools outside their doors and encouraged friends and relatives to sit and chat. In the winter, friends gathered around stoves and drank tea. At times of special need the visiting of friends and relatives was especially significant. It fulfilled and re-created material obligations, materialized *ganqing*, and hence metonymically reproduced *guanxi*.

As my own experience demonstrated, illness was an important occasion for visiting and embodying concern. Many considered the *ganqing* created in illness visits as actively contributing to curing the sick. The temporary misfortunes of the Zhang family can serve as an example. Mr. Zhang's grandson, Ying, had broken his leg. Originally it didn't affect Mr. Zhang too much. There were lots of people visiting his grandson, so he could go out if he needed. However, then Mr. Zhang's wife got sick. He said, "After Ying broke his leg, she worried so much she didn't eat right. Then she got a fever." With two close relatives sick in different households, his visiting burdens were doubled and he couldn't go out any more. Many fellow villagers visited the boy. Mr. Zhang divided his time between Ying and his wife. Mr. Zhang's two daughters, who had long been married and were living in different villages, took turns visiting their mother. They came on alternate days. After two weeks Zhang's wife got better, and he started going out again.

If an old person became seriously ill, friends, relatives, and fellow villagers visited from all around. They often brought gifts of food and were given tea to drink. As mentioned in the introduction, my visit to the family of a stroke victim led to some of my closest field relations. During that visit the house was full of visitors. One of the victim's sons told me that his relatives had come out of filial piety and respect (*xiao* and *zunjing*). He said, "Old people's lives haven't been easy, they suffered a lot to bring us up, so we are very happy that everyone could come today." The wife of the stroke victim seemed surprisingly relaxed. I suggested, "This must be worrying for you." She replied, "Why should I worry when so many people have come to visit?" For this woman and her son, the *ganqing* and *guanxi* created by so much visiting allowed an otherwise depressing situation to become somewhat positive.

Ellen Judd (1989), who also did research in Shandong Province in the late 1980s, writes of the important "affective and moral ties" (I would say *ganqing* and *guanxi*) between a bride and her natal home (*niangjia*) and argues that a woman's natal home and mother-in-law's home (*pojia*) make competing claims on their daughter's time and services. This tension was directly relevant to visiting practices. Women often returned to their natal villages to socialize, embody concern for sick parents, participate in rituals, or just help out. Some women took turns working each others' fields so that each would have regular opportunities to return to their natal villages. However, in contrast to Judd's emphasis on the competitive aspect of these relationships, I only once heard a woman complaining that her daughter-in-law was spending too much time at her natal home. More often I heard the calculation that a daughter-in-law's natal visits could improve affinal *guanxi*.

Figure 6   Neighbors assisting with house construction.

The larger life projects of house building and marriage provided opportunities for the exchange of favors and *guanxi* building that were neither matters of daily activity nor formal ritual. Almost all marriages in 1988–90 Fengjia were negotiated through matchmakers (*meiren*). Households relied heavily on their networks of friends and affinal relations to help find spouses. The successful location of a marriage partner often led to a long-lasting *guanxi* between the new couple's families and the matchmaker. Villagers also invoked *guanxi* when undertaking large construction projects (figure 6). For example, one household decided to enlarge the gate to their courtyard so that they could more easily move a newly acquired horsecart in and out of their yard. The project involved tearing down the old gate and adjacent brick wall and building new ones, including an ornate frontpiece. The family acquired the building materials and informed their friends and neighbors. On the arranged day, scores of young and middle-aged men came over. Households friendly to the family in question all tried to send someone. Some households also sent women who helped serve tea and informal meals when the men took breaks. The project was finished in one afternoon and seemed as much a social occasion as a building project.

Patterns of regular interhousehold help varied extensively among families. Practical needs and abilities dictated the availability of opportunities to exchange favors and create *guanxi*. However, a few examples can illustrate the more typical sorts of exchange. One childless, elderly widow looked after her neighbors' grandchildren and in turn received help with her fields. A household that ran a commercial vegetable garden took advantage of their frequent market trips to shop for their neighbors. In turn, they asked for help when the labor demands of vegetable gardening exceeded household capacity. Once, I watched an old man spreading his wheat out in the street to dry. A sudden change in the weather threatened to soak his grain, but a half dozen men and women from neighboring households came running over and managed to sweep it up before the rain began in earnest. He told me his son had done the same for his neighbors on other occasions.

The exchange of *ganqing* within households likewise depended on particular circumstances. The taking over of certain chores by a family member—say, clothes washing for a daughter-in-law or draught animal care by a grandfather—constituted an interdependence that continually re-created the *guanxi* of that household. Special care in the performance of more personal duties—preparing bath water for a tired and dirty farmworker, mending a cherished shirt, or cooking a favorite dish—embodied particular *ganqing*. Tensions between household members could be alleviated or exacerbated by the manner in which such duties were performed. Perhaps most basically, eating together (both in the sense of consuming the same dishes at the same time and in the sense of utilizing foodstuffs purchased from a collective budget) constituted household relationships. Not only was sharing meals a matter of spending time together and collectively enjoying the fruits of family labor, it also was an occasion for specific contributions to the family economy through frugality. By eating less expensive items or by consuming only what would have otherwise been wasted, particular family members, often older ones, embodied *ganqing* for (and made claims on) the other members of their household.

Certainly the everyday exchange of favors within and between households has always been a practical matter contextualized in the ever-changing socioeconomy of the present. The daily patterns of *guanxi* production were quite different during the precommunist era of household land tenure and the Maoist era of collectivized farming. They also vary from village to village. Judd (1994:202–212) demonstrates how patterns of interhousehold help in three other Shandong villages during the 1980s varied with each village's economic base. During my 1992 visit to Fengjia, I sensed that an increase in household entrepreneurship was again inducing changes in the patterns of interhousehold exchange. A man building a chicken factory relied on friends and relatives to raise

capital and find a construction team, yet he would not directly call on
them for labor. He purposely hired an out-of-village construction team
to build his factory and paid them cash. Another woman who had just
opened a store told me it was wrong to ask friends for help in running
a profit-making enterprise. However, she also said that her friends and
neighbors were her best customers. These two entrepreneurs both relied on friends, relatives, and fellow villagers in some aspects of their
businesses but avoided them as sources of labor. In contrast, the commercial vegetable gardener described above continued in 1992 to call
on the labor of his fellow villagers in exchange for shopping services.
In brief, the creation of *ganqing* through the exchange of favors should
not be viewed as an unchanging essence of Chinese village life. Especially over the past half century, the types and organization of labor in
Fengjia have been changing rapidly.

Kinship Terms and Names

Routine terms of address also constituted an everyday method of *guanxi*
production. When I was in Fengjia, all older relatives were called by relational kinship terms. This form of address was considered respectful
and was an acknowledgment of the obligation that junior people owed
to their older relatives. Language learning itself started from kinship
terms. Small children were constantly being told "call that man *shushu*"
(father's younger brother) or "call her *yiyi*" (mother's sister) and re-
warded if they managed to use the correct form of address. The term
ren qin (to recognize or acknowledge relatives) was closely related to
kinship terms. When a child began to call a friend of his father's "*shushu*," the child could be said to have "recognized" (*ren*) that man as a
relative. In Fengjia, the title teacher (*laoshi*) was also used like a kinship term. One man said, "Once they teach you, you call them *laoshi*
for their whole life." At times, children addressed their parent's teachers
with the terms for paternal grandmother or grandfather (*nainai, yeye*).

In some settings the use of a kinship term could be highly charged. I
spent the first day of the Chinese New Year with a woman who was old
both in terms of actual years and in terms of generations (the woman's
late husband had a generational name as old as or older than anyone
else living in the village).[5] That morning the village secretary, who in age
was only twenty-five years younger than this woman but who belonged
to the generation three levels below her, came and paid his customary

respects. After he left, she said, "Secretary Feng is so good to me. Did you see that he called me great grandmother [*laonainai*]?"

Recent Chinese films provide several more examples in which the emotional climax comes when one character acknowledges a relationship by calling another by a relational kinship term. In the movie *Old Tales South of the City Wall* (*Cheng Nan Jiu Shi*), a woman who thinks she has found her abandoned daughter prepares to run away with her, but just before they are about to go she realizes the young girl has not yet addressed her. She says, "You still haven't called me, call me just once (*Ni hai mei jiao wo, jiao wo yi sheng*)." The child calls her "Ma" and they run off in a haze of rain and confusion, only to be run over by a train. The stepson's use of "father" in Zhang Yimou's *Ju Dou* and the young boy's use of "maternal grandfather" in Sun Zhou's *Heartstrings* (*Xin Xiang*) provide equally compelling and perhaps better known examples.

In Fengjia, kinship terms were extended to everyone older, regardless of surname. Families of different surnames worked out generational equivalencies so that usages between different family members would be consistent. Fei Xiaotong (1939:90–91) noted a similar pattern in a Yangtze Plain village during the 1930s and suggested that attached to each kinship relation is a certain attitude and level of respect that is extended to each person addressed by a given kinship term. In Fengjia village, Fei's explanation also illuminates. When paying respects to one's older relatives on the Chinese New Year (by going to their houses, addressing them by the appropriate kinship names, bowing, and wishing them well for the new year), "fictional" kin relations were given the same respect as "actual" ones.[6]

Like many of the practices discussed in this book, Fengjia use of kinship names echoes the *Analects of Confucius*. "Confucius says . . .

> When names are not properly ordered, what is said is not attuned; when what is said is not attuned, things will not be done successfully. (Book 13.3, cited in Hall and Ames 1987:269)

Usually referred to as the "rectification of names" (*zheng ming*), the principle elaborated in this passage is interpreted by David Hall and Roger Ames as follows: "Acceptance of a name as appropriate involves a disposition to act. Language is dispositional and the ordering of names is per se an ordering of dispositions" (1987:299). In brief, names do not serve as "labels" for unitary, individual subjects; rather their usage implies a "disposition to act" that is appropriate to the *guanxi* that their usage reproduces. In some places party activists may also have been concerned with this implication. In Shen Rong's fictional account of a Chinese village in the late 1970s, a party cadre questions the extension of kinship names to those with bad class labels (Shen 1987:302). The logic is similar to Fengjia's cultural revolution ban on interclass funeral weeping. Practices that created *ganqing* between members of different classes were suspect.

Though residents of Fengjia generally addressed each other with relational kinship terms, they also had names, and it is worthwhile to consider how they were used. At "twelfth-day parties" (*guo shier tian*, banquets held twelve days after birth or shortly thereafter), parents gave their babies a *xiaoming* (baby name). Thereafter all villagers of an older generation or of the same generation but older in years, used this name to address that person.[7] When children entered school, their first-grade teacher, sometimes with the help of their parents, also gave the child a *xueming* (school name). For school purposes and all official purposes outside the village, a person would be known by his or her school name. Only fellow villagers would know one's baby name and only one's elders could use it. Some villagers also had nicknames, but only close friends of the same generation, age, and gender would use them.

Daughters-in-law and spouses were problematic in this method of addressing people. Since a daughter-in-law often came from outside the village, elders did not feel comfortable using her baby name. Because she was a family member, using her school name was inappropriate, and because of her youth a relational kinship term was too respectful. In the past the term *nizi* (girl or lass) was used to address daughters-in-law, but by the 1980s this term was considered abusive. After a woman gave birth to her first child, village elders and her husband would most likely call her (if the child's baby name were Cuicui) "mother of Cuicui" (*Cuicui niang*). The young mother might call her husband "father of Cuicui" (*Cuicui die*). Before the birth of her first child, some families called their new daughter-in-law "young lady" (*qingnian niang*); others began using a common urban form of address, also reportedly widely used in neighboring Jiuhu township, in which one says the woman's natal surname preceded by the word *xiao* (young or little). A few young people, purposefully rejecting other rural conventions as "feudal," called their spouses by his or her baby name.

One old man had a serious conversation with me about forms of address. Because his parents had died in their youth, he had raised his younger brothers himself and had had no children of his own. Thus, he could not call his wife mother of anyone. He told me that the term *nizi* was abusive, and went hand in hand with the slave-like position of daughters-in-law, and discrimination against women in general, of the old society. I then asked him what he called his wife. After some thought he replied, "Me and my wife are completely equal. If I need to get her attention I say 'hey,' and if she needs to get my attention she also says 'hey.'" Especially for older people, first names were not appropriate to use when addressing one's spouse.

During my first summer in Fengjia I spent a fair amount of time up-dating our version of the village's household registration booklet. Com-piled in th early 1980s, the booklet listed the head and members of each household in the village. Old women were often listed by their natal surnames and the character *shi,* a word that might be translated by the French usage née. When looking for such an elderly woman, I would first go to the house where I thought she lived. I would ask (for example) if Zhang Shi or "Mrs. Zhang" (*Zhang Taitai*) was there. Usually, even when I posed it to the old woman for whom I was looking, the question led to utter confusion. I found that my best strategy was to first find some younger relatives of the woman and then ask if their eighty-year-old grandmother was around. After finding her, it was still difficult to confirm her name. When asked who she was, the woman might point and say "I'm his mother," or "She calls me 'grandmother.'" At best, after going over the household registration booklet with me, a younger, literate relative might tell me "Yes, that must be her." As these people were generally being very helpful, I did not consider these instances purposeful obstinateness toward a rude foreigner. Rather, I believe these women had either forgotten their names or could not comprehend any-one attempting to address them by one. Officially, all they had left was a natal surname. Moreover, for perhaps decades (since their own elder, natal relatives had died) they had been called nothing but relational kinship terms.[8]

Rubie Watson (1986) suggests that the use of kinship terms to address rural women reflects their deficit of "personhood." Naming practices in Fengjia suggest a reframing of Watson's analysis. Though Ha Tsuen, the village in the New Territories of Hong Kong where Watson did her research during the late 1970s, and Fengjia are separated by both a dis-tance of over a thousand miles and distinct political economic contexts, several parallels in naming practices emerge. Watson is surprised that Ha Tsuen villagers address both older men and older women only with kinship terms. She attributes this practice to older men's diminishing role in controlling family and corporate resources and suggests that for both men and women to be addressed with kinship terms is to lose personal power and be defined by their relationships to others. Certainly kinship terms do define people in terms of relationships. However, I believe they do so in a positive and power-producing manner. If a child calls her parents "mother" and "father," while the parents use the child's given name, should we conclude that the child is more of a person than the parents? If a daughter-in-law calls her mother-in-law by a kinship term, should we conclude that the mother-in-law has no power? The circumstances that denied many Chinese rural women official names and power are not identical with the processes by which women earned kinship names and an intrafamilial power.

In Fengjia, old women's lack of names admittedly reflected their lack of educational opportunities and a shielding from the privilege/burden of interacting with bureaucracies that would need to label one with a name. However, in the context of everyday village life, being called by relational kinship terms instead of a name was considered a privilege. Furthermore, lack of clarity about names was not limited to old women (though it was most extreme with them). Several times I came across ten- to thirteen-year-old children who did not know their parent's first names. In addition, I often ran into the problem of what character to write for a given name. One villager would state that the character written in the household registration booklet for their name was incorrect. Others might join in and there would be a discussion among several literate people about which of several homonyms was the correct character for a given person's name. Even the village household registration booklet occasionally contradicted itself, using different characters (all homonyms) in different places for the same generational name.

What then is the significance of this looseness about names and corresponding emphasis on relational kinship terms? First of all, it indicates the importance of using relational terms of address as a practice of *guanxi* production. Every time a relational kinship term is uttered, a specific relationship—and the *ganqing* and material obligation it should involve—is re-created. The fact that in many village contexts relational terms of address are used to the exclusion of names demonstrates the emphasis placed on *guanxi* production in general.

Secondly, the type of subject construction that relational kinship terms enact likewise reflects the *guanxi* construction involved. A name stays the same no matter with whom one is speaking. It remains attached to a single body and implies a single, continuous, and unitary subject. In contrast, a kinship term may apply to any number of bodies of the same gender and approximate age; further, a single body may be called many kinship terms by different people on different occasions. The subject created is neither individual nor unitary. Each time one utters a name, one implies the existence of, and reproduces, a single or discrete subject who is labeled by that name. A kinship term instead reproduces a (hierarchical) relationship.

Tani Barlow (1989a:1–15) has noted the tension created by early-twentieth-century Chinese feminism, in which a biologized, universal "female" (*funu*) was appropriated from Western discourse to oppose the oppression of women as subjects created through the Confucian discourses of relational kinship. In rejection of the gender hierarchies implied in Confucian relational kinship terms, early-twentieth-century Chinese feminists wrote of women as "females" rather than as wives, mothers, or daughters. In so doing, they attempted to replace a contradictory, relational subject with a unitary, individual one. We can view the tension between kinship terms and names in Fengjia similarly. When young couples call each other by their names because other conventions are too "feudal," they are rebelling against a system of terminology in which hierarchies (of age as much as gender) are implied every time one addresses someone. At the same time, however, they are replacing a contradictory, relational subject with a unitary, individual one.

The difference between names and kinship terms also separates the sphere of the bureaucratic workplace from that of village life and work. Local officials who were on familiar terms called each other by their surnames preceded by "old" or "young" (*lao* or *xiao*), depending on the age difference. In introductions they were referred to by their surname and title. In contrast, Fengjia residents often introduced me to their relatives by saying "He calls me *shushu* [father's younger brother]" or "I call her *gugu* [father's sister]" (*Ta jiao wo shushu* or *Wo jiao ta gugu*). This usage is doubly significant. Not only is a kinship term used instead of a name, but the verb "to call" is used instead of the verb "to be." In introducing someone as "she whom I call *gugu*" rather than "she who is my *gugu*," the importance of *calling* someone a kinship term as a practice of *guanxi* reproduction is clearly indicated.

To sum up, using kinship terms, visiting and helping out, and embodying *ganqing* in specific human emotions all involved Fengjia residents in the daily production and reproduction of *guanxi*. Like other practices of *guanxi* production, these everyday actions involved a type of subject construction that was shifting and contested—a personhood subject to the claims of others, that in turn made its own claims. The next four chapters examine Fengjia *guanxi* production in more formal contexts.

2 Guest/Host Etiquette and Banquets

"No," said Chao Gai. "Since ancient times 'the strong guest must not exceed his host.' Strong I may be, but I've only recently arrived from distant parts. I cannot assume high command."

Lin Chong pushed him into the leader's chair. "This is the time. Don't refuse."...
[After two pages more of discussion and deferral, the first four leaders are seated in the first four seats.]

"Song and Du should now be seated," said Chao Gai. But Du Qian and Song Wan absolutely refused. They begged Liu Tang, Ruan the Second, Ruan the Fifth, and Ruan the Seventh to take the fifth, sixth, seventh, and eighth places respectively. Du Qian then accepted the ninth chair, Song Wan the tenth and Zhu Gui the eleventh.

From then on, the positions of the eleven heroes were fixed in Liangshan Marsh. ... Oxen and horses were slaughtered as a sacrifice to the gods of Heaven and Earth, and in celebration of the reorganization. The leaders ate and drank far into the night. They feasted in this manner for several days.
(*Outlaws of the Marsh*, Shi and Luo 1986:135–138)

When asked about the importance of seating at banquets, a retired cadre said, "etiquette emphasizes respect for position" (*lijie jiangjiu zunjing dengji*), and suggested that I read *Outlaws of the Marsh*, a classic novel about Song dynasty rebels.[1] Several sections of the book, including the passage quoted above, devote considerable attention to practices of seating. Seating was also important in the guest/host etiquette and the banquets of 1988–90 Fengjia, though the hierarchies and *guanxi* involved differed considerably. This chapter examines how Fengjia residents constructed and manipulated *guanxi* and hierarchies through practices of banqueting and guest/host etiquette.

The etiquette of banqueting (*yanxi*), hosting (*zuozhu*) and guesting (*zuoke*) involved skills important to all types of *guanxi* production. Though most used these skills on occasion, some people, because of their talent and position, banqueted, guested, and hosted more than others. Those highly skilled in these areas were valued by their friends and families. When describing a sixty-year-old woman who was often asked to accompany guests at banquet tables (*peike*), another woman said, "She really knows how to talk, guests are comfortable with her." Emily Martin (Ahern 1981:32) has similarly noted the importance of "knowing how to talk" among Taiwanese religious practitioners who wish to construct *guanxi* with their gods. Though no one in Fengjia spoke to me about talking to the gods, the need to speak skillfully to guests clearly extended to village government. When asked for descriptions of Party Secretary Feng's responsibilities, most villagers included "receiving guests" (*jiedai keren*) on their list. Indeed, Secretary Feng spent much time banqueting and hosting other officials in the village guest house. In brief, the skillful practice of banqueting, guesting, and hosting was both admired and seen as necessary to village business.

Guest/Host Etiquette

In Fengjia, hosts managed the going and coming of guests through a large array of kinetic, positional, dispositional, and verbal practices, all of which worked to construct *guanxi* through the positioning of guest and host and the embodiment of respect and/or friendly feelings. If possible, hosts received guests upon arrival at the outside gate and saw them off to the gate when they left. If the host was not outside and the gate was open, guests often walked into the courtyard (see figure 7), calling out the name of their host. In such cases the guest was greeted in the courtyard. Visitors who were neither close friends nor family members were almost always seen off, as villagers lived by the saying "It is impolite not to see guests to the gate" (*Busong menkou, bulimao*). Between 1990 and 1992 several households built screen walls (*yingbi*) in their courtyards. These small walls allowed villagers to leave the outside gates to their houses open without worrying about people in the street looking into their courtyards. The screen walls I saw were all decorated with painted tiles showing pine trees in a mountain setting with the words "Guest-Welcoming Pine" (*Yingke Song*). The evergreen quality of the pine, one screen wall owner explained, "expressed that the guest is forever welcome, that the *ganqing* of welcoming the guest will never end."

The comings and goings of guests were further marked by various polite formulas. While being seen off, guests often insisted "It's not necessary to see me off" (*bubisong*). This humble gesture both indicated

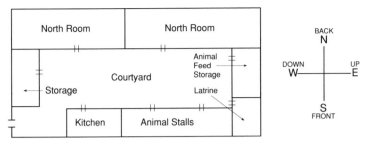

Figure 7   Common Fengjia house layout.

one was not worthy of respect and was a request to be treated informally, implying that one's *guanxi* was relatively close. As guests prepared to go, hosts often said "Sit and chat" (*zuowanwan*). This saying was sometimes taken as a literal invitation. However, it was also used in situations when everyone knew the guest must go. In these cases the saying indicated that one would like to devote more time to hosting one's guest, and that one considered hosting one's guest an important priority. Guests often countered by insisting that their host was busy, implying that there were more important activities for that host than receiving such a humble guest. These polite sayings and actions all served to create good *ganqing* and, hence, to improve *guanxi*. At the same time, however, being overly formal was a way of keeping guests at a distance. As the Chinese sociolinguist Bi Jifang has noted, in close family relationships even the use of everyday polite formulas like "Thank you" (*xiexie*) and "Excuse me" (*duibuqi*) would be taken as purposeful distancing or sarcasm (Bi 1990:18–19).

House orientation also informed etiquette. People slept, lived, and received guests in one of the "north rooms" (*beifang*) of houses. As they faced south, these rooms caught the sun's winter rays and avoided those of summer. Thus, they were comparatively comfortable. However, this orientation was not just a method of climate control. It also embodied the cardinality of the village and guest/host etiquette.[2] When verbally orienting a place or object in the village relative to oneself, one could use either the four cardinal directions or the directionality of seating guests. The wooden chairs used for receiving guests, called *kaoyi* (literally chair with a back to lean against), were almost always placed against the northernmost wall of the north room, facing south (see figure 8). The eastern chair was called "upper" (*shangyi*) while the western one was called "lower" (*xiayi*). Thus, one could refer to things to one's south as either "on the southern side" (*zainanbian*), or "to the front" (*zai-*

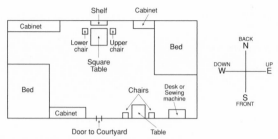

Figure 8   Furniture for receiving guests in north room.

qiantou), where front, regardless of the direction one was facing at the moment, referred to the direction faced when sitting in a wooden guest chair. Likewise, north could be referred to as "to the back" (*zaihoutou*), east as "toward the top" (*zaishangmian*), and west as "toward the bottom" (*zaixiamian*).

Slight variations of the furniture arrangement pictured above were used to receive guests in many of the houses in 1988–90 Fengjia. However, when collecting furniture for soon-to-be-married couples, some families bought sofas and easy chairs instead of wooden guest chairs and square tables (*fangzhuo*, which are placed between the guest chairs). The older style of furniture thus acquired the label "traditional" (*chuantongde*, a term whose significance is examined in chapter 9). Another exception occurred in houses where the "traditional" furniture was present but was so covered with sacks of grain etc., that one had to find other places to sit. The residents of such houses whom I saw were older couples whose children had all left town, and who did not often receive guests.

If there was functional "traditional" furniture, hosts led guests to the upper chair and then sat in the lower chair. If the guest was an honored one (as opposed to, say, a friend of a child) and several hosts were present, the senior adult (usually) male sat in the lower chair. When I made my rounds of the village, I would always be placed in the upper chair (figure 9). On several occasions, as various members of the host family came and went, there was a constant shuffling of occupants of the lower chair. If an older male relative of the current "host" entered the room, the current occupant of the lower chair would surrender his seat, reclaiming it if the older relative left. Some families were more strict about this format than others. In one case a brief argument broke out. I was conversing with a young man who spoke excellent Mandarin. His older brother entered the room and squatted near the lower chair.

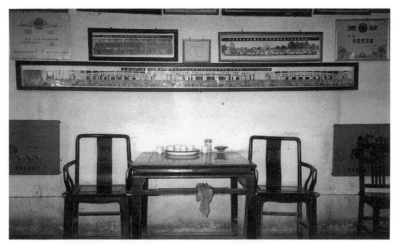

Figure 9   Guest and host furniture in party headquarters.

He too started to speak with me, but his Mandarin was worse and I constantly needed the interpretation of the younger brother. Seemingly irked by his younger brother's ease of communication, the older brother indicated that the younger brother should give up his seat. After some protest the younger brother gave way.

This disagreement reflects the dynamic described in the sentence quoted earlier, "etiquette emphasizes respect for position." Other villagers described this dynamic as a problem of *mianzi* (face).[3] In pairing hosts and guests, *mianzi* worked in two directions. It both conferred respect upon the guest and constructed intrafamily (or intraunit) hierarchies. Having enough *mianzi* to "face" someone implied that one had the authority to represent one's group in a manner similar to, or at least congruent with, the person one was facing. By having the oldest, most respected, and most authoritative member of one's family act as host, Fengjia families could suggest that their guests were people of significant authority and were worthy of significant respect (figure 10). In so doing, they created good *ganqing*, and established *guanxi*. On the other hand, by occupying the host seat, a senior male could also claim to be the most authoritative person of his family.

As Zito points out in her discussion of banquet seating in the eighteenth-century novel *The Scholars*, "*mianzi* hardly implies equal status, but rather functions as a site from which hierarchical communication is possible" (1994:119). In *The Scholars*, to sit with someone at the same table indicates that one's *mianzi* is good enough to "face" and

Figure 10   Couple with granddaughter seated on guest/host furniture.

hence communicate with one's fellow banqueter. In Fried's ethnography of Chu County (Anhui Province) in the late 1940s, banqueting together and *mianzi* conferral are likewise closely connected. The boss (*laoban*) described by Fried does not allow those whose status is too low to banquet with him (1953:78–79). In the case of the two brothers, the family's father's recent stroke had just caused the leadership of the family to become a relevant issue. Before, the father could have occupied the host chair; now, who occupied this chair had implications for family leadership and decision making. Claims to authority within the family manifested themselves in arguments over how best to confer *mianzi* upon and hence create *ganqing* and *guanxi* with the honored guest who had come all the way from America.

When men were not present, women in some families would act as host to my guest; in others they would not. In these latter families, even if there were no men in the room, women would not sit opposite me in the lower chair. One of these women said it was a matter of *mianzi*. She feared that I would perceive her occupation of the host chair as not giving me enough *mianzi* and hence as being disrespectful. However, most villagers described sexual segregation, especially in banquet seating, as a matter of "tradition" and convenience rather than *mianzi*.

Once I attempted an experiment. Upon arriving at a young teacher's house, I quickly sat in the lower seat. Without hesitating, my host sat down in the upper seat and we had an interesting conversation. After about an hour his father (who lived in a separate household) came in to give a brief message and left. After his father left, the teacher related that his father had reprimanded him for seating me in the wrong seat. He said that old folks in the countryside felt that only men should sit in these seats, but that in the city it wasn't that way. He added that there should be "equality in seating between men and women" (*nannu tongzuo*) and that the two chairs were the same anyway. But, he concluded, we might as well switch or the old folks would say that he didn't understand etiquette (*budong limao*).

At large ritual gatherings, scores of guests came from near and far. As guests were received, a representative of each group (usually the eldest male) was seated in the upper chair. If one group had two significant representatives, the host might lead them to the upper and lower chairs, while the representative of the host household sat wherever was convenient. As new guests came, there would be a constant deferring of seats.

Distance, as well as age, played an important role. A guest who had come from far away received the most deference. By traveling a long distance, such guests go to considerable trouble to attend a given event. This sacrifice creates good *ganqing;* hosts participate in this *ganqing* by extending extra deference. In addition, "guest" fellow villagers often acted as host to guests from out of town. In such instances, fellow villagers made claims about their own *guanxi* with the host in relation to the *guanxi* of guests from out of town. Here "distance," or lack thereof, was seen as indicative of the closeness of one's *guanxi* as well as one's degree of physical proximity. At one wedding a nearby cousin debated a brother who lived far away over who should defer their seat and, thereby, act as host. In so doing, they made competing claims about whose *guanxi* was closer.

After everyone sat down, hosts almost always offered tea, cigarettes, and sometimes small snacks like melon seeds, watermelon (during the summer), and (especially at weddings) candy. Hosts did not ask guests if they wanted these tidbits, and guests were expected to gracefully accept them. The informality of asking if someone wanted something and refusing it if one didn't was reserved for everyday situations among friends and relatives. Informality implied a close *guanxi*. A demand for informality from a distant guest was both rude and prohibited the *guanxi*-producing practices through which distance could be overcome. Cook Feng explained that people don't smoke and drink alone and told me a popular local saying, "wine and tobacco aren't split among households" (*jiuyan bufenjia*), implying that one shouldn't be too possessive with wine and tobacco. As media of *ganqing,* tobacco and wine had to be shared to be effective.

During my first summer in the village this practice presented me with a problem. As long as I drank tea, I could use my foreignness to excuse my inability to smoke. However, during one period stomach problems convinced me to also avoid tea. In my next household visit, I insisted that I didn't smoke and didn't want tea. Though tolerant enough not to be mad, my host commented "How *can* you both not smoke and not drink tea? If you don't smoke and don't drink tea, what do you do?" I had made myself a social cripple. By not accepting cigarettes and tea, I was refusing to participate in the creation of good *ganqing* and hence in the establishment of *guanxi.* I quickly learned to always accept tea, but also found it was not necessary to drink much.

One day a cornstarch factory worker explained to me the proper way to receive tea and cigarettes. He said that when someone gives you a cup of tea or a cigarette or lights your cigarette, you should receive it in one hand and hold the other hand next to but not touching it. This gesture indicates cooperation in the creation of good *ganqing.* He said that only when the item "should" be given anyway, as in the case of a son pouring tea for his father, is the gesture not important.

Though central to the procedures of receiving guests, the sharing of cigarettes especially was not limited to this context. The etiquette of giving, receiving, and lighting cigarettes was important anywhere they could be carried. The giving of cigarettes was especially important in courting officials. Cigarettes were almost always offered in office settings (often by the person visiting the office). On occasion I saw visitors to various offices open a new pack of cigarettes, give one to an official, and leave the pack on the desk. On other occasions I witnessed "etiquette battles" in which several parties simultaneously offer to give and light cigarettes. Official and personal *guanxi* were negotiated and produced in part through the etiquette of cigarettes.

Banquets

In 1988–90 Fengjia, banquets were often the first step in the establishment of *guanxi.* Banquets marked the first meetings of affinal relatives in wedding and engagement parties as well as the arrival of official guests to the village. However, before banquets took place, intermediaries had usually conducted negotiations to determine the propriety of the *guanxi* in question. In the case of marriages, matchmakers negotiated before the engagement party (*xiang qin*). In the case of new relationships with the village as a whole, or with village factories, introductions and negotiations mediated by middlemen determined the appropriateness of a relationship. In either case, a prior determination of the propriety of a *guanxi* occurs. If a *guanxi* were inappropriate, then the two parties would have trouble "facing" each other at a banquet table. The rejection of a relationship at a banquet table would destroy any *ganqing* that the banquet was supposed to create and would result in a loss of *mianzi* for the rejected party.

Banquets were usually preceded by the formal reception of the guest. In a personal banquet the guests' reception usually proceeded as described above. Hosts showed their guests into the house, sat them in the upper chair, and gave them tea, cigarettes, and snacks. In official receptions, guests were received in a room designated for that purpose and given tea and cigarettes. The village's most formal guest room, located in the party headquarters, contains an elegant framed couplet of calligraphy that reads: "The ocean contains close friends; the corners of the earth are like next-door neighbors" (*Hainei cun zhiji; Tianya ruo bilin*).

All banquets present the problem of determining who sits where. The local term for banquet, *yanxi* (used widely throughout China), itself illuminates this importance. The second character of this word, *xi*, means "seat" or "place" at a formal gathering like a banquet or in a political organ like the People's Congress.[4] The convergence of banquets and politics here reflects the importance of banquet seating to negotiating hierarchy, social relations, and power. The eleven heroes of Liangshan Marsh permanently reorganized their leadership positions by arranging banquet seating. Though Fengjia banquet procedures did not constitute political hierarchies so directly, banquet seating was still negotiated and was still relevant to problems of reproducing and recreating specific hierarchies.

At banquets given by families in their homes on ritual occasions, Fengjia residents used square banquet tables arranged for groups of eight. At one large wedding a dozen such tables were needed. The hosts set up the tables in the north rooms of their own and their neighbors' houses. A fellow villager took charge of arranging who sat at which table. Men and women were segregated, and people from the same family or place were seated together. For each table of guests the host

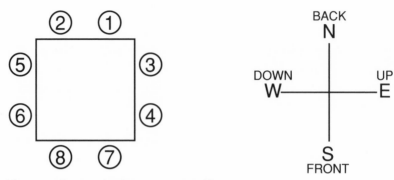

Figure 11   Banquet seating at a square table.

assigned a person or two to act as host representatives (*peike,* literally the person who accompanies guests). Usually fellow villagers served as host representatives, as relatives had other ritual duties. The host reps were chosen to match the most honored guest at each table in age and sex. The ranking of seats is pictured in figure 11. Depending on the circumstances, many seating arrangements were possible. The simplest arrangement occurred when there were six guests of one sex from one family and two host reps. In this case the guests most frequently sat in age order in chairs one to six while the host reps sat in age order in seven and eight. It did not matter if the youngest guests were younger than the host reps. However, occasionally even in this situation there were attempts to defer seats. At one wedding banquet I saw a host rep seated in one of the head two chairs with the oldest guest placed in the other. At this table the significance of the banquet had shifted. Instead of acting as a representative of the host (which constructs the other banqueters firmly as guests), the host rep used this banquet to establish his own relationship with the guest family.

Whenever I saw two guest families seated at the same table, serious negotiation took place. The guests milled about the table, discussed who should sit where, and tried to understand each other's intentions. Arguments about distance from host, age, and positions within family were all offered. Host reps sat in the seventh and eighth chairs and tried to mediate. On one such occasion one family had two representatives older than the eldest of the other family. The negotiations became particularly tricky. Should the eldest two men at the table occupy the first two chairs or should each family's eldest representative occupy the first two chairs? The families argued for more than five minutes and I had to leave before the issue was resolved. Because the expressions of respect embodied in seating order could be interpreted in terms of age hierarchies, distance hierarchies, and *guanxi* between families, the issue was complex and ambiguous.

The seating of future daughters-in-law and sons-in-law was particularly interesting. When a future son-in-law attended a banquet at his parents-in-law's house, he was often given the first chair even when the other guests at the table were older than he. In contrast, when future daughters-in-law participated in banquets, they usually took their age-order seat among their fiancé's female relatives. Since future daughters-in-law are almost always young women, their seating position was generally quite "low." The difference reflects the logic of patrilocality. Sons-in-law are and will continue to be from different villages and patrilineal units and thus are likely to be constructed as guests in banquet seating arrangements. Daughters-in-law will switch to the host's village and patrilineal unit and thus may be constructed as members of the host hierarchical unit.

The placement of sons-in-law in the most honored guest position often had further significance. An older man with three married daughters told me that if one loved one's daughter, it was important to treat one's son-in-law especially well. That way the son-in-law would feel obligated to be good to her. A young father provided a complementary example. He said that if you get mad at your wife and want to yell at her or hit her, you would think about how good your parents-in-law were to you. If you were bad to her, you would not be able to face them. In this way, people say, the *ganqing* you have with your relatives can keep you from doing bad things. Thus, like most practices of *guanxi* production, the seating of a son-in-law may be seen as managing the specific (and potential) obligations of a relationship through the manipulation of *ganqing*. Giving him the most honored seat helps create appropriate *ganqing*.

The tables used in official village banquets held in either the village guest house or the village committee building were round rather than square. There was no fixed number of seats per table; large groups could be broken into separate tables or crowded together at one table. When village leaders held banquets for delegations to the village, seating arrangements did not construct a guest/host opposition by placing guests in the most honored positions and hosts in the least. Instead, representatives from each recognized unit shared the head seats. Thus

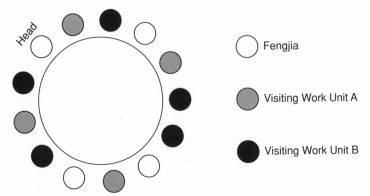

Figure 12   Banquet seating at a round table.

for example, a banquet of thirteen people including village leaders and members of two visiting work units might have been seated as pictured in figure 12.

Before sitting down, village officials and their guests usually discussed who would be the primary representative of each group. The primary representatives then sat next to each other; their seats became the head of the table. Others then negotiated their seats with much deferral. The farther a seat was from the head of the table the less important it was. Though the primary representatives were usually the leaders of their own units, intraunit hierarchies were not always strictly observed. Rather, who the primary representatives were depended on the nature of the *guanxi* being constructed. For example, if one unit wished to introduce a new member to work with the other unit, this new member would be constructed as the primary representative for that banquet. Or, if the purpose of a banquet was to patch up a relationship between arguing members of two units, the arguing members plus a mediator would be constructed as the primary representatives. In short, in interunit banquets, interunit *guanxi* were constructed by seating representatives of each group next to each other at the head of the table.

In matching primary representatives or matching host reps to guests, the problem of face (*mianzi*) was again relevant. As mentioned earlier, having enough *mianzi* to "face" someone implied that one had the authority to represent one's group in a manner similar to, or at least congruent with, the person one was facing. If a provincial-level official came to the village to negotiate village agricultural practices, it would make little sense for him to negotiate with someone who did not have the authority to change such practices. Since in Fengjia of the late 1980s only Party Secretary Feng, and perhaps agricultural specialist Zhang Lin, had such authority, no one but these two would have the *mianzi* to face such an official as the primary representative at a banquet table. In banquet seating the possibility of and need for achieving a given *guanxi* was central. Villagers arranged seating to produce *guanxi* between individuals who had the authority and hence the *mianzi* to represent their unit or household at the appropriate level.

Once everyone was seated, the banquet proper could begin. All of the banquets I saw had servers. The village hired a cook and a waiter to work its official banquets. At personal banquets, fellow villagers handled the cooking and serving. The servers generally brought out the food as it was cooked and kept liquor glasses full. As soon as one drank from one's glass, it would be filled again. The food was brought out in plates that were placed in the middle of the table. In general, individuals had only a small empty bowl, or perhaps just their chopsticks and liquor glasses. Pieces of food were picked up from the plates in the middle and immediately eaten, or temporarily placed in one's small bowl. Banquets were generally divided into two parts. In the first, people toasted each other and ate food between toasts. After the primary representatives or most honored guest and host rep decided that everyone had drunk enough, a last toast was made, in which everyone emptied their glass. The host representative would then tell the servers to take away the glasses and bring out the "main food," usually steamed bread or dumplings. In contrast to the meat and vegetable dishes, each person received his or her own portion of this food. In the second part of the banquet, people continued to eat food from the plates on the table as well as their own steamed bread and/or dumplings.[5]

During the late 1980s, banquet foods were materially and symbolically rich. Recently built greenhouses allowed for year-round vegetables. Most personal banquets followed a twenty-plate format: eight large plates (usually hot dishes), eight small plates (mostly cold dishes), and four bowls (usually soups). The two sets of eight plates was sometimes called "double eight dishes" (*shuang ba cai*). Since the *ba cai* rhymes with *fa cai* (good fortune), this arrangement was doubly propitious. At the start of the banquet, most of the cold dishes were already on the table. The rest were brought in during the course of the banquet. The host rep would urge the banqueters to eat the choicest morsels from the most recently arrived plates while they were still hot. Not all of the dishes were solely for eating. At weddings a big chunk of pork fat was almost always served as one of the large plates, but was never eaten. The fat embodied wealth and surplus.[6] A whole fish with its head pointed to the east was also served at weddings. The words for fish and surplus (*yu* in the second tone) are homonyms. This dish, though also embodying wealth and happiness, was eaten.

Eating and drinking during banquets was collective and negotiated rather than a matter of individual hunger or taste. Especially at banquets in which *guanxi* were just being established and people did not know each other well, people drank only during toasts and ate only what someone else put on their plates or indicated they should take with their chopsticks. Likewise, cigarettes were smoked only when offered and lit by someone else. Host representatives were responsible for orchestrating, or at least initiating, eating, drinking, and smoking. At personal banquets the host reps usually started off with several toasts and encouraged the guests to eat from various dishes between toasts. If the banquet remained stiff and formal, all such initiatives were taken by the host rep. The guests' role was one of accepting or resisting the host reps' suggestions. At interunit banquets or at personal banquets where guests and hosts shared responsibility, countertoasts and offers were often made by the guest representatives. In the most cooperative instances, complete interdependence was ritually achieved. Guests and hosts were focused entirely on the eating, drinking, and smoking of others and depended entirely on others for their own satisfaction.

Cooper (1986:183) describes cooperation and deference in eating etiquette in Hong Kong in terms of Taoism and Confucianism:

> At the macro level of China's great tradition, one finds such behavior characteristic of the *chun-tzu*, the individual skilled in the *li* (etiquette, rites and ceremonies). He is also skilled in the art of *jang*—of yielding, of accomplishing without activity, of boundless generosity, of cleaving to the *li*. There is even something of a Taoist resonance in all this, getting at things indirectly, without obvious instrumental effort.

However, in some cases the hosts and guests had no personal *guanxi* before the banquet, and the event remained stiff and formal. The guests resisted most of the host reps' suggestions and thereby refused to depend upon the host reps for satisfying their wants. At the end of the banquet, the host reps could similarly refuse to involve their own desires in the banquet. By pretending to eat until the guests finished and then having the servers abruptly remove all the plates, the host reps could indicate that they had eaten only to accompany the guests and that their own needs were not involved. Though such stiff formality could indicate an ambivalence toward the construction of a certain *guanxi*, we should remember that the attendance of the banquet in itself was a positive *guanxi*-constructing act.

Drinking was important to banqueting for many reasons. For the most part, men drank *baijiu*, a strong clear liquor, while women and youths drank *hongjiu*, a sweet, red fruit wine. Most saw these drinking habits as the only significant difference between men's and women's banqueting habits and as the reason for the "traditional" sexual segregation in banquet seating. Though predominantly male intervillage and county-level official banquets would include women if necessary, most village and county cadres felt that single-sex banquets were more convenient. Cadres paid close attention to who drank how much and felt uncomfortable if different types of liquor were mixed at the same table. Different types of liquor ended the equivalence of a toast in which both parties drank one cup. Thus, gender-marked drinking habits obstructed the smooth use of alcohol at sexually integrated banquets. Since the public political sphere was dominated by men, gendered drinking patterns contributed to the continued exclusion of women from important political posts. However, at least within the village, such segregation not only shut women out from male *guanxi*-making activities but also shut men out from female *guanxi*-producing activities. Women created their own networks within Fengjia and between Fengjia and their natal villages. Like village men, well-connected Fengjia women could rely on their networks to secure help in times of need, to locate and evaluate potential spouses, and to borrow money for small family enterprises. The *guanxi* of these spheres of activity were consolidated through all-female *guanxi*-producing activities, such as the giving of cloth and quilts (discussed in chapter 3) and all-female banquet tables. As Weiner (1976) has argued about the segregation of men's and women's gift-giving spheres among Trobriand Islanders, women's control over certain spheres of relationships gives them a source of power that is both envied and feared by men. In Fengjia, I twice heard men complain that their wives' many *guanxi* made them too independent.

Both men and women used drinking to break down excessively formal postures. Skillful host reps coaxed their guests to drink and relax. Toasting materialized respect, while drinking deconstructed the boundaries that distinguished guests from hosts, thus allowing *ganqing* to flow. The local saying "exchange feeling by toasting" (*jingjiu jiao qing*) sums up this use of drinking. At an official banquet a county-level cadre told me that close friends and acquaintants just establishing a relationship drank more than others. He added that refusing a toast was the equivalent of refusing to give *mianzi,* the starting point for relationships. At personal banquets I observed similar patterns. Once I attended a banquet held for the older brothers of a bride and groom. The groom's older brother (the host) explained his aggressive toasting to me. He said that drinking a lot helped make the guest "happy" (*gaoxing*) and thus established the *guanxi* between them. After such a banquet established their *guanxi,* he said, the two brothers-in-law could become more informal (*suibian*) in their interaction.

However, though drinking was a practical method of creating *ganqing,* at some banquets it became a competitive game. In an attempt to get other banqueters drunker than themselves, hosts and guests could initiate drinking games, and try to make toasts that resulted in others drinking more than they did. For example, if there were two host reps and six guests, the first host rep could simultaneously toast all six of the guests while the second host rep just watched. The second host rep would toast all the guests later. After the two toasts, each of the guests would have drunk two glasses while each host rep would have drunk only one.

The drinking responsibilities of (the almost always male) officials whose job it was to foster *guanxi* between work units were considerable. In Zouping, cadres compared their drinking capacities by specifying the exact number of ounces (*liang*) of white liquor (*baijiu*) they could hold. Two men both confident of their superior capacity might try to drink each other under the table. Several times I saw officials drink themselves sick at banquets. In a fictional account of Shaanxi cadres during the 1980s, a newly appointed official earns the wrath of his family because his new job compels him to get drunk as often as two or three times a day (Jia 1992:415–416). At times, unit leaders delegated their drinking responsibilities to subordinates. When they made or accepted a toast, they would tell a subordinate sitting at the same table to drink it for them. Once, I saw an official play a drinking game during which his subordinate had to drink every round he lost. On another occasion, I saw an official of one county-level unit try to get a worker in a province-level unit to drink for him. Though supposedly cooperating on a mutual project, there was much tension between the units. The provincial worker refused the order to drink, thus also refusing the direct authority of the county unit's leader. When I left Fengjia, the two units were still having difficulty in their relationship.

An article in the newspaper most widely read in Fengjia, *Village*

Masses (1989a), gives a fascinating account of the role of drinking in cadre life. As it is consistent with my own observations, I present the article here without consideration of how its didactic purposes may have influenced its construction.[7]

Capacity for Liquor, Capacity for Courage, Capacity for Work

The charm of liquor is growing. In the China of a commodity economy that is developing daily, liquor, already more than a mere commodity, has become a lubricant for the people's political life. In one county where they were preparing to select a township party committee secretary, there were three suitable candidates. Qualifications, experience, ability, and spirit were all comparable, and those in charge of the selection could not decide. Then, one person suggested a drinking contest. The result was that the victor, who drank one *jin* (.5kg) of *Erguotou* liquor [a type of white liquor] without getting drunk, was appointed the next day.

Don't be surprised about this. The primary work of whoever occupies a head position in a township or county, a "parental official," is to revitalize the local economy. The consequence, since this task necessitates economic exchanges, economic exchanges entail banquets, and banquets require drinking, is none other than China's special characteristic: giving and taking, guesting and hosting, greeting them when they come and seeing them off when they go—how could this be done without getting drunk?

And it is not that all officials can drink a lot, in this matter there is also a factor of courage. A friend who works at the township level complained that the hardest work of village officials is to accompany guests at banquets. Even if a responsibility system for accompanying guests' drinking has not been set, as soon as you enter a dining hall, your body is not your own. Setting up the liquor glasses seems like killing one's way to the battlefield—all selfish ideas and ulterior motives are flung to the back of one's brain. The great poet of the Tang dynasty, Li Bai, could after drinking create with poetic inspiration. Nowadays "parental officials," though without poetic inspiration, can also create greatly when inebriated. With magician-like drinking ability, they often win the approving words of satisfied guests. Before leaving, these full-bellied guests sell 80 or 100 tons of product at production-target [i.e., state-regulated and therefore inexpensive] prices. No wonder people say that a cadre's official responsibility is eating and drinking, and that a leader's drinking capacity is his working capacity.

Courage and drinking capacity as a special measuring stick of those climbing the political ladder has a close relationship with the present sociopolitical climate. In the years of the Great Leap Forward, brave braggarts succeeded and got rich. During the Cultural Revolution, brave looters came to the fore. Now brave drinkers get along well. As a result, drinking problems are the viruses of current cadres and policies, interfering with the implementation of the economic system reforms while eroding the body of the party in power. Morality and ability should be the basic standard for selecting cadres. We should not allow negative social inclinations to influence the party's cadre system. If we don't thoroughly liberate all levels of leaders and cadres from the shackles of liquor, the giant wheels of reform can veer off track.

The presentation of banquet drinking as a sometimes onerous task that officials undertake to engender *ganqing* and thereby secure privileges for their local units mirrors my own view of the importance of banqueting to local *guanxi* production. The role that drinking white liquor plays in cadre selection demonstrates how gender-specific practices of *guanxi* production exclude women from the official sphere. The success of (presumably male) cadres with "magician-like drinking ability" in eliciting favors from their guests further points to the socially coercive aspects of *guanxi* production. The "battlefield" of the banquet table exposes one to the *ganqing* manipulations of one's host.

The article's critique of cadre drinking as a "virus" of current policies that interferes with the implementation of economic system reforms raises another point. There has been considerable tension between the official policies and propaganda of the CCP and the banqueting behavior of local officials. Like gift giving, banqueting can be used to form *guanxi* whose material obligations take precedence over the policy preferences of the CCP-led state. If, for example, the central organs of the CCP want certain local units to provide land to public works projects or to pay extra grain taxes, local cadres could use their *guanxi* with higher level officials to try to protect the interests of their home villages. As Mayfair Yang (1989a, 1994) argues, *guanxi* are often constructed to bypass the policy directives of the party state. Consequently, official propaganda often attacks the banqueting (and gift giving) of local officials as either feudal or corrupt.

However, though the banqueting of local officials may be inimical to the interests of the state's center, they do not necessarily counter the interests of local people. Other newspaper accounts of cadre banqueting portrayed it as a corrupt pleasure of the privileged that aroused the fury of the masses—a presentation quite opposite to the opinions I heard expressed in Fengjia.[8] As mentioned above, those I interviewed saw it as a necessary part of official work, as part of forming *guanxi* that protected the interests of the village. Wilson (1994) and Xu (1992) likewise describe the practical benefits that rural people can derive from cadre banqueting. At least during the 1980s, Fengjia residents saw the banqueting of their officials as a necessary activity.

The attempts of the party to curb cadre banqueting during the 1980s and early 1990s have been numerous but seemingly ineffectual. After the Tiananmen Massacre in June of 1989, Fengjia received a directive suggesting that cadres limit their banqueting. Village leaders told me that they had received several such directives before and that they always reacted with caution, curbing their banquets for at least a month or so. In the spring of 1995, the party's Central Commission for Discipline Inspection announced regulations banning cadre participation in banquets with any "influence seekers" (*China News Digest* 1995). Less than a month earlier the *Canton Evening News (Yangcheng Wanbao)* wrote that cadres' yearly public expenditure for banqueting amounted to twelve billion American dollars (*World Journal* 1995). In the memories of Fengjia villagers, only during the height of the Cultural Revolution—when Red Guards attacked any practice that could be labeled feudal, capitalist, or corrupt—was cadre banqueting severely curbed.

3 Gift Giving

❋

Perhaps more directly than any other method, gift giving constituted *guanxi*; by giving gifts, villagers managed (created and re-created) relationships. Since *guanxi* were simultaneously matters of material exchange and human feelings, the material exchange of gifts directly generated *ganqing* and *guanxi*. The Chinese term *zuo ge renqing* illustrates this implication. Literally it means "to make human feeling," but in common use it refers to giving a gift or doing a favor or, more specifically, giving a gift or favor for the purpose of establishing or improving *guanxi*. In gift giving, the relation between *ganqing* and *guanxi* worked as a linking force between past, present, and future. *Ganqing*, the feeling of the present, elicited memories of relationships past and begat *guanxi*, the material obligation for future exchange.

To present a complete picture of gift giving in the Fengjia of 1988–90, and to contextualize the case studies and analysis that follow, I begin with an account of the types of gifts villagers gave and the occasions on which they gave them. In no sense, however, should this background be taken as a set of "rules." As both Pierre Bourdieu (1977, 1990) and Annette Weiner (1976:220–222) argue, resorting to "rules" as an explanation detemporalizes practice, and time is central in gift giving. The time lapse between gift and countergift defines gift giving as a social form. It is the possibility that a gift might not be reciprocated that gives the gift its moral weight. Social custom, the relationship between giver and receiver, or even the lives of the parties involved could end or change abruptly during the time lapse between gift and countergift. Consequently, gift giving produces a contingent social field rather than reproduces a static social structure and is an art rather than a science.

Moreover, as many scholars have noted, "traditional" gift-giving practices have been anything but static under CCP rule in both rural and urban China (Walder 1986; Miao and Lu 1987:16; Mayfair Yang 1988). In Fengjia, as in the Heilongjiang village described by Yan (1993) and the fictional Shaanxi village depicted by Jia (1992:321), increases in the standard of living during the 1970s and 1980s allowed villagers to invent new gift-giving opportunities, expand gift-giving capacities, and extend gift-giving networks. Yet, though change was continuous, it was only against the background of what was held to be usual in 1988–90 that individual gift-giving acts took their significance, and that actors' motives and strategic artistry become apparent.

Perhaps an example can further illustrate my approach. If, at a series of weddings, a certain category of gift givers all give the groom the same type of gift, one may conclude that at that time, under those historical circumstances, that type of gift was usual and that all of these gift givers, following their own aims and strategies, decided to give the usual rather than an exceptional gift. One may not conclude that there was a "rule" for a certain category of gift givers to give that type of gift at weddings. Indeed, in 1988–90 Fengjia, as in the fictionalized village portrayed by Jia (1992:471), the size of gifts and relationships of givers was public knowledge and a matter for much discussion. Thus, the "usual gift" was well-known and was treated in practice as a background for specific gifting decisions.

Gifts

In 1988–90 Fengjia, most gifts fell into five categories: cloth, clothes, food products, "congratulatory gifts" (*hexili*), and "gift-money" (*renshiqian*—literally, person-event-money). Foodstuffs (*shipin*) were the most common gifts. During the late 1970s and 1980s Fengjia residents began giving more expensive foods like bottled fruits, sweets, and cookies instead of grain or steamed bread, though in a few contexts it was still most appropriate to give steamed bread. On some occasions specific food gifts were fairly standard. For example, when celebrating the birth of a child, eggs were given to the new mother to help her recuperate. In general, giving foodstuffs showed concern for someone's health; when visiting the elderly or the ill and mothers who had recently given birth, food products were appropriate gifts. Likewise, food given in ancestral offerings embodied concern for the well-being of ancestors.

Cloth was almost always given by women to women. Money, equivalent to the value of the cloth that would have been given was sometimes substituted; however, on those occasions it was said that the meaning of this money was "cloth," differentiating it from the money that was given as "gift-money." Parents gave clothes to children or children-in-law.

Figure 13   Jingzi *(glass-framed artwork) on display at a store in the county seat.*

Congratulatory gifts were given by friends to the groom and/or his family on the occasion of his wedding. They included practical items like thermoses and decorative wall hangings — either paintings, cloth with congratulatory messages attached, or a type of glass-framed artwork (*jingzi;* see figure 13). Like Chinese paintings given to a patron, the inscriptions on congratulatory gifts usually included the giver's name, the occasion, and the date. Glass-framed decorations were often displayed in villagers' homes years after the event for which they were given. Similarly, urban work units and village committees throughout Zouping County displayed glass-framed decorations that they had received from other units.

Gift-money was given to the head of a household on the occasions of weddings, engagement parties (*xiang qin*),[1] "dowry parties" (*song hezi*), and twelfth-day parties. The prominent use of cash as a gift contradicts Western sensibilities which, except between parents and children, deem money an inappropriate gift. As Bloch (1989) points out, the need for Western anthropologists to explain the significance of cash gifts in foreign locales says more about the symbolism of money in the West than elsewhere. We place gifts in the realm of kinship, sentimentality, and morality, and cash in the realm of commodity exchange. We deem it tactless to inquire of a gift's monetary value and idealize gifts as inalienable (cf. Weiner 1994). As the essence of alienability and countability, cash is the least appropriate gift.

In contrast, Fengjia residents had no compunctions about discussing the price of gifts. More than once I heard young men brag of the congratulatory present that they had bought for their newly married friend, saying something like "That glass-framed decoration cost 60 yuan and only one other friend chipped in on it with me." Likewise, parents preparing a dowry proudly pointed out which items had been newly bought and told me the price. When a dowry was delivered, people crowded around to check out the quality and quantity of furniture.[2] Moreover, dowries were not the only sort of gift whose value was publicly assessed. Gifts were never wrapped and were given in front of everyone who happened to be there at the time. Congratulatory gifts had the *giver's* name written on them in big letters, and were displayed for everyone to see. In brief, assessing, bragging about, and displaying the value of gifts was a popular, public activity. Because gifts were about *guanxi,* and *guanxi* involved both sentiment and material obligation, both giving monetary gifts and assessing the monetary value of non-cash gifts were reasonable behaviors.

Gift-giving Occasions

Food products could be given any time one visited friends or relatives, but were almost always given when visiting during spring festival, visiting old relatives when they were sick, or visiting the families of friends or relatives who had recently passed away. Over spring festival, older friends and relatives gave money (about 2 to 8 yuan) to preteen children.[3]

Fengjia residents held birthday parties for old people and one-year-old babies. To an old person's birthday party friends usually brought food. To a child's first birthday party, relatives usually brought eggs (twenty to fifty in number or ¥4 to ¥10 worth) and some twisted sticks of fried dough called *mianhua*. Female relatives also brought cloth. Fellow villagers and friends could bring cloth, fried dough, or both.

At twelfth-day parties people from outside the village usually gave gifts on the day of the feast, while fellow villagers gave any time in the month after the baby was born.[4] Gifts were of two sorts. Close friends and relatives, who were allowed into the mother's room to see the baby, gave money to the mother *for* the baby. Other people gave presents of eggs and fried dough sticks to the head of the household (usually the mother's father-in-law) *for* the new mother. The mother's female, natal relatives attended these events in large numbers and gave generously of both money and food products. If the family was given more eggs than they could use (as was usually the case), the surplus was sold at local markets.

Engagements and weddings included numerous gift-giving occasions. The first or second time that the prospective bride and groom met,[5] the man usually gave a "meeting gift" (*jianmian li*) which in 1989 amounted to ¥300 to ¥400, the value of a rather expensive watch. By accepting this gift, the bride-to-be accepted the match. The families then scheduled an engagement party. On such occasions the woman, her matchmaker, and several of her elder female relatives (including sisters, sisters-in-law, or aunts, but *not* her mother), went to the man's house and inspected his family's house, land, and property. After a banquet the matchmaker introduced the bride-to-be to all of the man's elder female relatives, each of whom gave her a gift of cloth. That evening or the following day, the fiancé, either in person or through the matchmaker, gave the woman's household part of the brideswealth, usually about ¥1,000. This occasion was also a public declaration of the engagement (*biao tai*). The fiancé's household notified their friends and fellow villagers, and many came over in the days preceding the event and gave the head of his household some gift-money.

The next day the fiancé and his matchmaker usually went to the woman's house for a *ren qin* (recognition of relatives). On such occasions the man met his fiancée's parents, ate a meal, and was given his own "meeting gift" of ¥300 to ¥400. At this point the couple was considered engaged and waited until they reached legal age (twenty-two for men and twenty for women) to marry. During the engagement period the woman was expected to make four formal visits a year to her fiancé's house.[6] During such visits the man first went to the woman's house, perhaps bringing some food gifts to give to her parents. The woman's parents might give him ¥30 or a set of clothes. Upon returning to the man's house, the woman and her future parents-in-law exchanged similar gifts. She then ate a meal at their house before he took her home.

After the couple became old enough to legally register for marriage (local officials allowed people to add a year to their age after each January 1, so most people registered in early January and held their weddings before spring festival), they went to the township marriage bureau and registered. If their registration was approved, the groom gave the bride the rest of the brideswealth (usually about ¥2,000 more) and the families went about arranging the wedding. The bride and her household generally used the brideswealth to buy furniture for the dowry, often adding to it themselves.[7] The groom's household also might buy additional furniture. Which household bought what furniture and exactly how much the brideswealth should be were topics subject to much negotiation. Thus these figures are only approximations. They are, however, comparable to those reported elsewhere in rural China during the 1980s (Fei 1986:5; Thireau 1988:308; Yan 1993:196). That everyone I spoke to reported figures in the same range perhaps indicates the lack of class differentiation during the 1980s in Fengjia. In general, friends and relatives of the bride's family delivered the dowry the day before the wedding. The groom's family feted the deliverers and gave them each gifts of ¥5 to ¥10.

The day before the wedding the bride's household sponsored a dowry party. At that time many of the bride's family's fellow villagers, friends, and relatives gave the head of the bride's household gift-money. In addition, the bride's aunts and her maternal grandmother's family usually gave her quilts or quilt covers to go with her dowry.

The wedding ceremony itself was sponsored by the groom's household. Fellow villagers gave gift-money to the head of the household. As on the day of the engagement, all of the groom's elder female relatives gave gifts of cloth to the new bride in addition to the gift-money that they gave to the head of the household. The personal friends of the groom, from both inside and outside the village gave the groom congratulatory gifts. These could be quite expensive (as much as ¥60), though often several friends would join to buy one present. In 1988–90 the village committee likewise gave one of these presents to each groom in the village. In the wedding of the son of an official who worked in the township seat but lived in the village, friends of the groom's father also gave congratulatory presents. The groom's family invited all who pitched in on congratulatory presents to "hexijiu" (drink the wine of happiness)—the final event of the wedding day. At most of the weddings I went to, three separate records were kept: one for the congratulatory presents, one for the fellow villagers' presents, and one for other gifts. Finally, a present of noodles was often given to the bride by women who had previously married out of (and into) the same village as the bride. One such woman told me this gift embodied sympathy for the new bride's awkward situation. The bride's family gave no gifts to the groom's family on the day of the wedding.

Talking about Gifts and *Guanxi*

The language used to talk about gifts and *guanxi* likewise points to the congruence between feelings of friendship and economic exchange in *guanxi,* and the elements of virtuosity and timing in the art of gift giving. The term *laiwang* (coming and going) when referring to *guanxi* could mean the exchange of gifts, the exchange of visits, or the exchange of *ganqing* (human feeling) between friends. When talking about how to deal with *guanxi* and gift giving, people often used the phrase "*zenme lai zenme wang*" meaning to treat people as they treat you. Sometimes I would be confused by this phrase and ask if it referred to reciprocal visiting, the exchange of gifts, or feelings and attitudes toward the other person. Almost always the reply was "It's all the same" (*yige yisi*). Descriptions of *guanxi* as being close (*jin*) and, therefore, having a high level of *ganqing* and being reliable (being able to count on it for material support and favors) also overlapped in several situations. For example, in response to the question "Who will you get to deliver the dowry?" the two most common replies were someone who had a close *guanxi* and someone who was reliable (*kekaode*). After a while I began to realize that people were using these terms interchangeably. As with *laiwang,* when I asked what was the difference between these two terms, I got the reply "It's all the same" (*yige yisi*). The language here is certainly not a local phenomenon. In his investigation of the political uses of *guanxi* and *ganqing* in a rural Taiwanese township during the early 1970s, Bruce Jacobs (1979) reports the use of practically identical phrases.

Finally, consider the following descriptions of people who gave or received unusually many or unusually few presents. Of a teacher who received about ¥1,200 in gift-money on the occasion of his youngest daughter's marriage, several men commented, "He handles his *guanxi* very well." Of a young man who received relatively few congratulatory presents on his wedding, one said, "He does not handle *guanxi* very well." In these statements not only is giving gifts directly related to handling *guanxi,* but the dimension of skill is also clearly indicated. A few days after the 1989 spring festival I went to see a local official, accompanied by a couple who were going to town on another errand. The official's wife gave the woman some foodstuffs as a present. The woman resisted accepting them, but the local official told his wife to "just put them in the car," thus forcing the gift. On the way back everyone seemed quite pleased and the woman's husband said of the official, "[He] is very polite and really knows how to make friends." Again, the skillful use of gifts to establish friendly feelings was praised as artistry.

Case Studies

This section discusses cases emblematic of the full range of gift-giving practices I saw in Fengjia. At most ritual events, the hosts set up an accounting table and kept lists of who gave what gifts. My knowledge of these cases comes from reviewing such lists. At first I was surprised that people would share these lists with me, but I later surmised that many villagers enjoyed discussing their gift networks; they viewed them as accomplishments. Moreover, as Yan (1993:45) comments, gift lists were sometimes used like photo albums; they commemorated family reunions and were meant to be reviewed.

The first case is the wedding of a young man whose education ended after junior high school and whose family did no work outside of farming. As a result the groom and his family had no connection with a large network of classmates or coworkers. Thus, most of the people who came to the wedding were relatives and fellow villagers. However, the groom's father had four brothers and the groom himself was popular in the village. Sixty people gave the head of the household a total of ¥350 in gift-money. Most people gave ¥5, but the groom's four paternal uncles each gave ¥10, while one of the groom's maternal aunts gave ¥20. When I asked why she gave more than everyone else, the groom said because she was especially close to his mother. All of the groom's elder female relatives also gave the bride ¥7 to ¥8 worth of cloth. In all, seventy-five people gave or pitched in on congratulatory gifts. The largest single giver was the groom's best friend (a fellow villager and classmate in junior high school) who gave a large glass-framed decoration by himself.

A second case involves the dowry party for the youngest daughter of a retired teacher. The daughter had graduated from college and had just been assigned a teaching job in the prefectural seat. Her father said she was the first woman in the village to marry a man of her own choosing (though she and her husband still relied on matchmakers to handle the wedding arrangements). The young woman had three older brothers who had already married and were living in separate households in the village. The bride's classmates and coworkers were going to throw a separate party for her when she returned to the prefectural seat, and thus they were not present at this event. However, in addition to relatives, many of the father's former coworkers and students came. I did not get an exact total, but approximately ninety people gave over ¥1,200 in gift-money. Many of the bride's older female relatives also gave quilts for her dowry. Monetary gifts ranged from ¥5 to ¥20 for fellow villagers and from ¥20 to ¥30 for close relatives. Three exceptional gifts of ¥200 each were made by the bride's three older brothers. They said that they were beginning to carry out the duty of supporting their father in his old age (*shanyang*). On two other occasions I also saw sons who had already moved out of their parents' homes giving their elderly parents large amounts of gift-money.

When asked why so many gave more than the usual ¥5, people gave two sorts of answers. One was because this retired teacher handled his *guanxi* with others especially well (*ta guanxi gao de man hao*). The second was that people were just repaying him in the same amounts that he had given them on various earlier occasions (*zenme lai zenme wang*). When I asked for help in resolving the differences between these statements, Teacher Feng pointed out that there really was not any difference. To have good *guanxi* with people and to exchange a large quantity of money on various festival occasions were parts of the same process.

A third case is a twelfth-day party that celebrated the birth of a baby boy to the wife of a young teacher who still lived with his parents in one household. In general, gift giving at these events was on a smaller scale than at weddings or dowry parties. Guests gave eggs and fried dough sticks to the teacher's father (as a present to the young mother) and/or gave money to the young mother (for the baby) when they went in to see the newborn. In all, about fifty people gave gifts. Most gave twenty eggs, but the relatives from the young mother's natal home (*niangjia ren*) gave thirty eggs each. Most people gave ¥3 to ¥5 when they saw the baby, but one man gave ¥10. This man was the father of the fiancé of the teacher's younger sister. The teacher said that he gave more than others in order to help establish (*jianli*) the *guanxi* between his family and that of his son's fiancée.

The final case regards the decisions of a young man about whom to give to and how much to spend on congratulatory gifts. I give him the pseudonym Ming. In a two-day span, three men were to be married. One was from the same team as Ming;[8] moreover, this groom's bride was from the same town as Ming's own fiancée. The other two grooms were from different teams and had no particular *guanxi* with Ming. All were slightly older than he, so none of them had been Ming's classmate.

At first Ming was just going to chip in with two other friends to buy a painted glass decoration for the groom from the same team. However, after more careful consideration Ming decided to chip in on a present with three other friends for one of the grooms not on his team, and to buy an expensive painted glass decoration with just one other friend for the groom who was on his own team. Ming explained his decision: now people were buying more and more presents. Though he didn't feel obligated to buy one for the groom from the other team, some of his friends were buying him one, thus making this groom the friend of a friend from the same village. By chipping in on this present, Ming could confirm this *guanxi* and have one more friend. So "giving was better than not giving." In the case of the groom from the same team, Ming said that he had just discovered that his fiancée was friends with this groom's bride. Since in the future his own wife and his teammate's wife would bring their families closer together, he decided to buy an expensive present.

Discussion

Perhaps the first point that could be made is that the closer the *guanxi* the bigger the gift. Close relatives tended to give more than friends, and those who wished to claim a close friendship gave more than those who didn't. Whenever I asked why one person gave more than another, the answer almost invariably was "because so and so's *guanxi* is closer." However, this point is potentially misleading. On the one hand, the correspondence between closeness of *guanxi* and size of gift should be seen as constitutive and not simply representational; a large gift did not merely "stand for" the unchanging reality of a close *guanxi*, it constituted or reconstituted the *guanxi*. To not give the gift would have altered the *guanxi*. Gifts, in their embodiment of the desired closeness of a *guanxi*, helped construct that *guanxi*. On the other hand, there was more to the constitution of *guanxi* than gift size; a person could not create a *guanxi* ipso facto with anyone at any time just by giving a large gift. The circumstances and timing had to be right. When Ming gave the husband of his fiancée's friend a large congratulatory gift, he seized an opportunity to strengthen a *guanxi* that, because of other circumstances, had the potential to be deepened. Thus large gifts constituted close relations, but not in and of themselves.

In any case, this capacity of gifts to realize *guanxi* allowed several types of action to be taken through the giving of gifts. On the one hand, by giving identical gifts, givers could claim an equality among themselves in their *guanxi* with the gift receiver. In each case where I saw sets of brothers giving gifts to their father or one of their other brothers, they always gave the same amount. For one to give more than the others would declare one of the relations to be closer than the others. On the other hand, by giving more than is typical, one could acknowledge or assert the closeness of a *guanxi*. Thus, when deciding how much to spend on congratulatory gifts or how much gift-money to give, Fengjia residents considered how close the *guanxi* was (which perhaps had been defined on previous giving occasions), how close the *guanxi* could be, and how close they wanted it to be. This calculation was then viewed in a comparative fashion vis-à-vis what others were giving. Likewise, when relatives from a woman's natal home gave more eggs than anyone else on the occasion that marked the birth of the woman's child, they asserted that their *guanxi* was close enough to be counted on, and should be counted on as a first resort, if the woman for some reason needed any help. As discussed above, to say their *guanxi* could be counted on was also to say that it was very close.

There were at least two general strategies that households adopted in gift giving. One was to use records to keep track of what others had given them in the past, and when the occasion arose, to give back the exact equivalent of what had been given. Several of the households I spoke with used their records in this way. Others took a more expansive strategy. They always tried to give more than had been given to them. One man, who was an official in the township seat, went so far as to say that one should strain one's economic capacities to give as much as one could to as many people as one could. When his youngest son got married, this man received so many congratulatory gifts that even after hanging them in all the rooms of his own house and each of his three son's houses, he still had piles left over. My general impression was that those whose work necessitated social networks outside of the village (such as local officials and the teacher whose youngest daughter's marriage is discussed above) were more likely to have this sort of expansive style than peasants whose work kept them involved mainly in village and family social networks.

In addition to managing the closeness of existing *guanxi*, gifts were also used in establishing new *guanxi*. The marriage process was the prime example of this use of gifts. Marriage was not just a relation between husband and wife, but rather between two families. To allow for the establishing of *guanxi* between various households of both families, the engagement process created many opportunities for different people to give different gifts. As discussed earlier, the groom gave gifts to the bride, the bride's parents gave gifts to the groom, the groom's parents gave gifts to the bride, and the groom's elder female relatives gave gifts to the bride. These gifts were both numerous and large. In addition, if one of the two families had an event in which people give gift-money, the other family would send a representative to give some. On three separate occasions (including the twelfth-day party discussed above), the person who gave the most gift-money at a given event was the father of the fiancée of a member of the host household.

Next consider the giving of cloth to the bride when she was introduced to her husband's older female relatives. Recall the importance of kinship terms in the defining and acknowledging of *guanxi*. In both the engagement ceremony and the marriage ceremony, the bride was likely to be formally introduced to her older female relatives. I saw this introduction done twice and was told that it was a part of every marriage ceremony and most engagement ceremonies. Thus many people went through it twice. Even in a wedding where the family had abandoned most of the ceremony on the grounds that it was "feudal," this formal introduction still took place. In it each of the groom's elder female relatives gave the new bride a piece of cloth. As each gave her a piece of cloth the groom's mother introduced them, saying, for example, "This is your *gugu* [father's sister]. You call her *gugu*." The bride then responded by addressing her new relatives with the appropriate term.

Though I cannot say how widespread this exact ceremony was, Isabelle Thireau describes a similar custom in rural Guangdong:

> Chinese custom requires the bride to worship her husband's ancestors and pour tea to her parents-in-law and other relatives as soon as she enters her new house. Raising a cup of tea with both hands, she offers it to her mother-in-law saying "Mother-in-law please drink . . . Everyone who is offered tea naturally gives the bride in return a red envelope with money or jewelry. This custom has persisted until today. (1988:309)

Rubie Watson (1986:626) similarly emphasizes the ritualized exchanges of kinship terms in rural Hong Kong wedding ceremonies, though in the ceremonies she describes only men gave red envelopes (R. Watson 1981:602). In a fictionalized account of a Shaanxi village during the 1980s, Jia Pingao (1992:289) depicts a ritual for creating adoptive "dry" (*gan*) kinship relations. In it the adoptive father-to-be prepares many gifts and carries them to his future adoptive child's house. Upon arrival, the child's mother accepts the gifts and the child bows down, kowtows (see chapter 4), and utters the kinship term "adoptive father" (*gan die*). In all of these accounts, the construction of new kinship relations involves the exchange of a respectful use of a kinship term (by the younger) for a gift (from the older).

The role of the gift in the establishment of the kinship relation here is to create the obligation and thus the basis for respect that the younger generation owes to the older. As Bourdieu (1977:171–197; 1990:105) writes of gift giving everywhere, and as I was told in both Fengjia and elsewhere in China, the most insulting thing one can do upon receiving a gift is to return a gift of exactly equal value within a day or two. A gift given from one person to another creates an outstanding obligation and, thus, *guanxi*. To immediately return a gift in kind is to immediately erase the obligation and thus negate the *guanxi*.

In the case of kinship relations between older and younger, an ideal *guanxi* is that of the older caring for the younger until maturity, thereby establishing an obligation that is repaid through respect and care in old age. In establishing the new kinship relations of affinal ties, elders gave gifts in an attempt to create an obligation that would be the basis for the respect granted in the use of relational terms of address. The gifts of cash and clothes from the bride's parents to the groom and from the groom's parents to the bride, and the gifts of cloth from the groom's elder female relatives to the bride all served this purpose. Furthermore, the number and size of gifts was roughly congruent with the extent of the deference the older hope to elicit from the younger. Gifts from the groom's parents to the bride were the largest because the deference they desire from their daughter-in-law would be expected on a daily basis. Other *guanxi* in which either contact was less frequent or the difference in age was only one of years and not of generations, were marked by smaller gifts. The most distant affinal relationships marked by kinship terms, such as those between older and younger brothers-in-law, lacked gift giving altogether but did involve *guanxi*-constructing banquets.

Sinological anthropologists have long argued over whether monetary gifts to the bride's family before a marriage were best viewed as purchasing the bride's labor, and hence called "brideprice," or as endowing the new couple through the dowry, and hence called "bridewealth" or indirect dowry (M. Cohen 1976; Freedman 1966; Goody 1990; Han and Eades 1992; Yan 1993). Sociologists of rural China have tended to see these gifts as bride prices that purchase all, or part of, the bride's labor power. Parish and Whyte (1978:180–192), for example, argue that high bride prices especially indicate the complete transferral of the bride from one family to another and consequently the end of all obligation on the part of the daughter to her natal family. Building on Whyte and Parish's work, Chan, Madsen, and Unger (1984:189–191) argue that in Chen Village, Guangdong Province, because brides who married in their natal village continued to provide labor and resources to their natal families, the rise of intravillage marriages led to a reduction of bride prices. I believe the language of *guanxi* and *ganqing* provides a more satisfying way of examining the problem. In 1988–90 Fengjia, there were high "bride prices" in both inter- and intravillage marriages. I would say that these gifts should be seen as a *guanxi* claim on one's future daughter-in-law, while spending a lot on the dowry should be seen as a counter claim. As mentioned earlier, Ellen Judd (1989) argues that a woman's natal home and mother-in-law's home (*pojia*) made competing claims on their daughter's (daughter-in-law's) time and services. The giving of more eggs than anyone else by people from the mother's natal home at twelfth-day parties likewise contributed to these competing claims. Describing marriage gifts as a form of payment misses the eventual transfer of wealth to the younger generation in addition to portraying kinship relations as little more than commodity transactions. Describing marriage gifts as a form of endowment accurately captures the transfer of wealth to the younger generation but misses the *ganqing* and *guanxi* debts the young couple owes to both sets of parents. Understanding marriage payments as part of the never-ending cycle of creating, manipulating, and relying upon *guanxi* and *ganqing* gives a more accurate picture.

The obligation-generating role of gifts was also related to the style involved in the different types of gifts. Cash and/or clothes, as given to the younger generation in the engagement process and as given by villagers to each other on various occasions as gift-money, created an unfulfilled obligation that could only be properly repaid at a future unspecified date. As such, Fengjia residents used these gifts to create and maintain *guanxi*. Food, given to the elderly, the ill, and women recuperating from childbirth acknowledged that an already existing obligation could be counted on in time of need. A notable exception to this scheme were the sizeable gifts in cash in the form of gift-money given by sons who had already moved out of their parents' house to their parents on the occasion of a younger sibling's marriage. This cash actually was part of the repayment of the debt owed to one's parents.

Cloth given by older women to younger women also acted to establish *guanxi*. However, as a gift given only by women, cloth had further overtones. Cloth required the labor of women to become useful. Cloth given to the bride on her wedding was often made into clothes for the bride by her mother-in-law. Hence, gifts of cloth utilized a medium crucial to labor exchange and labor obligations among women. In many respects cloth was a medium of *guanxi* production controlled almost exclusively by women. Weiner and Schneider (1989) argue that cloth cross-culturally constitutes significant gendered media of material and symbolic exchange. Chapter 5 returns to the implications of this control.

The value of gifts used in establishing new relationships illuminates another aspect of *mianzi* and its relation to *ganqing*. Michelle Rosaldo (1984) has defined emotions as embodied thoughts. In the case of *ganqing* in Fengjia gift giving, these thoughts were both memories of past *ganqing* flows and promises for the future. The prominent display of gifts in families' homes as well as in the village committee building, announced the extent of the hosts' *guanxi*, of their potential network for future material exchange, and visibly embodied the memory of *ganqing* past. When relationships were just being established, no memories of past *ganqing* flows existed. Without a preexisting relationship, non-related rural families lacked *mianzi* to face each other and allow *ganqing* to flow. Hence, intermediaries must be used. By establishing obligations that took time to fulfill, the extensive giving at the beginning of relationships created a period of indebtedness during which flows of *ganqing* could begin. In this sense such giving created *mianzi*, which in turn acted as a starting point for *guanxi*. After the establishment of affinal *guanxi*, the intermediaries could be bypassed.

In conclusion, I return to the most basic claim of part I: that *guanxi* unite material obligation and *ganqing*. This chapter describes many gift-giving practices. Some created *guanxi*, some altered *guanxi*, some maintained *guanxi*, and some acknowledged *guanxi*. Some of these *guanxi* were hierarchical family *guanxi*, while others were (more or less) egalitarian *guanxi* between friends. This diversity in *guanxi* corresponded to a wide range of gift-giving practices. However, despite this diversity, or rather at the basis of this diversity, was congruence between material exchange and *ganqing*. There was a congruence between the size of gifts, the burden of obligation, the strength of feeling that either existed or that the parties hoped to develop, the closeness of the *guanxi*, and the dependability of the *guanxi*. In pointing out this congruence, I do not want to assert that there were no instances of unfilial sons, of daughters-in-law who hated their mothers-in-law, or of people who manipulated *guanxi* purely for material gain. In fact, avoiding such occurrences was a reason for maintaining good *guanxi* through wise and faithful gift giving. Rather the point is that the significance of giving and accepting gifts, and the resulting strategies for managing *guanxi* through the giving of gifts, invoked a world in which these assumptions, this congruence, held true. In this sense, gift giving in 1988–90 Fengjia was an example of the types of strategies and practices that exist when congruence between material exchange and *ganqing* are assumed.

4 "Kowtowing"

The Chinese word *ketou,* usually translated as "kowtow," means literally "to knock one's head" and refers to a bodily gesture in which one performs a kneeling bow and (at least in Qing dynasty court ritual) touches one's head to the ground.[1] The sycophantic connotations of the English usage reflect Western misunderstandings of the *ketou* in imperial Chinese practice. James Hevia (1994:118) demonstrates the grip of this misinterpretation when he quotes a 1988 review of Bertolucci's *The Last Emperor* in which even so preeminent a sinologist as the late John K. Fairbank describes the "full kowtow" performed in the opening scene as a "ritual of abject servitude." Hevia traces Fairbank's interpretation to misunderstandings of the *ketou* by eighteenth-century English diplomats and merchants.

Carma Hinton's documentary, *Small Happiness,* filmed in another North China village during the 1980s, likewise presents the *ketou* in a less than positive light.[2] In the wedding scene a relative of the groom reads a list of the groom's ancestors' names aloud. The bride and groom, standing side by side, kneel on a mat after each name is read. The groom kneels without assistance. In contrast the bride, though seemingly willing to kneel on her own, is pushed down repeatedly. A rowdy crowd of the groom's relatives, friends, and neighbors watches, talks, and laughs. At the conclusion of the scene, Hinton cuts to a series of interviews with young local women. They assert that there is little choice but to *ketou* in one's wedding ceremony. If one didn't *ketou* voluntarily and quickly, one would be pushed.

The scene is ambiguous. However, as part of a movie about the difficulties of rural Chinese women, Westerners might easily read these *ketou* as forced displays of servility. Indeed, in classes where I presented the film many students did just that. Certainly the violence of such forced *ketou* served patriarchy by usurping the bride's initiative. However, I would argue that the "abject servitude" interpretation of *ketou* is inappropriate even in this case. While not advocating forced *ketou* at weddings nor diminishing the difficulties of Chinese rural women, I would like to suggest that this widespread judgment of the *ketou* properly explains neither why modern northern Chinese villagers, both male and female, perform *ketou* on many occasions, nor why brides are averse to performing *ketou* at their weddings.

This chapter presents the *ketou* of 1988–90 Fengjia as a type of *guanxi*-producing practice that enables villagers to structure and restructure subjectivities. I suggest that the *ketou* is an act of social creativity rather than self-destruction, that its performance empowers the one who performs it rather than displaying his or her abject servitude, and that it is more often performed by socially confident individuals than the weak.

Let me begin by reiterating the terminology of Sun Lung-kee (1987), described in the introduction. For Sun, the *xin* or heart/mind and locus of individual motivation is always defined socially through the *ganqing* of *guanxi*. In addition to constituting individual heart/minds, *guanxi* also generate the boundaries (ever shifting) of the group of people whose "magnetic field of human feeling" (*renqingde cilichang*) constitute individual heart/minds. In short, *guanxi* generate both the individual and the social; it is through the managing of *guanxi* that *ketou* subjectify.

Ketou in Fengjia

In 1989, Fengjia residents distinguished two types of bodily decorum: a bow (*jugong*) and *ketou*. A bow involved bending from the waist while standing. A *ketou* was a bow of the head while kneeling on one or both knees. Though any kneeling bow counted as a *ketou*, on at least two occasions I saw elder villagers do a fuller *ketou*, which included three bows in each of three directions. When asked why younger villagers didn't do this style of *ketou*, one old man responded "because they never learned how," an explanation that can be accepted literally as far as it goes.

Before 1949 there were no bows in Fengjia, only *ketou*. When the CCP came to power they wanted to end arranged marriages in the countryside. As part of this effort, they encouraged changes in the wedding ceremony itself, including the substitution of bows for *ketou*. In the (re)invention of ritual life that occurred after the restrictions of the Cultural Revolution ended, villagers continued the use of bows in wedding ceremonies. Though it no longer demanded the substitution of bows for *ketou,* the post-Mao state still pronounced arranged marriages illegal. Thus, parents still needed to claim the degree to which they controlled their children's spouse selection was not "arranging" a marriage.[3] By asserting that the marriage was a matter of "free choice," bows by the bride and groom (as opposed to *ketou*) helped make this claim.

Other than the claim that bows make about "free marriage," I view post-1978 bows and *ketou* as similar. Both constructed *guanxi* in a similar manner, and both were seen by local nonpeasants as "feudal" practices. Both count as a type of *bai,* a verb I translate as "to embody respect for." In a wedding the bride and groom *bai* various groups of people by bowing; on other occasions people *bai* by performing *ketou.*

In Fengjia, I observed *ketou* or bows on four occasions: ancestral offerings, funerals, weddings, and the Chinese New Year (aka spring festival, *chunjie*). I also observed *ketou* in regional Buddhist temples located outside of Fengjia. Each temple had statues of its own combination of Buddhas, bodhisattvas, and arhats. Those wanting to create a *guanxi* with a specific Buddha, bodhisattva, or arhat usually approached the image of that being, knelt down on a pad provided for the purpose of performing *ketou,* performed a full *ketou,* and placed some money in a nearby donation box. In brief, in Buddhist temples people combined *ketou* with gift giving in a ritual practice specific to the production of *guanxi* with Buddhist beings. As Ahern (1981) describes in her discussion of Taiwanese religion, humans manage relationships with "gods, ghosts and ancestors" through the same methods that they manage *guanxi* with each other.

In the ancestral offerings performed in 1988–90 Fengjia,[4] one or more adult members of a family, sometimes accompanied by a male child, walked out to a point near the site of that family's ancestral grave. They usually brought a basket containing yellow paper and some food (cooked noodles or dumplings) and liquor, drew a circle with a cross in the middle, wrapped some of the food in the paper and lit it, knelt down and performed *ketou* while saying the relational kinship names of those ancestors who were on their minds. After the paper was burnt, they got up, poured out some liquor, and scattered some of the remaining food on the crossed circle, and left.

Funerals were long and complicated. Here it is enough to note that in 1988–90 Fengjia most funerals had a time for male friends and relatives to *ketou* in family groupings in front of a memorial image of the deceased, and a time to *ketou* collectively at the place where the ashes were buried. In addition, the morning after the funeral the immediate family of the deceased (men and women) usually went door to door through the entire village performing a *ketou* to whoever happened to be at home at each house. This latter occasion was the only time I heard of elders presenting a *ketou* to youth. Close relatives usually visited the grave again and performed *ketou* three weeks, five weeks, one hundred days, and one year after the funeral.

In marriage ceremonies there could be both bows and *ketou*. During most 1988–90 Fengjia wedding ceremonies, an offering table was set up in the courtyard of the groom's family's home. Usually the father of the groom (or some other elder male relative if the father were dead) first performed *ketou* before the table. Then the text of the wedding ceremony was read: "Embody respect for heaven and earth, embody respect for your ancestors, embody respect for your father and mother, embody respect for your friends and relatives, embody respect for each other" (*bai tiandi, bai zuxian, bai dieniang, bai qinqi pengyou, huxiang bai*). In descriptions of modern wedding ceremonies by older men and women, after each "embody respect for" the bride and groom should bow before the offering table. However, in the eight ceremonies I saw, the bride never bowed before the offering table, while some of the grooms bowed and others did not.

In Fengjia no one forced either the groom or bride to bow. After the ceremony was read, firecrackers were lit and the couple was considered married, *ketou* or not. In general there was no fuss over the issue. However, in one ceremony there appeared to be considerable tension. In this case the groom's aged paternal grandmother was still alive. Out of respect to her, throughout the day the family included in the wedding every custom and symbolic display the old woman could remember. Other guests constantly commented how they had never seen such and such before and had no idea what it meant. When the time for the ceremony came, the old woman first burned some paper and then did a full *ketou;* her son, the groom's father, then also did a full *ketou* (figure 14). However, as the ceremony was read, the bride not only did not bow but, by wearing sunglasses and folding her arms, managed to look defiant rather than embarrassed as most brides do. The groom also just stood there, but in contrast appeared mortified, constantly glancing back and forth between his bride and father. Perhaps in this wedding, because they were so consciously inventing tradition, the family elders especially hoped the young couple would bow.

The final *ketou* discussed here are the *bainian* (embodying respect on Chinese New Year, aka spring festival). On spring festival in 1989 most

Figure 14   Groom's father performing ketou *at wedding.*

families got up before dawn. Upon rising, the younger family members performed *ketou* to members of the older generation in the family. Then, at most houses, *jiaozi* (dumplings) were cooked, firecrackers set off, some paper with *jiaozi* in it was burnt for the ancestors, and breakfast was eaten. After breakfast, people walked around the village to *bainian* (i.e., perform *ketou*) to anyone in the village who was older by both years and generations. People went around the village both singly and in groups. Except for mothers with small or infant male children, these groups were segregated by sex. Unmarried women and girls (who were expected to marry out of the village) did not participate.

I spent the Chinese New Year in the house of an elderly woman who, whether one calculated by age or generations, was one of the oldest people in the village. Hundreds of people came to *ketou* that morning. The activity ranged from ceremonious to rushed and superficial. One old man, almost as old as this woman in years but a generation younger, came over and talked for almost an hour (visitors who came during this interval also performed *ketou* to him) before performing an elaborate *ketou*. On the other extreme was a group of about twenty high school boys. The leaders rushed in and said "we've come to *bainian*," knelt down, and quickly left. The rest, unable to fit in the room, milled about the courtyard and in some cases even failed to *ketou*.

Although most of the villagers came over to *bainian*, some did not. One man who failed to appear was a township official who, though he held a "peasant" household registration (*hukou*), didn't consider himself a peasant. Significantly, when his own sons married, this man did not include those parts of the ceremony that he considered "feudal," including the parts where bowing or *ketou* would take place. In this instance, the official was refusing to participate in a peasant subculture (discussed in chapter 9) of which he considered the *ketou* a part.

During the several days after spring festival most Fengjia residents went to other villages to *bainian* their elder affinal relatives. They brought food gifts, performed a *ketou,* and were treated to a banquet. In all of these spring festival *ketou,* almost as soon as the performer touched his or her knee to the ground, the person to whom the *ketou* was directed urged the performer to get up quickly (*kuai qilai*).

Ketou as *Guanxi*-Producing Ritual

Of the *ketou* in the ancestral offering, Teacher Feng said, "Before it was a superstition, now it generates a meaning/feeling" (*Guoqu shi mixin, xianzai biaoshi yige yisi*). This statement, though apparently simple, says much about what *ketou* and ritual were in 1988–90 Fengjia. In earlier times, ancestor worship was efficacious because of the agency of dead ancestors. In the late 1980s, when most dismissed (at least to me) the agency of dead people, the *ketou* of the past was called a superstition. The *ketou* of the 1980s' ancestral offering may have copied earlier forms, but its significance was new.

The second part of the statement is more complex. The term, "to generate a meaning/feeling" was also used to describe what one did when giving a gift. What gift giving, the *ketou,* and ritual all had in common was that they were all types of *li* (gift as *liwu, ketou* and ritual as forms of *lijie*) and were all ways of working on (creating, maintaining, and improving) *guanxi*. Since *guanxi* were matters of both *ganqing* and social and material obligation, the translation "meaning/feeling" is necessary. The meaning/feeling generated both the idea of what the material obligation involved in the relationship was or should have been, and the *ganqing* of the relationship.

Others described the *ketou* as an embodiment of *jingyi,* a word commonly translated as "respect." However, this translation is accurate only if one emphasizes that this respect is not abstract admiration, but rather a *ganqing* that accompanies the social and material obligation extant within a concrete relationship. During the Cultural Revolution, those with class labels of rich peasant or landlord were prohibited from performing *ketou* at the funerals of poor and middle peasants. If *jingyi* meant only an abstract sort of admiration, as we often take respect to mean, then during the Cultural Revolution landlords might well have been forced to *ketou* at poor peasants' funerals. However, this respect implied a concrete relationship, and the embodiment of it in a *ketou* helped to constitute that relationship. The CCP's ban of landlord *ketou* at poor peasant funerals was an attempt to prevent the formation of (and deny the existence of) cross-class relationships.

The *ketou*'s meaning/feeling or respect constituted relationships and hence, following Sun Lung-kee, both individual heart/minds and "magnetic fields of human feeling." As such, performing a *ketou* could be a powerful act, and in Fengjia it was more likely an assertion of social initiative than an expression of "abject servitude." In fact, several villagers described both the prohibition of landlord *ketou* during the Cultural Revolution and the "tradition" of allowing only men to *ketou* at funerals as restrictions on privileges of the relatively powerless.

Understanding the *ketou* as a type of *li* that worked on *guanxi* and thus on both individual and collective subjects allows us to consider exactly how *ketou* constituted the social world. I submit that *ketou* formed *guanxi* between people by declaring them to be members of the same (hierarchical) group. Recall that *ketou* during spring festival were divided into separate periods for immediate family, village, and affinal relatives. This partition allowed the separate formation of each group. Unmarried women did not perform *ketou* at the village level because it was not clear what village they would belong to after marriage. Performing a *ketou* to one's dead ancestors (in the 1980s deprived of extraworldly agency), though clearly also a form of mourning and an expression of filial piety (*xiao*), was an affirmation of the relationship of the one performing *ketou* to all living members of the family (i.e., the descendants). Likewise, performing a *ketou* to the recently deceased at a funeral was both mourning, filiality, and a reconstitution of the relationships among all of those who performed *ketou* at the same funeral.

At weddings, brides moved from one family to another. Though women usually maintained strong ties with their natal families, at her wedding a bride's primary *guanxi* began shifting from her parents' family to her husband's. At weddings the bride theoretically should have bowed with her husband five times (to heaven and earth, to the ancestors, to mother and father, to friends and relatives, and to each other). If carried out, these five bows would have constituted the bride's relationship to her husband in five ways,[5] announcing them both to be members of the same five subgroups: the entire social world (*tiandi*), the husband's patrilineal family extended indefinitely in time both toward the past and future (*zuxian*), the immediate family of the husband and his father and mother (*dieniang*), the living extended family of the husband projected outward in space by affinal ties and friendships (*qinqi pengyou*), and the immediate family to be constituted by the new bride and groom (*huxiang bai*). The groom's father's *ketou* before the offering table likewise reconstituted his relationships within the patrilineal family.

The hesitancy of brides to *ketou* at their weddings was a very ambiguous act. Even within the context of a single wedding, multiple interpretations are possible. Most said that brides didn't bow at weddings because they were embarrassed (*buhaoyisi*). Some said this embarrassment itself was a "traditional" disposition for brides to assume at weddings. Chapter 9 addresses this sort of emphasis on tradition. Here consider the only woman I met who, by self-assuredly bowing at her wedding, "violated" this "tradition." The young woman in question was well educated (a high school graduate), a hard and able worker, handsome, and outgoing. She said in a boastful but jocular manner, "If you have no shortcomings, you're not afraid to bow even if they [i.e., your new family and friends] are all strangers." Her interpretation again portrays the *ketou* as more of a social initiative than a burden. Only the self-confident dared to boldly assert new relationships with people they didn't know well.

However, other interpretations of wedding bows (or lack thereof) are possible. The timing of the husband's father's *ketou* and resultant reconstitution of the extended patrilineal family was important. By performing a *ketou* just before the ceremony proper, the father focused attention on the bride's changing of membership in patrilineal units. In another interpretation, the wedding bows could then be seen as asserting that the bride was related to her original family only as an affine and not as a member of the same patrilineal unit. A bride's refusing to bow could be seen as resisting this assertion.

Recall that the day before a daughter was to be married, her family usually sponsored a dowry party in which the friends and relatives of the bride's family came over and gave presents both to the bride's family and for the bride's dowry. Because they were about to "lose" a daughter, this event was generally a very sad time for the bride's parents.[6] Immediately after spending a day with parents expressing their sadness at "losing" their daughter, a bride may not have been up to generating the meaning/feeling that would reconstitute her family membership. To do so would have been a slap in the face to her parents.

Here, again, Judd's (1989) discussion of the competing claims that a woman's natal and marital families make on her are relevant. A new bride's heart/mind is almost structurally guaranteed to be troubled by this contradiction. Stockard (1989:22) likewise explores this tension in the Canton Delta, while Blake (1978, personal communication) suggests that in southern China the bride's acting embarrassed, singing marriage laments, and refusing to *ketou* were standard parts of the wedding ceremony that ritually expressed her ambivalence toward leaving her natal family.

In any case, whether one interprets a specific case of reluctance to bow at a wedding as the embodiment of a "traditional" disposition, as a hesitancy to assert one's new relationships, or as a resistance to the negation of one's natal (*niangjia*) relationships, the refusal to bow was only temporary. After a period of time that allowed for a reconstruction of their heart/minds, new brides began to participate in rituals that required performing *ketou* before their husbands' families'—now also their own families'—ancestors.

Every Fengjia resident participated in particular (though openly defined) social groups, particular "magnetic fields of human feeling." Contradictions among these groups could manifest themselves in a hesitancy to *ketou*. The organization of spring festival *ketou* (different times for constituting relationships with different groups), the five separate bows during the wedding ceremony, and the refusal of brides to *ketou* at their weddings all point to these distinct positions.

So far, I have described the *ketou* as a form of *li* that worked by re-creating the membership of social groups, thus acting upon both the group as a whole and the relationships among members of groups. However, performing a *ketou* to live people (as opposed to ancestors and the recently deceased), added another dimension. Here, Bourdieu's concepts of timing and disposition clarify (1977:5–15). When, during the village-level spring festival *ketou*, an old man spent an hour talking with an old woman and then performed a full *ketou*, he not only affirmed a *guanxi* as a fellow villager like any other fellow villager but also worked on his personal *guanxi* with her. Likewise, when members of the younger generation of an immediate family performed *ketou* to their elders, and the elders urged them to quickly rise, individual *guanxi* were mended. Hence, the following statement made to me by a township-level official at a spring festival banquet: "When a daughter-in-law performs *ketou* to her mother-in-law over spring festival, and the mother-in-law tells her to quickly rise, all of the year's contradictions can be resolved in one minute, the family can reunite and resume production." With proper timing, the dispositions that *ketou* revealed could be artfully employed to regenerate *guanxi*. In the book *Shandong Folk Customs* (*Shandong Minsu*), local ethnologists offer a similar explanation for the continued practice of *bainian* in rural Shandong: "the reason the activity of *bainian* continues is that it is able to deepen *ganqing*, eliminate estrangement, and adjust interpersonal *guanxi*" (Fang et al. 1988:6). As in other practices of *guanxi* production, the generation of good *ganqing* re-created specific interpersonal *guanxi*.

5 Weddings, Funerals, and Gender

To the Chinese girl the practical introduction of Christianity will mean even more than to her brother. It will prevent her from being killed as soon as she is born, and will eventually restore her to her rightful place in the affections of her parents.
Arthur Smith (1899:341)

The more one knows Chinese life, the more one realizes that the so-called suppression of women is an Occidental criticism that somehow is not borne out by a closer knowledge of Chinese life.
Lin Yutang (1977 [1936]:139)

Since 1975 this optimistic view of the accomplishments of the Chinese Communist Party (CCP) in liberating women, and of the changes women have experienced, has been gradually dispelled. With the almost simultaneous publication in 1983 of Women, the Family, and Peasant Revolution in China *by Kay Ann Johnson,* Patriarchy and Socialist Revolution in China, *by Judith Stacey, and* The Unfinished Liberation of Chinese Women, 1949–1980 *by Phyllis Andors, this view has been effectively laid to rest.*
Emily Honig (1985:329)

[T]he predominant representation of Asian women as meek and mild silently suffering objects of policy is often the product of scholars' and publishers' blinkered and culturally biased notions of liberation and appropriate female behavior. In the Chinese case, one can also say that the notion of the passive and oppressed traditional woman was also an idealized form in the patriarchal discourse of the Imperial period as well. Moreover, the passive and oppressed Chinese woman has become a commodity subjected to historical bias on the part of the post-1949 redactors.
Louise Edwards (1992:59)

How to write of gender relations in rural China? Does the Western presentation of the subordination of Chinese women support a global feminism, or does it merely justify Christian proselytizing and imperialist intervention? Is the presentation of the strength and power of Chinese women resistance to imperialism, a rejection of feminist analyses, or the broadening and development of feminist thinking?[1] Beyond the political question of how representations of Chinese women are used is an epistemological one: can one assess the position of rural women in Chinese society at all? The literature on the subject divides sharply over the extent of patriarchy in both pre- and post-1949 China. For example, while Kay Ann Johnson (1983) suggests that a patrilineal, patrilocal kinship system kept and continues to keep Chinese rural women firmly subordinated, Jack Goody (1990) argues that focusing on the lineage system has obscured the links of women to their natal families and the power they derived from these links.

Johnson and Goody may disagree about the extent of patriarchy in rural China, but both point to the relation between a patrilineal, virilocal kinship system and the subordination of women in patriarchal power relations. For Johnson, the marital movement of women from one family and village to another marginalizes them in both settings. Because they will move out of their natal families, parents invest less in daughters than in sons. Because they are newcomers in their husbands' families and villages, they lack the stature to compete with men who have consolidated intravillage *guanxi* for more than twenty years. For Goody, because women receive property from and maintain ties to their natal families, the system is not strictly patrilineal, and the power of women is not entirely subordinated to patriarchy. Indeed, one might argue that by positioning themselves between families and villages women can occupy a strategic position. Ellen Judd (1994) presents an intermediate position. Though she acknowledges the importance of female connections, she emphasizes the factors that limit their influence. Not only do men monopolize all of the important political posts and live amongst their brothers and fellow villagers, but notions of propriety that restrict young women's extrahousehold activities further limit female *guanxi* production. In all of these works the role of women's *guanxi* is pivotal. For Judd, women produce *guanxi* but are prevented from consolidating relationships that would drastically increase their social influence. For Johnson, women are isolated and therefore powerless, while for Goody they productively embody the links among families.

I am ambivalent about both the political implications and epistemological possibility of proclaiming either the subordination or liberation of women in 1988–90 Fengjia. I saw instances of women asserting their power and of men dominating women. I wouldn't begin to know how to weigh one against the other. However, though firm conclusions about the positions of women may be impossible,[2] the analysis of gender relations is central to any study of kinship (Collier and Yanagisako 1987) and hence to that of the production of *guanxi* in rural China. Previous chapters have pointed to the separation of women's and men's *guanxi*-producing practices in gift giving, performing *ketou,* and banqueting. This separation both constrained and empowered women. In this chapter I examine how funerals and weddings engendered women's and men's *guanxi* production, and some of the implications of this gendering for the status of women.

During weddings and funerals in the late 1980s, Fengjia residents managed *guanxi* on a large scale. Both rituals included gift giving, banqueting, performing *ketou,* guest/host etiquette, uses of relational kinship terms, and other ritually specific practices of *guanxi* production. In both rituals men's and women's roles differed sharply. More importantly, this differentiation both isolated and linked women and thus both defied and constituted gender difference and patriarchy. The contradictory nature of these rituals manifested itself in the ambivalent subjects they constructed. As Sun Lung-kee would remind us, magnetic fields of human feeling are always overlapping and conflicted. Moreover, these subjects were simultaneously gendered and cross-gendered. Though ritual *guanxi* production was generally sexually segregated, villagers were always already constituted by cross-gendered husband/wife, sister/brother, mother/son, and father/daughter *guanxi*. Women drew on power derived from their *guanxi* with male household members in dealing with nonhousehold women as they drew on power derived from extrahousehold intrafemale *guanxi* when dealing with their menfolk.

Weddings

In 1988–90 Fengjia, weddings marked the establishment of a new household, the ambiguous and perhaps partial transfer of the bride from one family to another, and an opportunity for the groom's family to reconstitute *guanxi* with a wide range of people, including members of the bride's family. To the extent that weddings created an alliance between the bride's and groom's families and that women played an active role in the creation of these *guanxi*, weddings empowered brides and other women. Insofar as they separated the bride from her old family while subjugating her in a new one, they were patriarchal affairs. I discuss first the portions of the wedding that were most promising for women and end with the least.

FEMALE-CENTERED *GUANXI*

Han Min and Jerry Eades (1992) point out that in rural Anhui during the 1980s brides' families increasingly found themselves able to make heavy demands on the grooms' families during marriage negotiations. Han and Eades attribute the empowerment of brides' families to the increased importance of affinal ties and women's productivity under the responsibility system. In Fengjia too, brides' families seemed to have the upper hand in marriage negotiations. The parents of boys often complained about the difficulty of finding spouses for their sons, while the parents of daughters seldom worried. They said that nearby villages, which were not as stable and prosperous as Fengjia, contained many unmarried and increasingly desperate men. Indeed, according to the 1990 census among the adult (fifteen years and older) population living in rural Shandong, there were 5.8 million men who had never married, but only 4.5 million women (State Statistical Bureau 1991:405). In Fengjia most parents managed to find brides for their sons at an early age, though it was an expensive proposition. Brides' parents used the power derived from a lopsided marriage market to insure the future welfare of their daughters. They typically demanded that the groom's family build a separate residence, or at least set off several rooms from the groom's parents' residence for the new couple. They also tried to find sons-in-law who lived in villages close to Fengjia so that they could maintain close *guanxi* with their daughters. Indeed, several villagers said that marriages within the village (between families of different surnames) were becoming increasingly popular.[3]

In addition to demanding a new residence, the brides' families negotiated the purchase of the material goods to outfit it. The groom's family bought some, while others were included in the bride's dowry. The families had to work together to insure that the couple did not end up with, say, two beds but no cabinet or three televisions and no bicycle. However, both sides usually bought more than the negotiated minimums. The bride's family tried to spend considerably more on the dowry than they received in the betrothal gift. A typical dowry might include several large pieces of furniture, such as a bed, dressers, desks, tables, chairs; perhaps a TV, radio, bicycle, and/or sewing machine; and some everyday household items like toiletries and clothes. Some families also included large sums of cash. Thus, brides' families adopted a double strategy. On the one hand, as argued in chapter 3, they gave large dowries in order to maintain a claim on their daughter. On the other hand, they demanded that the husband's family make an even larger investment by establishing a *separate* residence for the new couple. The house was not considered a gift. The building of a separate residence was simply a minimum condition for securing a bride in 1988–90 Fengjia. Indeed, it created the possibility of the new couple's independence from the groom's parents rather than binding them together. Most couples in 1988–90 Fengjia formed separate households (*fenjia*) from the groom's parents within six months of marriage, if they were not already separate from the day of their wedding. Thus, brides' families endeavored to create as bilateral a condition as possible for the new couple. The young bride and groom not only lived separately from the groom's parents but they were also indebted to both of their families. Because of the marriage market, grooms' parents had little choice but to accept these terms. Moreover, because many grooms' families wanted to borrow money, exchange labor, or otherwise rely on their affinal *guanxi,* such arrangements were not entirely disadvantageous to them either.

Indeed, though marked by tension and some divergence of interest, successful marriage negotiations were also a trust-building venture. The wedding ceremony itself provided opportunities to consolidate *guanxi* built on this trust. The day before the wedding the bride's family arranged for some close friends and relatives, usually five to ten men and women, to load the dowry onto horsecarts and deliver it to the groom's family's house. Friends and neighbors of the groom would crowd around the groom's house in anticipation of seeing and making an evaluation of the dowry. When the dowry arrived, the groom's family helped unload it while the people who delivered it were banqueted, at separate tables for men and women, in the groom's family's home. Often the groom's family gave cash gifts of ¥5 to ¥10 to each of the people who delivered the dowry. The groom's family thus established *guanxi* with some close friends and relatives of the bride's family. In addition to the dowry, the bride's family sent large quantities of *laohuoshao,* a type of cookie made from flour and jujube dates sent by the husband's family, onto which was imprinted the double happiness motif.[4] Like the dowry, the *laohuoshao* was composed by the bride's family with raw materials supplied by the groom's family for the benefit of the new couple. Both products embodied the two families' cooperation. On the day of the wedding three separate banquets allowed various members of the bride's and groom's families to consolidate *guanxi*. These banquets included tables for the bride's mother and the groom's mother, the bride's elder brother(s) and the groom's elder brother(s), the bride's matchmaker and the groom's matchmaker, uncles and nephews of the bride and representatives of the groom's family, and the bride's sisters-in-law and groom's sisters-in-law.

For the bride herself, the wedding included not only occasions for constructing *guanxi* with the groom's elder female relatives but also opportunities to reaffirm *guanxi* with women from her own family and village. The day before the wedding at the dowry party (*song hezi*), friends and relatives of the bride and her family visited and gave presents both to the bride's family and for the bride's dowry. Gifts given for the bride's dowry included daily-use products like thermoses and toiletries and beautifully decorated bedding consisting of quilts and a type of thin mattress (*ruzi*). The bedding was made and given by the bride's natal elder female relatives. In some families only women who themselves had given birth to both sons and daughters made this bedding. As such, it embodied hopes for fertility. However, in most families all of the bride's elder female relatives contributed bedding regardless of their personal childbearing histories. In many dowries there were so many quilts and mattresses (once I counted over thirty) that the new couple could never use them all.

These gifts placed *guanxi* claims on the bride that both competed with and complemented the claims made by the bride's affinal elder female relatives. As counter-claims to the resources and person of the bride, they challenged the initiative of the groom's female relatives. However, by enlarging the bride's own *guanxi* network, they extended the pool of *guanxi* resources to which these women had access. In so doing they placed the bride at a nodal point of a network that spanned at least two villages. With their gifts of noodles, Fengjia women who came from the same natal village as the bride reinforced these networks. Because many Fengjia "daughters-in-law" came from a few nearby villages and attended the same junior high school, some women entered Fengjia with a network of friends they had known as children. Thus, these women were not as isolated as those portrayed by Johnson (1983) or even Judd (1994). Though the relative exclusion of women from the *guanxi*-producing activities of public political life reinforced patriarchy, sexually segregated networks also consolidated spheres of female dominance. Women controlled the *guanxi* and hierarchy of these spheres of activity through all-female *guanxi*-producing activities like the giving of cloth and quilts, and all-female banquet tables.

A focus on the importance of women's networks, or even on the ways in which these networks are limited (Judd 1994), suggests a rethinking of Gayle Rubin's (1975) classic reading of Lévi-Strauss's (1969) *Elementary Structures of Kinship*. While Lévi-Strauss proposed that the origins of the incest taboo, kinship, and culture could be found in the exchange of women between groups of men, Rubin saw the roots of patriarchy in this same "traffic in women." Rubin argued that the social relations produced by such a kinship system ensure that men have rights in female kin that women have over neither themselves nor their menfolk. These social relations in turn produce a gendered psychology in which men desire to have women while women desire to be possessed. Since this psychology reproduces patriarchal social relations, this kinship-based patriarchy has continued even in societies where kinship itself has ceased to be of critical political and economic importance. Rubin concludes that ending patriarchy requires modifying the child-raising patterns that produce the gendered psychology. Kinship in Fengjia, as well as the material presented by Judd, suggests other strategies, especially in places where kinship carries critical socioeconomic weight. Rather than focusing on early childhood experiences that supposedly permanently structure a gendered psyche, one could analyze the shaping of social relations themselves. How are women's kin networks constrained or empowered? How is marriage structured as an exchange *of* women *by* men? What keeps even patrilocal marriages from being a mechanism for women to extend their own networks for their own purposes? Insofar as Fengjia parents sought to consolidate the social positions of their daughters, and as Fengjia women formed their own intervillage networks, some alternative starting points for the empowerment of women were already apparent.

AMBIGUOUS TRANSFER

If Fengjia kinship in 1988–90 was not strictly patrilineal, neither was it bilateral. Kinship terminology distinguished between one's son's children (*sunzi, sunnu*), who shared one's surname, and one's daughter's children (*waisheng*), who were placed in the same category as one's sister's children. Village land was allocated to enable agnatically related households to have adjacent plots. Perhaps most importantly, except for intravillage marriages (which were still a minority in 1988–90 Fengjia), brides did move to their husbands' villages. To account for the ambiguities of practical kinship in multisurnamed villages, Judd (1992) suggests describing such kinship as androcentric rather than patrilineal. Whatever the terminology, Fengjia wedding rituals simultaneously celebrated the auspicious establishment of a new household and insinuated the transfer of the bride out of her natal family and into the groom's family. As the examination of wedding ceremony *ketou* demonstrated, this ritual process was fraught with ambiguity and contradictory intent. A more complete portrait of wedding day events confirms this view.

In most 1988–90 Fengjia weddings, the groom's family sent a bridal procession to the bride's house early in the morning. Some families sent borrowed cars, others bicycles or tractors or horsecarts. In one case, the father of the groom arranged for a former student (the father had been an elementary school teacher twenty years earlier), who was now a driver living in a town a hundred kilometers away, to supply and drive the car used in his son's wedding. Whether bicycles, cars, tractors, or horsecarts were used, the groom's family always decorated the vehicles with red paper. The groom, accompanied by three or four older and younger male relatives, rode together to the bride's house. They usually brought a red flag and a gong. Upon entering and exiting their own village, the bride's village, and any village in between, they got off their vehicles and walked slowly through the streets loudly banging the gong. After arriving at the bride's house, they were shown into a north room and given a banquet. Typically, the bride's family arranged for a male of suitable age to accompany the diners (*peike*) while the bride and her family remained in another room.

Meanwhile the groom's family finished their preparations for the wedding. They arranged the furniture and other dowry items in the new couple's bridal chamber (*dongfang*).[5] They also posted wedding couplets on all of the doorways and completed whatever other ritual preparations were necessary for the arrival of the bride. Such bride arrival rituals varied markedly; some families dismissed them entirely, while others included every ritual their elders could remember, even if the specific significance of a given ritual action was not clear. Preparations for the bride's arrival included, in one family or another, placing bricks covered with red paper on the roof of the main gate, hanging firecrackers in the main gate, spreading hay in the bridal chamber, burning paper money, placing a saddle in the doorway, and pasting red paper on the windows of the bridal chamber, among others.

Back at the bride's house, the groom's party finished their breakfast banquet while the bride put on her red wedding outfit. Then the bride, accompanied by a couple of young boys (younger brothers, nephews, or family friends) called *yajiaoche* (literally, "sedan chair guarantors"), returned to the groom's village with the bridal procession. The bridal procession banged their gong on the way home as they did on the way there. After the bridal procession left, the wedding guests from the bride's family prepared to go. The bride's family's wedding party usually included two or three male relatives older than the bride but younger than the bride's father, and two or three female relatives older than the bride but younger than the bride's mother. In the weddings I saw, the bride's parents never attended. The wedding party brought some candy, steamed bread, peanuts, and/or other food products to be placed on the wedding ceremony's ancestral offering table. They traveled to the groom's house separately from the wedding procession.

Elisabeth Croll (1981) has emphasized the continuity between post- and pre-1949 bridal processions. She notes that even if bicycles or cars are substituted for sedan chairs, the bride was still picked up by a vehicle in a procession sent by the groom's family. She argues that what is significant is that the bride does not go to the wedding under her own power. The picking up of the bride by a vehicle sent by the groom's family constructs the marriage as an event controlled and arranged by the elders of the two families. Martin Yang (1945), whose work Croll draws on, describes the pre-1949 sedan chair as a symbol of marital legitimacy. That the parents had arranged the wedding was part of what made the marriage legitimate. The CCP, after gaining control of the countryside, banned sedan chairs in an attempt to reduce parental control of marriages. Croll's reasonable argument is that continued parental control of marriage in the countryside is reflected in the continued use of wedding processions.

However, Fengjia residents saw it somewhat differently. They felt the elimination of sedan chairs was a significant change. Many older residents emphasized that youth did have more of a say in post-liberation marriages than before. One older woman (who had been married before 1949) commented that when one rode in a sedan chair, one was all alone, in the dark; in contrast, when one rode in a car, one rode with other people.[6] She added that young wives could return to visit their natal family more easily than before. Her comments resonate with Robert Weller's (1984) description of the journey from the bride's house to the groom's as creating a ritual state of liminality, in between membership in two households. At least on a psychological level, perhaps riding alone in the dark was more conducive to constructing liminality. More importantly, this woman saw cars as making a more ambiguous statement about the nature of the transfer of the bride. After a car ride, the bride could visit her natal home more easily.

Some of the rituals enacted upon the bride's arrival in the groom's village seemed concerned with effecting the bride's transferal, while others had more to do with blessing the new couple. In two of the eight weddings I saw, the groom's mother walked around the bridal procession vehicle three times counterclockwise while burning some spirit money. One of these women said this burning brought good fortune. In other weddings small stools were brought out so that the bride would not step directly from the vehicle onto Fengjia village ground. Weller (1984), among others, has argued that this action prevents the possibility of dirt from the bride's natal village contaminating the groom's village and thus helps effect the bride's transferal to the groom's village and family. In all the weddings I saw the bride's arrival drew a big crowd. People (mostly women) gathered around to catch a glimpse of their new fellow villager. Typically it was difficult to do, as the crowd around the vehicle was too large. Furthermore, the bride usually bowed her head and covered her face with a scarf. Denied their initial glimpse, the crowd of onlookers followed as the groom's mother led the bride from the vehicle to the main door of the groom's house. Often, as she entered the main door, friends of the groom who were standing on the roof of the doorway lit firecrackers and threw candy at the bride. The bride would then be shown into the bridal chamber, where she remained until the ceremony proper. The onlookers packed into the bridal chamber too, still eager for a glimpse. Often the bride continued to hide her face. Twice I saw male villagers intervene at this point and force the bride to remove her scarf and look at the crowd. In all cases the crowd eventually got their glimpse and dispersed.

While waiting for the ceremony, much could happen to the bride. Often, other young Fengjia women who had married out of the same natal village as the bride came to the bridal chamber with bowls of noodles and tried to console her. Sometimes male teenagers came in and taunted the bride in anticipation of the blatant harassment they would carry out later that night. Eventually the female members of the bride's family's wedding party arrived and entered the bridal chamber to console the bride.

At noon, the wedding ceremony proper (described in chapter 4) was held. In the weddings I saw, the male guests from the bride's family never entered the courtyard to see the ceremony. They remained inside a north room, drinking tea and smoking, and waited for the post-ceremony banquet. The female guests from the bride's side accompanied the bride to the courtyard, but stood well to the side. The bride's guests thus registered their collective ambivalence regarding her incorporation into the groom's family; but note that the women played more of a mediating role than the men. After the ceremony proper came the ceremony in which female cloth gifts were given and kinship names were introduced (described in chapter 3) and the wedding banquet. In the afternoon most of the guests dispersed while the bride and her wedding party returned to her natal home. The bride returned later that night with her mother and older brothers for a final banquet.

DIFFICULT ENDING

From the bride's perspective the worse part of the wedding occurred after that final evening banquet. Then her mother and older brothers returned to their village and teenaged boys from the groom's village arrived and began the *naofang* (literally "stirring up the bridal chamber"). Notably, none of the bride's natal *guanxi* were present; she was completely isolated. During the *naofang,* the teenagers tried to extort candy, jujube date cookies (*laohuoshao*), money, and cigarettes from the bride by twisting and painfully squeezing her hands and arms. In all of the *naofang* I saw, the bride came prepared with a lot of candy, etc., and tried to maintain a jocular attitude, but also always broke down at least once and cried. The groom usually appeared mortified. On one occasion a groom went to another room and lay down with tears in his eyes. Other grooms passed out cigarettes and candy nervously and quickly, trying to divert extorters from their wives. Only once did I see a groom intervene on the part of his bride. One young man told me "the groom is afraid that people will say he dotes too much on his wife." In general, around midnight the groom tried to end the *naofang* and start the last event of the long wedding day, the *hexijiu* (drinking the wine of happiness ceremony). Usually several close friends of the groom, who would be in their early twenties, came for this event. However, the rowdy teenagers from the *naofang* remained. At the *hexijiu,* the friends of the groom toasted the newlyweds and tried to get them to touch or kiss while the rowdy teenagers looked on. After a final toast everyone left and the wedding day ended. One *naofang* and *hexijiu* that I observed proceeded as follows:

The room was crowded with teenaged boys (the high schools and junior highs were now on vacation) who would corner the bride and take turns demanding candy, *laohuoshao*, cigarettes, and money, and extort them by squeezing and twisting her hands. She tried her best to laugh along and put up resistance (by refusing to give out things until a given boy actually twisted her hands or at least demanded and threatened many times), but several times she ended up crying. One of her crying spells lasted several minutes, during which one of the older boys tried to talk her out of it by claiming that it was all in jest. Nobody showed much sympathy, including her husband who ran around passing out cigarettes, avoiding the people who were abusing his wife and looking very anxious. The boys who weren't extorting candy shot the breeze and did a lot of play fighting, creating a generally rowdy atmosphere. Several times the groom's older sister walked in and looked like she wanted to help but couldn't do anything. One of the bride's girlfriends (from the same natal village) tried to come in, but the boys wouldn't let her. A mother of one of the younger boys came and dragged him home. One of the groom's friends said it might have been worse if I had not been there.

This went on from about nine to midnight, at which point the groom brought out a whole bunch of candy and convinced everyone it was time to *hexijiu*. He set up eight chairs around a square table with some sweet red wine and four plates of cold food. The friends of the groom argued over who should sit where. Finally six of them agreed to sit down. The bride and groom sat together at the north end of the table with the groom in the upper chair. Next the friends, in clockwise order, began making toasts and "presenting problems" (to the bride and groom), such as eating a piece of meat at the same time, that would make them touch or kiss. A particularly difficult one involved blowing a cigarette into an empty beer bottle. The bride and groom had to hold their heads cheek to cheek and blow steadily and softly at just the right pressure to move the cigarette. Several times one of them blew too hard and the air pressure made the cigarette pop out, forcing them to start over. The bride looked extremely mortified. She did not want to come too close to kissing her husband in front of all of these strange boys and men. Her hands trembled when she picked up her wine glass (perhaps they hurt too much from the twisting). After each of the six friends had made one toast (and presented one problem), the groom made a final toast thanking everyone for coming. Everyone left.[7]

The *naofang* isolated and subordinated the bride in more ways than one. In a village where age hierarchies could be important, she was forced to submit to boys younger than her. By suggesting that neither her former natal connections nor her new husband could support her, the event magnified her isolation. The *naofang* also prevented the groom from privileging his new *guanxi* with his wife over his old relationships with fellow villagers. Margery Wolf (1972, 1985) has described rural women's inability to depend upon their husbands' support as a source of subordination. In the *naofang* this disposition was ritually imposed. To use the words of Sun Lung-kee, the magnetic field of human feeling of husband and wife was attacked by the magnetic field of human feeling of the young male villagers. These two fields battled for primacy in the groom's heart/mind.

In their totality, 1988–90 Fengjia weddings reshaped *guanxi* in three, somewhat contradictory directions. First, they separated the bride from her natal family and village and incorporated her into the groom's. Second, they formed a larger alliance between the bride's and groom's families. Third, they created a new, independent nuclear household. Exactly which of these three streams was dominant depended both on the specific wedding in question and the social vantage within the wedding that one occupied.

Funerals

Perhaps the world over, and certainly throughout China, grief is a powerful emotion that can be used to consolidate political and social groups of various types. Aware of this potential, CCP officials, like their imperial predecessors (see Rawski 1988), have manipulated funerary arrangements with great care. The deaths of political leaders touched off both the 1976 and 1989 Tiananmen movements. The entombment of Mao Zedong involved internal party debates at the highest level (Wakeman 1988). In the Inner Mongolian city of Huhhot, CCP cadres, like their predecessors, guard the tomb of Wang Zhaojun (a Han concubine who married a Mongolian prince) as a symbol of Han/minority ethnic unity. In each of these instances communal mourning has been manipulated to construct widespread but diffuse social solidarities.

In addition to their focus on such diffuse mourning subjects, official Chinese funerals also involved subtle and numerous reconstitutions of specific social hierarchies. For example, just as Fengjia elders did not attend the funerals of those with younger generation names, so party leaders avoided the funerals of their subordinates. When former president Li Xiannian died in 1992, Deng Xiaoping merely sent condolences and did not attend the funeral. Party organizations at all levels have committees to determine the level of grandeur of every nonpeasant party cadre funeral. Who attends whose funeral, how big it is, and where everyone stands are carefully orchestrated and closely watched details. Jiang Zilong's (1991) short story "Yin-Yang Succession" (*Yin-Yang Jiao-jie*) gives a fascinating fictional account of such funeral committee work.

Through the embodiment of grief, care of the dead, banqueting, *ketou,* wailing, and other means, 1988–90 Fengjia residents also used funerals to manipulate *ganqing,* social hierarchies, and magnetic fields of human feeling. In Fengjia these hierarchies and magnetic fields of human feeling constituted gender and kinship. Women were positioned as daughters and daughters-in-law while men were constructed as sons. More so than weddings—where both women and men gave gifts, attended banquets, and bowed—funerals organized men and women in separate types of ritual actions: women wailed, while men performed *ketou.* This segregation of ritual actions suggests a slightly different approach to the problem of gender. Rather than examining women's and men's networks in terms of their scope and influence, this section asks whether the *guanxi* women produced were at times qualitatively different from those of men. Indeed, Emily Martin has suggested that women and men bring entirely different worldviews to rural Chinese funerals:

> [I]t is possible to glimpse the outlines of two strikingly different ideologies of life and death. In the preeminently female ideology, women see life *and* death in birth, *death* in marriage, and a cycle of change from death to birth to death in funerals. On the female side we see emphasis on the unity of opposites, denigration of separation (recall the bride's lament over her separation from her family), and celebration of cyclical change. On the male side we see constant efforts to separate opposites, to maintain and make oppositions steadfast, and desire for eternally unchanging social status. (Martin 1988:173, emphasis in original)

As Martin would note, *guanxi* construction in Fengjia funerals gendered men in tightly defined hierarchies and women in undifferentiated groups. However, the degree to which this ritual gendering reflected or produced social relations is difficult to ascertain. In this section I present how Fengjia funerals constructed gender and examine the social significance of this gendered ritual.

Funerals in 1988–90 Fengjia also invoked a world populated with the spirits of deceased ancestors. Most dismissed a literal belief in spirits as "superstition" (*mixin*) and were reluctant to discuss the topic at length. By analyzing funerals in terms of the construction of *guanxi* and gender, I provide a this-worldly interpretation; however, I don't wish to

deny the extra-worldly dimension. Indeed, it seemed to me that many
Fengjia residents, especially elder ones, concerned themselves with both
secular practice and spiritual accommodation. That residents themselves saw funerals as places for building *guanxi* was evident in the cate-
gorization of the funerals of aged villagers as "happy events" (*xishi*).
Weddings were called "red happy events" (*hongxishi*), while the funerals of old people were "white happy events" (*baixishi*). In both white
and red happy events, families took pride in the numbers of people who
attended, and described well-attended and well-run ones as "ceremonious" (*longzhong*). The funerals of youth who died before their time
were not considered "happy events," and were painful, poorly attended,
and "unceremonious" functions.

The funeral of an aged villager who died of natural causes was usually
organized by two men: the head of the deceased's team (*duizhang*) and
a master of ceremonies (*siyi* or *zhuchiren*) selected by the deceased's
family. The master of ceremonies was usually a close, elder fellow villager, as family members had other specific ritual duties. The team
leader took care of nonritual matters. He got the village committee to
write a death certificate; he looked into the situation at the crematorium (i.e., when was the next possible time to cremate the body); he
sent messengers to invite whomever the family asked him to (both inside and outside of the village); and he appointed people to buy and
cook the food for the funerary banquet. The master of ceremonies arranged the ritual itself. He made sure people wore the proper clothes;
he prepared the ritual props; he told family members how to perform
their ritual roles; he invited groups of men to *ketou* in the proper order
and generally directed the ceremony.[8]

Different relatives had different ritual roles. The filial descendants
(*xiaozhe*) always included the patrilineal male descendants of the deceased—that is, sons, sons of sons, and their sons. One family also included the unmarried daughters of the deceased's son. All filial descendants wore white robes and hats, while male filial descendants shaved
their heads. Relatives who could trace a common ancestor with the deceased within five generations wore white strips of cloth around their
waists and on their shoes, or at least tied around their ankles.

After the death of an aged relative at home, the family notified their
team leader and chose a master of ceremonies. They told the team leader
which relatives outside of the village to contact. The team leader also
contacted the crematorium. If the deceased was not survived by any
members of an older generation of his family, then the deceased's family

pasted strips of white paper on the doorways of households with a common ancestor within five generations. They pasted five strips on filial descendants' households' doorways, and three strips on the doorways of households within five generations. If the person died in the evening, and it was not possible to contact the crematorium, then the family stayed up all night with the body, and out-of-town relatives would be notified that the funeral would not occur until the following day. Upon learning of the death, the deceased's daughters (who were most likely to live in other villages) performed *ketou* to their parents-in-law before taking their children to the funeral. If these daughters were already by the side of the deceased at death (which was quite possible since daughters often returned to their natal homes to visit extremely sick parents), they returned home to perform this *ketou* and collect their children.

William Jankowiak (1993:289) describes how urban women in Huhhot during the 1980s paid more ritual attention to their dead mothers than to their dead mothers-in-law. He frames his observation in a discussion of the growing power of women in a practice of kinship that had become more bilineal and neolocal than patrilineal and virilocal. The funerals of 1988–90 Fengjia positioned women in two families, and prevented them from blatantly favoring their own parents. Women and their children attended their parents' funerals, but only after performing *ketou* to and, thus, reaffirming their *guanxi* with, their parents-in-law. Women also attended the funerals of their parents-in-law, while men did not.

In any case, after notifying the necessary people, the family washed the deceased's hair, body, and feet and dressed him or her in a new set of clothes, putting a few items of special significance in the pockets. In one funeral, for example, an old calligrapher's family put a writing brush and some paper in his pocket. In another, a Christian woman had a small prayer book in her pocket. While the family prepared the body, close friends and relatives within the village began arriving. The family next performed the "calling of the spirits" (*jiao hun*).

To call the spirits, everyone went out into the courtyard of the deceased's house. The deceased's eldest son (or whichever man had been supporting him in his old age if the deceased had no sons) turned a chair upside down in the courtyard, climbed on it, and faced southwest where the Chinese netherworld (*fengducheng*) is traditionally located. Then he said three times "Mother (or Father) is coming up to the family" (*niang [die] shang jia lai*). Finally, the family members burned some spirit money and everyone present wept.

If the funeral was to be on the same day, relatives from out of town began to arrive at the home of the deceased. The women wailed loudly whenever they entered and exited the village. Several fellow villagers (arranged by the team leader) formally received guests from outside the village. The master of ceremony busied himself with the ritual preparations. He set up an offering table in the north end of the courtyard with perhaps four plates of ritual food — fruit, candies, and cake. On a piece of yellow paper, folded into the shape of a funerary tablet (a rectangle with a triangle on top), he wrote the name of the deceased followed by the words "spirit position" (*lingwei*) and placed it on the offering table, propping it up so it could be read.[9] He made sure the male filial descendants shaved their heads and that people were wearing the proper clothes.

After all the close relatives arrived, the family held the *zhilu* (showing the road) ceremony. The son of the deceased again climbed on the upside-down chair, this time holding a carrying pole (*biandan*). He used the stick to point toward the southwest while saying three times "Father (Mother) goes to the southwest, brightly illuminate the road" (*die [niang] shang xinan, mingguang dalu*). Then all of the onlookers wept again.

Next, three or four men, usually an immediate family member of the deceased and a few fellow villagers, used a tractor-pulled covered cart to take the body to the crematorium. Some of the elderly disliked the fact that bodies were cremated instead of buried whole. They both felt that cremation was disrespectful and feared that the burning was quite painful. The crematorium was in a town twenty miles away, and the round trip took at least four hours. In the meantime the guests were banqueted.

Those who went to the crematorium would return several hours later with the funerary casket holding the ashes of the deceased. They placed the casket on the offering table, and laid out a mat before the table. Male friends and relatives of the deceased then performed *ketou* in front of the offering table, in order of the closeness of their *guanxi* with the deceased. In these *ketou*, men first performed three standing bows, then knelt down and performed three *ketou*, then wept, and finally stood up and performed three more bows. The first group to bow would be the filial descendants. While bowing, they held "mourning sticks" (*kusang bang*), made of foot-long pieces of sorghum stalks tied together with white paper, in their hands. The next group to bow consisted of the surviving male descendants of the deceased's parents-in-law (if the deceased were a man) or the surviving male descendants of the deceased's natal family (if the deceased were a woman). Next came the "honored guests" (*guike*). These were new relatives, such as the in-laws-to-be of an engaged filial descendant. Then came other relatives, in order of the closeness of their *guanxi*. Finally came close fellow villagers. After the fellow villagers completed their bows, the filial descendants bowed again. The filial descendants then performed a *ketou* to the fellow villagers to invite them to participate in the funerary procession (*chubin*).

In preparation, some male fellow villagers went out to the deceased's ancestral land and dug a small grave for the casket of ashes. The filial descendants, *waisheng* (the sons of one's sisters, daughters, or granddaughters), and close fellow villagers then walked out to the grave in the funerary procession. Usually, the eldest son of the deceased carried the funerary casket, the eldest grandson carried a "flower umbrella" (*huasan*), and the *waisheng* carried flower wreaths (*huaquan*), while the rest of the filial descendants carried their mourning sticks. In the funerals I witnessed only men participated in the funerary procession; women remained at the edge of the village and wailed. The men sometimes wept aloud as they walked slowly to the grave site. When they got to the grave, the deceased's eldest son placed the funerary casket in the grave and then fell down kneeling and weeping. The fellow villagers filled in the grave and built up a mound over it. Everyone else placed their flower wreaths, flower umbrellas, or mourning sticks on the burial mound and fell down kneeling. All the participants then performed several *ketou* together. After these *ketou*, the filial descendants and *waisheng* walked around the grave three times clockwise and three times counterclockwise. Once I saw the filial descendants tear up their white hats and throw them on the grave. Finally everyone walked home. One man said the filial descendants made sure not to turn their heads and look back when returning from the funerary procession.

After the funerary procession, the out-of-town guests returned home. The women among them wailed as they left the village. The next morning, the immediate family of the deceased rose early and went door to door throughout the village. They knocked on each door and performed *ketou* to whoever answered it. If no one answered, they went to the next house and did not bother to return. Both men and women participated in this round of *ketou*. This practice was called "thanking the guests" (*xieke*) and was described by one villager as a means of notifying everyone in the village of the death.

The death of a senior member of a family necessitated the readjustment of intrafamily hierarchies, and interfamily relationships. If the deceased were male, a new man became the family member with *mianzi* adequate to represent the family in creating *guanxi* with other men and in male domains like the bureaucratic world. Eldest sons were thrust into this position with their central roles in the "calling the spirits" and "showing the road" ceremonies and in the funerary procession. The death of a senior woman likewise required the women of the family to reorder their *guanxi*. However, the funerary ritual itself provided no special role for newly senior women. In either case, the new family ritually reformed its *guanxi* with friends and relatives from both inside and outside of the village. Men and women banqueted (at segregated tables); men performed *ketou* in differentiated, agnatically related groups; and women wailed communally. As in Martin's depiction (1988), men formed mourning subjects in distinct groups with hierarchically ordered *guanxi* to the family of the deceased. Those subjects whose *guanxi* was closer, or in the case of the "honored guest," whose *guanxi* was new and thus especially worthy of attention, performed *ketou* first. In contrast, the women mourned collectively and formed a gendered subject that seemed unconcerned with intra- and interfamily hierarchies. In both their mourning practice and lives, women never belonged to just one family.

Yet, it would be easy to push such an analysis too far. Even in funerals there were times for all participants, male and female, to weep together. The construction of *guanxi* involved both men and women in multiple and contradicted magnetic fields of human feeling. Fengjia residents' lives and loyalties were not organized as simply as funerary rituals made them out to be. Moreover, funerals were organized by masters of ceremony; they were not spontaneous outbursts of *guanxi* production. A self-awareness about purposefully passing on tradition (examined in chapter 9) dictated how masters of ceremony orchestrated sexually segregated mourning activities. Participants in funerals were concerned with following the master of ceremony's directions, an "orthopraxy" (J. Watson 1988) of sorts, as well as with reconfiguring *guanxi*. By organizing men in groups with differentiated dress and *ketou* order, masters of ceremony purposefully continued practices that have their origins in the codified mourning grades of the Ch'ing dynasty. These grades stood in problematic relation to both the legally defined kinship rights and obligations of Dengist China and the practical production of *guanxi* in 1988–90 Fengjia.[10] The ideology of gender embodied in these funerals likewise seems problematic. The extent to which women in 1988–90

Fengjia were less concerned with problems of hierarchy than men remains an open question.

Of imperial funerary ritual Evelyn Rawski remarks that "ritual constituted a structure in which individual feelings could be expressed in purposeful deviations from the norm" (1988:248). In the funerals of 1988–90 Fengjia, women and men embodied grief and constructed *ganqing* as well as they could within the ritual structure organized by the masters of ceremony. That men's and women's *guanxi* could not be reduced to the relationships constructed in funerary ritual suggests a distance both between Ch'ing dynasty and Dengist law and between jural and practical kinship. That a gendered analysis of funerals in Martin's terms works as well as it does suggests that the official patrilineal kinship of Ch'ing dynasty China still had some relation to kinship as practiced and imagined in 1988–90 Fengjia and, perhaps, that funerals orchestrated by older male masters of ceremony helped to reproduce such kinship.

6 Feeling, Speech, and Nonrepresentational Ethics

Rawski's statement that imperial funerary ritual "constituted a structure in which individual feelings could be expressed in purposeful deviations from the norm" (1988:248) must be interpreted in the context of a *ganqing* ethics of emotion. In many Western contexts the statement would be understood as a matter of making ritual space for the expression of the spontaneous, authentic, innermost feelings of a grieving individual. However, in Rawski's analysis the emperor's "expression of feeling" is more about *guanxi* propriety than about authentic individual expression. By displaying greater grief for his parents than his concubines, the emperor publicly affirmed a hierarchy of *guanxi* in which parents were more important than wives. Since Confucian ideology held that the emperor is to a minister as a father is to a son, this hierarchy also implied the emperor's own preeminence. The emperor's embodiment of filiality both affirmed his right to the throne (as the chief mourner of his imperial parents) and reinforced the hegemony of a statist Confucian ideology. In my invocation of Rawski's analysis, I mean to suggest that Fengjia residents also manipulated *ganqing* within the ritual sequences organized by specialists. In Fengjia too, the ethical dynamics of this manipulation were more about relationships than about emotional sincerity.

In this chapter I wish to extend the contrast between a representational and a *guanxi* ethics of expression as far as possible. Such a contrast enables a more accurate translation because it unmasks hidden assumptions that individuals of different backgrounds bring to a communicative exchange. In the West, an ethic of accurate representation entails both emotional "sincerity" (accurately representing inner feelings in outward expression) and "honest" speech (accurate verbal representation). This chapter examines various Chinese contexts (in Fengjia and elsewhere) in which a Western ethic of accurate representation is not taken for granted—hence the title "Nonrepresentational Ethics." In this last chapter of part I, I push my interpretive framework as broadly as possible, including examples from past and present, rural and urban places, and popular and official life. However, I have chosen the phrase "Nonrepresentational Ethics" to prevent this broad approach from suggesting that I hold an essentialist view of Chinese ethics. By emphasizing the *lack* of a set of Western cultural assumptions, I bring these examples together in terms of the similar problems they pose to Western translators, not because of an essential similarity among the Chinese contexts themselves. As Gadamer (1975, 1976) argues, translation requires unpacking one's own assumptions as much as describing foreign ones.

In their examination titled "The Cultural Construction of Emotion in Rural Chinese Social Life" (1990:180), Sulamith Heins Potter and Jack M. Potter also argue for significant divergence between American and rural Chinese assumptions about the ethics of emotional expression. However, they suggest that emotion is simply irrelevant to relationships in rural China, a view quite the opposite of my own, where *ganqing* is a central component of *guanxi*. Thus, I begin my examination of ethical problematics with a critique of the Potters' analysis.

Potter and Potter never say what Chinese terms they are translating as "emotion" or "to feel." As Russell and Yik (1996) point out, many Chinese words might be translated as emotion or feeling, including *ganqing, qinggan,* and *qingxu.* If one further considers that the Potters were translating a rural Cantonese dialect and I a rural Mandarin one, one might assume that part of our divergence lies in the difficulties of translation. However, though linguistic problems may contribute to our differences, the range of examples they give to support their argument clearly overlaps with the materializations of *ganqing* I have described in previous chapters. Moreover, the examples they describe are explicable within my own framework. Thus, I proceed with the caveat that the Potters may not have been referring specifically to *ganqing.*

Potter and Potter emphasize that in the United States personal emotions "legitimate" social relationships. A marriage, for example, would be illegitimate if not based on feelings of love. These emotions are supposed to be spontaneous and sincere; to feign love for the purpose of gaining a spouse would both be immoral and leave a flimsy basis for one's marriage. In contrast to writers who emphasize the importance of spontaneous emotion in the West,[1] Potter and Potter claim that the Western need for "sincerity" eliminates true spontaneity. Instead, they argue, there exists a complex system of psychological repression and denial that allows one to maintain an "emotionally appropriate self"

(1990:181). In contrast, they contend, for rural Chinese emotion is irrelevant "to the creation or to the perpetuation of social institutions of any kind . . . [E]motions are not thought of as significant in social relationships . . . (and) are thought of as lacking the power to create, maintain, injure, or destroy social relationships" (1990:183). Since rural Chinese people believe "how I feel doesn't matter" (1990:183), they can be truly spontaneous, and give vent to anger and other unsocial emotions in almost any context. The Potters back their theory with observations of child rearing, in which crying children are neither scolded nor comforted. Supposedly Chinese children thereby learn that emotional outbursts are inconsequential. In addition to not controlling unsociable emotions, rural Chinese people are further said to have no special use for positive ones. When discussing family relationships, Potter and Potter claim that rural Chinese never speak of love. Rather, they emphasize work. Daughters, for example, work incredibly hard before they marry in order to affirm their relationships with their parents. They don't talk about how much they love their parents. In marriages, rural Chinese at best would speak of "good feelings." They quote one villager as saying "We Chinese show our good feelings for one another in our work, not with words" (1990:194), and conclude:

> From an outsider's point of view, the social world of the Chinese villager is characterized by an insistent emphasis on work, drudgery, and production. But work is the symbolic medium for the expression of social connection, and affirms relationship in the most fundamental terms the villagers know. (1990:195)

To back up their contention that emotions are irrelevant, Potter and Potter present several examples of rural people displaying negative emotions. They include public grieving over family tragedies and the past and present misfortunes of friends and relatives. They also include displays of anger, such as women screaming at the brigade officials responsible for implementing birth control policy. From these examples they conclude:

> The behavior of villagers who show these strong feelings is consistent with the idea that the expression of most feeling is not a significant act, in and of itself, rather than with the idea that affect is in some way intrinsically dangerous and to be concealed. The villagers would be perfectly capable of self-restraint, if they believed that open expressiveness were damaging to their social position. (1990:185)

The Potters further conclude that brigade officials tolerate outbursts of anger from villagers because they too see it as irrelevant.

I believe that Potter and Potter have missed entirely the significance of these displays of negative emotions. A public embodiment of grief and sorrow creates a collective *ganqing* with all of those who feel the same grief, including the victim and his or her close friends and relatives. In so doing, a collective subject, and a series of *guanxi* among the members of that subject, are formed. Likewise, women who yell at birth control officials embody sympathy for all of the members of those families who are hurt by a specific instance of implementation of the birth control policy. The significance of such yelling is not that these women believe emotions don't matter and therefore that yelling will not hurt their *guanxi* with the official; rather, it is the *ganqing* and *guanxi* that are created between the yeller and the people on whose behalf the yelling is done. That officials tolerate such abuse perhaps reflects that they too realize the yelling is more a matter of creating solidarity with a third party than personal abuse directed at them. Potter and Potter find rural people "vividly expressive" and consider that evidence of their seeing emotion as irrelevant. In opposition, I see the vividness of *ganqing* as evidence of its centrality to social relationships. The statement "How I feel doesn't matter" is better interpreted as a complaint about individual powerlessness rather than a general statement about the irrelevance of emotions.

Secondly, that rural Cantonese affirmed relationships through work rather than words merely shows the link of material obligation (embodied by working for others) and *ganqing* in *guanxi*. It has nothing to do with the "irrelevance of emotion." In one of the dowry parties that I attended in Fengjia, the parents of the bride sat together in one corner of the room with tears in their eyes. They were not interested in talking to me or anybody else. The daughter was also not interested in talking. She kept doing chores — dusting and fetching water. Both parents and daughter were creating and participating in the mutual *ganqing* of a *guanxi* they both wanted to continue. That *ganqing* was embodied in facial expressions and work rather than words made it neither less moving nor irrelevant to social relationships.

Finally, I should point out that in 1988–90 Fengjia children were not, as a rule, left to cry out their temper tantrums. If anything, I felt that Fengjia children received more attention than their American counterparts, though I did not carry out systematic research on this point.

In discussing the importance of sincere, *personal* emotions in America, Potter and Potter have at least pointed at the type of assumptions one must abandon to interpret the ethics of *ganqing* in Fengjia. *Ganqing* is not primarily an individual matter. Rather it is a type of feeling that must be conceived of more socially than psychologically (i.e., that is held to exist between and among people as much as within individuals' heads).[2] Furthermore, sincerity—at least a notion of sincerity that requires one's words and facial expressions to accurately represent the "inner" feelings of one's heart—is usually absent from *ganqing*. To be "sincere" with one's *ganqing* is to be serious about and to live up to the obligations incurred in the *guanxi* that *ganqing* involved. Both in and out of Fengjia, I heard Chinese people of various backgrounds criticize crass manipulations of *ganqing* in pursuit of material gain. However, even these criticisms had little to do with the "insincere" representation of inner, individualized feelings. What was wrong about that sort of *ganqing* was the inauthenticity of the *guanxi* created. In the venal sort of gift giving that these manipulations involved, the value of the gift given was negotiated to be exactly equal to the value of the favor extracted from the person to whom one gives the gift. As a result, the material obligation involved in the *guanxi* was erased soon after it was established. The *guanxi* and *ganqing* involved were intentionally short-lived.

In their critique of the Potters, Arthur and Joan Kleinman (1991) problematize the orientalism inherent in the Potters' presentation. By discounting exceptions, asserting homogeneity, and denying shared human qualities, the Potters risk "narrowing the humanity of the other and thereby of ourselves" (Kleinman and Kleinman 1991:286). Certainly Americans can emphasize the social import of emotions while Chinese at times discuss authenticity; yet the timing, methods, and contexts usually differ. Holland and Kipnis (1994), for example, discuss the "sociocentrism" inherent in American cultural models of embarrassment, while Leo Ou-Fan Lee (1973) provides a detailed discussion of the history of emotional authenticity in Chinese literature and philosophy. Lee describes how the problem of meshing sentiment (*qing,* as in *ganqing*) and propriety has been debated by Confucians, Buddhists, and Taoists since the Han dynasty. During the May Fourth era, a generation of Chinese writers influenced both by these earlier debates and by Western Romantics like Byron and Goethe created an iconoclastic literature that rejected the propriety of *li* entirely in favor of impulse, sincerity, sentimentality, and individual, subjective experience. However, as Lee points out, neither the early sentimentalists nor the May Fourth romantics held a dominant position. The former were contained by the hegemony of Confucian ideology while the latter, though quite influential for a brief period, were abruptly stifled or transformed by the communists' demands for a revolutionary literature.

In my own consumption of popular culture in Dengist China — including television, movies, short stories, and novels — I was often struck by an intense sentimentality, which I found first maudlin and later moving. Though this sentimentality perhaps reflected the influence of May Fourth romantics, I usually felt that it too had more to do with *guanxi* propriety than with emotional authenticity. By embodying powerful emotions, fictional characters demonstrated the strength of their commitment to socially legitimate *guanxi*. Popular stories of romance, like Qiong Yao novels and the television series *Blushing Grass* (*Hanxiu Cao*) (both imported from Taiwan), were full of passionate characters embroiled in complex situations that separated them from the objects of their attraction. What struck me was that these characters were never fickle. They endured decades or even lifetimes of separation without ever falling in love a second time or even reducing the strength of their initial passion. Whatever the complications of their situations, the monogamous commitment implied by their unwavering passion made their *ganqing* legitimate. Fickle characters were most often evil ones. In urban areas, where perhaps a majority of young people selected their own spouses, romance could be important (Jankowiak 1993). However, though such romance could be read as the epitome of emotional spontaneity, the tendency to construct romantic impulses monogamously indicated a practice of propriety as well. In Jankowiak's study of Dengist Huhhot, for example, romantic inclinations often involved lifelong attraction to a single love. Men and women who failed to marry their "first and true love" found their later marriages to be devoid of passion (1993:209).

While at Nanjing University, a friend of mine took a course designed for foreign students on women in modern Chinese short stories. On the first day of class the teacher (a Chinese man) gave the following introduction. He said that when teaching Chinese literature to Westerners, he has found it necessary to emphasize that characters, especially women, were morally evaluated primarily on their emotional reactions. He said that though Chinese readers take this for granted, Western readers often ignore this point and consequently find Chinese literature too sappy. I met many Chinese who felt that Americans were cold and unfeeling and who could not imagine living in American society. Though I don't necessarily agree with this assessment of Americans, I do think it reveals the lack of understanding of how to embody *ganqing* on the part of many Americans in China.

My own shortcomings in this area can serve as an example. Once in Nanjing I attempted to arrange a Chinese language tutor for an American friend of mine. After several rebuffs, I explained my problem to a Chinese friend. He said my approach had been too direct. He said that I couldn't just explain the tutoring needs of my friend and suggest a price, especially to someone I didn't know well. If the potential tutor accepted the arrangement, she would appear as someone who was interested only in money, who had no *ganqing,* and thus acted outside the bounds of *guanxi* propriety. He said I should work through intermediaries so that everyone could embody *ganqing* by doing a favor for someone that they knew well. The price could be suggested by one of the intermediaries as an aside along the way. Unappreciative of a concern for *ganqing* that would lead me to approach the problem as a matter of favors between friends, I appeared cold and aloof.[3] As with imperial funerals, the ethics of *ganqing* were caught up in *guanxi* propriety rather than problems of authenticity. Indeed, at the linguistic level, describing someone as having *ganqing* means that that person acts out of a concern for (specific) other people rather than the selfish yearnings of an individualized heart.

The importance and propriety of *ganqing* in many Chinese contexts are also gendered differently than in the West. Campbell (1987:225) discusses how Western patriarchal ideologies relegate human feeling and personal relationships to the realm of the feminine and politically unimportant. Most Chinese would see them as central, and Chinese men don't allow women to dominate these arenas. Though the professor of literature cited above suggested that women especially were judged on their *ganqing,* I was struck by the sentimentality of Chinese men. In both rural and urban settings I often heard Chinese men speaking of their friendship and *ganqing* for other men, and saw them do favors for, exchange unexpected gifts with, and hold hands with each other. None of these actions implied homosexuality; indeed, most reflected the utmost of *guanxi* propriety. Susan Brownell (1995:213–32) likewise discusses displays of affection between Chinese women without fear of lesbianism. If anything, especially in rural settings, it was exchanges of *ganqing* between men and women, even husbands and wives, that were beyond the boundaries of propriety and kept fully out of public view.

Nonrepresentational Speech Ethics

The above section described how a Chinese ethics of *ganqing* was more concerned with *guanxi* propriety than with accurate emotional representation; the ethical evaluation of emotional responses began from a consideration of the implications of those emotions for individuals' *guanxi* rather than from a consideration of their "sincerity" (accurate representation of their inner selves). This section suggests that a similar dynamic underlies the moral evaluations of speech acts in Fengjia. In situations in which middle-class Americans would emphasize "truthful" representation, Fengjia residents tended to base their moral evaluations on *guanxi* propriety or other forms of social pragmatics. The parallels between an ethics of speech and that of emoting reflects the fact that both language and feelings are means of communication that can be used to manipulate *guanxi*.

Consider the following common scene at the village's clinic. A four-year-old child was brought in with a fever. As soon as he entered the clinic door, he started crying. His mother began repeating "There won't be a shot, there won't be a shot [*budazhen*]" (children were almost always given a shot in this situation). After a brief examination, the village doctor carried the child into the back room for a shot. The child wailed the whole way, and the doctor and mother attempted to drown out his wails with a chorus of "There won't be a shot." This chorus continued until the shot was actually being administered at which point the doctor switched to his own monotone wail of "Aiiiii..." and then to "No more shots" (*budazhenle*) as he pulled out the needle.

I was struck by this scene because in my experience middle-class American parents would not handle the situation in the same way. They would consider this method of hushing the child to be "lying" and thus to be a "bad example" to set for the child. For example, Dr. Spock's manual, *the* classic how-to book of middle-class child-raising, suggests:

> The best way to get your child ready for each immunization is to be as honest and simple in your explanations as possible. Tell him that the shot will hurt, but that it will protect him from a sickness that would hurt much more than the shot. (Spock and Rothenberg 1992:239)

In Fengjia when I asked several parents if the *budazhen* method of hushing the child could be considered "dishonest" (*bulaoshi*), they all said no. This led me to a consideration of the word *laoshi* (usually translated as "honest"). Fengjia residents often complimented people as being very *laoshi*. When I asked about desirable qualities for a spouse, *laoshi* also often came up. After hearing several stories about *laoshi* people, I realized that *laoshi* almost always had an element of self-sacrifice. For example, if there was a very distasteful job to do, and several people got out of it by giving one excuse or another, the person who finally did it was more *laoshi* than the others. Being "honest" or "dishonest" was more than a matter of representation; it involved the *purpose* for which one used language. False representations were only "dishonest" if they were done for selfish purposes. Since, at least from the point of view of adults, giving children shots and reducing their anxiety about these shots were for the children's own good, "lying" about imminent shots could not be called "dishonest."

The *New Peasant Encyclopedia of Family Happiness* (*Xinnong Lejia Baike*), an advice manual on handling family relations that went through three printings in the 1980s, gives a plethora of advice on what to say in what sort of situation to improve one's intrafamily *guanxi*. Of language in general, it says:

> Speech is a tool for the exchange of *ganqing*. One sentence can make someone cry, another can make someone laugh. Let speech be the medium for transmitting *ganqing* to your interlocutor. [*Yuyan shi jiaoliuganqingdegongju. Yijuhua neng baren shuoku, yijuhua neng baren shuoxiao. Rang yuyan zuomeijie, ba ganqing chuandaogei duifang.*] (1985:100)

Here, too, a *guanxi* ethics for speech acts is directly invoked.

Nonrepresentational ethics have been prevalent in official speech acts of imperial and modern Chinese governments as well. Of state historiography in imperial China, Kenneth DeWoskin writes, "the historicity of events themselves is only incidental, a concern secondary to the moral purport and effecting power of the written words" (1991:46–47). During the Republican era, Lin Yutang wrote:

> In order to understand Chinese politics, one should understand Chinese literature. Perhaps one should here avoid the word literature (*wenhsueh*) and speak of *belles-lettres* (*wenchang*). This worship of *belles-lettres* as such has become a veritable mania in the nation. This is clearest in modern public statements, whether of a student body, a commercial concern, or a political party. In issuing such public statements, the first thought is how to make them nice-sounding, how to word them beautifully. And the first thought of a newspaper reader is whether such statements read nicely or not. Such statements almost

always say nothing, but almost always say it beautifully. A palpable lie is praised if it is told in good form. (1977 [1936]:223)

Whatever its roots in the rhetorics of earlier Chinese governments, the CCP's practice of propaganda is also typical of Leninist party-states. Katherine Verdery suggests that socialist regimes in Eastern Europe treated language and discourse as "the *ultimate* means of production. Through discourse even more than through practice, their rulers (hoped) to constitute consciousness, social objects, social life itself" (1991:430, emphasis in original). Paying little attention to the accuracy with which their rhetoric represented lived realities, socialist cadres' manipulation of language in both China and Eastern Europe at times approached the ludicrous. As Vaclav Havel sarcastically described it:

> Life in the system is . . . thoroughly permeated with hypocrisy and lies: government by bureaucracy is called popular government; the working class is enslaved in the name of the working class; the complete degradation of the individual is presented as his or her ultimate liberation; depriving people of information is called making it available; the use of power to manipulate is called the public control of power, and the arbitrary abuse of power is called observing the legal code; the repression of culture is called its development . . . the lack of free expression becomes the highest form of freedom; farcical elections become the highest form of democracy; banning independent thought becomes the most scientific of world views. (1988:30–31, cited in McCormick 1993:1)

Noncadre publics have occasionally attacked official languages for their lack of representational accuracy. Such attacks have been an effective strategy in the undoing of socialisms in Eastern Europe. Vaclav Havel's naming of the lies of socialism was a conscious and important element in his revolutionary strategy (McCormick 1993). Solidarity's resistance to the socialist state in Poland, as Kristi Evans describes it, similarly involved espousing representational accuracy.

> Solidarity's own ideology of language was based on the idea that language should directly and clearly reflect an externally constituted reality. This ideology, which is widespread in the Western world, is what Silverstein (1979) terms a reference-and-prediction ideology, in which the ideal operation of language is reference to objective reality. (1992:761)

At times, struggles within the CCP similarly hinged on philosophies of language. The Maoist aphorism "Seek truth from facts" (*Shishiqiushi*) became a common battle cry for heterodox campaigners within the party. In the late 1920s, Mao used it to oppose orthodox Marxist theories that denied the peasantry potential as a revolutionary class. During the Lu Shan Plenum of 1959, Peng Dehuai used it in opposition to politically correct but apparently distorted accounts of commune productivity in the Great Leap Forward. Deng Xiaoping used it to counter the "whatevers" orthodoxy of the Gang of Four.[4] However, unless already encoded in a new party orthodoxy, these battles rarely reached the public at large. CCP propaganda continually presented itself to the public as language with beneficial social effects. Rather than confronting such language straight on with questions of accuracy, the Chinese public has for the most part tended to either subvert it with humor or manipulate it for personal gain.[5]

Certainly these events are rather distant from Fengjia. However, party debates over "truth" are far from irrelevant. The CCP has often concerned itself with the ethics of local speech acts. During the Cultural Revolution, the expression of "revolutionary spirit" was far more important than representational objectivity. Under Deng Xiaoping, "seeking truth from facts" took a back seat to promoting "stability and unity" (*anding tuanjie*) as an ethical priority in speech. The following "editorial" heard in Fengjia on a radio broadcast in April of 1989 was typical of Dengist exhortations.

> Comrade Deng Xiaoping has recently emphasized the importance of stability and unity. In our daily life in villages and work units, some people seem to voice an opinion (*yijian*) on every subject no matter how disruptive it might be.... Don't be a person with too many "opinions." Don't do things that aren't useful to unity; don't say things that aren't useful to unity (*Buliyu tuanjiedeshi buzuo; buliyu tuanjiedehua bushuo*).

This propaganda both explicitly urged people to concern themselves with the social effects of their speech acts and, like most Chinese propaganda, justified itself by presuming to be a speech act with "beneficial" social effects. The point here is not to excuse CCP propaganda as either socialist necessity or a manifestation of deep-rooted "Chinese culture." Indeed, the self-serving nature of CCP propaganda made it "dishonest" (*bulaoshi*) by Fengjia standards regardless of its representational accuracy. Rather, the point is that the CCP state, like its predecessors, did *not* promote representational truth as an ethical priority.

In contrast, as Evans's (1992) citation of Silverstein (1979) suggests, "reference-and-prediction ideologies" of language have been "widespread in the Western world." Consequently, Western sociolinguists have long felt it necessary to emphasize that speech acts pragmatically in the social world and that representational models of language are hence limited (e.g., Gumperz 1982:9–29 and Levinson 1983). This fetishization of "truth" as representation with moral obligation, though beyond the scope of this project, is perhaps a more interesting historical problem than the sort of honesty lived in Fengjia. Certainly Foucault's (1973, 1978, 1980:194–229) explorations of the rise of confession as a technique of power/knowledge and the linkages of "biopower" with our "will to knowledge" are suggestive. As Foucault describes, the rise of confessional techniques in psychoanalytic practice (especially relevant to emotional representation) and the Cartesian separation of language and thought from the material world both have emphasized representational rather than pragmatic ethics and practices of speech acts. In China, on the other hand, ethics of *ganqing* and speech have been influenced by recent increases in the importance of practices of *guanxi* production as well as by statist prescriptions for socialist speech. In brief, the forces that have molded Western taken-for-granted notions of truth have not been as influential in China, and vice versa.

This chapter has emphasized the interpretive problematics of moving between representational and pragmatic ethics of speech and feeling. In conclusion, I would again caution against essentialization. Raised to the level of generalities, equations like the West is to representation as China is to social pragmatics become absurd. In the hands of orientalists they can become tools of imperialism. In 1894, for example, the missionary Arthur Smith portrayed "the absence of sincerity" as a Chinese racial characteristic curable only through the introduction of Christianity (Smith 1894). There have been many different versions of, and counterdiscourses to, representational and *guanxi* ethics of feeling and speech. Fang Lizhi's (1990) championing of the objective language of science in opposition to the hegemony of Marxism-Leninism-Mao Zedong thought is matched by American Marxist, feminist, and cultural studies scholars' insistence that no "scientific" investigation has ever been or could ever be apolitical. At a more mundane level Eve Sweetser (1987) describes the importance of "white lies" and "social lies" in American speech ethics. In both China and the United States, doctors avoid detailed discussions of cancer prognoses with their patients. In fact, it would be difficult even to imagine a place entirely devoid of either representational or pragmatic speech. What is significant is difference in the degree to which and the matter and contexts in which the two sorts of speech are moralized.

II *Guanxi* Versions

Introduction

I began my rendering of Chinese *guanxi* in English with an invocation of Mauss's "total social phenomenon." The value of Mauss's construct lies in its ability to illuminate the arbitrary and often inappropriate manner in which the Western division of academic disciplines classifies the social world. Art, religion, and politics, for example, are never neatly bounded activities located in the museum, the church, and the town hall—least of all in places without this architectural typography. More importantly, economics is not a sui generis, all-determining orb. More than any other discipline in Western academia, economics has developed into a disarticulated module of theoretical knowledge. The academic reification of economics reflects the bourgeois separation of material obligation from human feeling, the Western location of the former in the reified realm of contract and law and the latter in the whimsical field of personal spontaneity. Problematic in a Western setting, the separate analyses of economic and personal relationships becomes absurd where the two are combined as "total social phenomena."

However, Mauss's insight is easily abused. James Clifford describes how Mauss insisted that ethnographers "construct 'series and not panoplies'" and explains:

> Mauss used old terms precisely: a *panoply* is a full complement of arms, a suit of armor with all its accouterments. The term suggests a functional integration of parts deployed and displayed around a coherent, effective body. Mauss did not see society or culture this way. One should be wary of reducing his concept of total social facts (reminiscent of Freud's "overdetermination") to a functionalist notion of the interrelation of parts. (1988:63, emphasis in original)

As Mauss and Clifford were aware, a holism that rejects the disarticulation of human social life into separate realms is too often confused with a structural-functional outlook that portrays cultures and societies as homeostatically reproducing wholes.[1] By insisting on a diversity of uses for, conceptions of, and constructions of *guanxi,* I hope to debunk three related essentialisms — historical, causal, and psychological — upon which structural-functional approaches rely.

First, historical essentialism. A Radcliffe-Brownian (see especially 1952:178–187) structural-functional approach portrays the various "structures" of a given "society" (the kinship "system," the economic "system," the religious "system," etc.) like the organs of the biomedical human body — maintaining and complementing each other to homeostatically perpetuate the society as a whole. This approach is ahistorical in two senses: both the whole (the relation among the parts) and the individual parts remain static over time. Explaining "practices of *guanxi* production" or "Chinese conceptions of *ganqing*" in terms of their relations to an unchanging Chinese society or "traditional Chinese culture" invokes the part/whole language of structural-functional antihistory. To combat this tendency, I insist both that practices and conceptions of *guanxi* have evolved and that these practices and conceptions have multiple and shifting effects on other areas of Chinese social life.[2]

The construction of Chinese society or culture as a reproducing whole leads to a second sort of essentialism, the causal variety. To explain homeostatic reproduction, structural functionalists posit causal relations among the parts: that the economic system shapes religious beliefs in such and such a manner; that the kinship system shapes economic interaction in such and such a manner. The positing of *guanxi* as an independent variable in a field of causal relations would defer human agency to an abstract category of behavior. While the production of *guanxi* has political, economic, psychological, and social implications, I do not see these implications as caused by *guanxi* in an abstract sense. Rather, they are the consequences, often intended, of the actions of the Chinese subjects who form *guanxi.*

The privileging of *guanxi* as an independent variable in a causal field can lead to a third type of essentialism, the psychological variety. When *guanxi* are viewed as a key element in the homeostatic reproduction of a neatly bounded "traditional Chinese culture," *guanxi* become conflated with an essential "Chineseness." Those of a psychoanalytic bent, or who see cultures as defining characteristics of individuals within a cultural whole, give a physical reality to this Chineseness inside the brains of individual Chinese (e.g., Sun 1987, 1991; Pye 1981). Such psychologism not only denies the social nature of *guanxi*-reproducing practices, but also entails the following racial implications: that non-Chinese cannot participate in the production of *guanxi;* that Chinese cannot participate in personal relationships that differ from *guanxi;* and that practices of *guanxi* production produce a single, distinct type of Chinese subject. I resist psychologism by insisting on the social nature of *guanxi,* and the multiple kinds of subjects that manipulations of *ganqing* are able to create.

Two theoretical tools clarify the diversity of *guanxi* explored here: Hebdige's (1987) concept of versioning and the Foucauldian notion of subjectification.[3] Developed in his discussion of Caribbean music and culture, Hebdige uses versioning to refer to the multiple reworkings of a song, a theme, or a style that occur in the continual production and reproduction of music, writing, and cultural practices in general. In versioning there is always repetition and always something new; there are no single points of origin and there are no single examples that represent the pure essence of a given song, theme, or cultural practice. Versioning allows one to envision both change and continuity over time without positing an essence. Versioning allows one to see both local innovations and broad fields of continuity. Versioning makes psychological essentialism impossible.

For Foucault, the making of persons into subjects involves both the dividing and labeling practices of state institutions (which often rely on the classificatory schemes of social sciences) *and* the techniques by which people try to mold themselves.[4] In Fengjia, villagers constituted subjects through practices of *guanxi* production as the state delineated its own subjects by labeling villagers as members of a certain class, as "peasants" or "nonpeasants," and as members of particular households (*hu*) resident in a single village. Foucauldian subjectification debunks psychological essentialism in two ways. First, it involves a dialectic of making and being made that avoids a type of determinism which maintains that a one-way culture formats individual minds. Second, it enables one to see how different forms of *ganqing* can construct different types of human subjects. The involvement of *ganqing* in state discourses on class and residency endows local practices of *guanxi* production with wider significance. In addition to subject construction in personal relationships, villagers deploy "magnetic fields of human feeling" in national and international "imagined communities" (B. Anderson 1991) of class and ethnicity. In so doing, they help construct the subjectivities caught up in those communities.

The three chapters in part II do their best to historicize and diversify the picture of *guanxi* production drawn in part I. Chapter 7 narrates recent history in Fengjia, derailing the notion that *guanxi* have played a static role in village life. Chapter 8 explores the wide variety of conceptions and practices of *guanxi* in Chinese settings outside of Fengjia. Chapter 9 returns to Fengjia with a consideration of how state narratives of class and place have imbued constructions of *ganqing* with diverse subjectivities.

7 *Guanxi* in Fengjia, 1948–90

Both the methods Fengjia residents used to produce *guanxi* and the purposes for which they formed them evolved radically during the forty-plus years of CCP rule from 1948 to 1990. Though these transformations will hardly surprise those familiar with the history of the People's Republic, they are worth reviewing because they forcefully dispel any notions of there being a functionalist stability to the role of *guanxi* in village life. I divide my presentation of their history into three sections: the social organization of production, family strategies, and ritual activities. Each of these domains has been drastically affected by separate (though related) CCP policies—the social organization of production in the sequential movements of land reform, collectivization, and decollectivization; family strategies by marriage laws, birth control policy, and the destruction of lineage organization; and ritual life by policies to oppose "feudal superstition" and "destroy the four olds." In each of these domains, the villagers' reactions and adaptations to CCP policies, as well as economic development and technological change, have shaped the places of *guanxi* in village life.

Social Organization of Production

Sketching the social relations of production in Fengjia before the arrival of the communists and their 1948 land reform is difficult. Prasenjit Duara (1988:252) and Philip Huang (1985; 1995:114–115) argue that in most North China villages, class differences were not severe. In Fengjia most older residents denied the existence of any big landlords, but one said that some families had "slaves" (*nuli*). Two others described how their families had been quite well off in the years before 1945, but through some fortunate disaster had managed to go bankrupt before the arrival of the communists, enabling them to be categorized as "poor peasants" during the land reform. Regardless of their differences, all of these people agreed that disparities in wealth played at least some role in pre-communist Fengjia social life. Several described how they had worked as tenants on richer families' land. In his description of landlord-tenant relations in an Anhui Province county seat during this period, Fried (1953) describes *ganqing* as mediating the relationship between individuals of different classes. However, when I asked of the role of *guanxi* and *ganqing* in landlord-tenant relations in Fengjia, two former tenants insisted that such matters were completely without *ganqing*, involving only calculations of economic benefit. These men were appalled by my suggestion that labor exchanges in Fengjia of the late 1980s were anything like pre-communist landlord-tenant relations. "Working on someone's fields now," said one of them, "is a voluntary relation between family members or equals."

Whether pre-communist labor relations were as harsh as these men remembered, or those in the 1980s as gentle, we can imagine how the land reform transformed rural social relations. To begin, the redistribution of land ended the need for some villagers to work as tenants. Thus, one type of *guanxi* (landlord-tenant) was eliminated completely. More important still was the assignment of class labels that were to structure opportunities for thirty years.[1] In Fengjia most families were labeled middle and poor peasants, while a few received the rich-peasant label. This assignment of class labels did more than just reverse the fortunes of families in Fengjia, transforming the previously underprivileged into the newly privileged. It also shifted the basis of privilege from land ownership to state classification.

Indeed, the land reform can be viewed as a massive work of state classification and penetration. The assignment of classes and the redistribution of land required the geographic positioning and registration of every rural family in China. In his description of the reorganization of the land reform in Longbow village, William Hinton writes:

> The first step in any such reorganization had to be the creation of a new Poor and Hired Peasants' League. But before such a League could even be started, some determination had to be made concerning who were the poor and who were the hired. A detailed classification of the whole community therefore became mandatory and the thoroughgoing investigation which the cadres had earlier bypassed crowded all other matters off of the agenda. (1966:274)

The classificatory procedure was enormous and central. In addition to guaranteeing farm land to all rural Chinese, it transformed village membership into a matter of state record rather than lineage or family relations. When the CCP used these records to enforce the household registration (*hukou*) policies in the 1950s, rural Chinese people became more or less permanently bound to the place in which they had been assigned land. They lived out their lives in the administrative units (villages) into which they were born or married.

Fei Xiaotong (1939:180–185; cf. Chun 1985, 1991) argues that pre-communist Chinese peasants treated land more like a family heirloom than a commodity, selling it only under circumstances of dire need. The land reform, however, treated land ownership as a matter of state record and policy rather than family or lineage membership. The onset of collectivization completed this transformation. Though pre–land reform peasants may have been reluctant to sell their land, they could still do so in times of desperation or exceptional opportunity. The pooling of land into collectives ended this possibility. As collectivization was accompanied by the household registration policies, villager land relationships, like village membership itself, became state-determined and, from the point of view of the majority of rural people, intransigent matters.

Philip Huang (1985:32) describes the "semiproletarianization" that occurred in many North China villages during the first half of the twentieth century. As peasants left the land for at least part of the year in search of factory work, village insularity and solidarity decreased. In Fengjia many older men had in their pre-1948 youth gone to big cities like Jinan, Qingdao, and Shanghai seeking work or education. However, the household registration policies, which severely restricted rural/urban migration, ended this mobility. The majority of youth in the 1980s had never left Zouping County. Especially for men, the geographic scope of *guanxi* production narrowed sharply.

As state policy determined village residence and made it permanent, the category of relations known as "fellow villager" (*xiang qin*) grew in importance. Collectivization furthered this trend. Selden (1993) describes how the strict economic policies of the collectivized decades ended the extensive involvement of rural people in the extravillage marketing communities so well described by Skinner (1964–65). The decades of community stability and insularity enforced by these policies form an important background for Fengjia *guanxi* production during the 1980s. When I was in Fengjia, distantly related individuals continued to describe each other as fellow villagers or team members much more often than as family members. This form of address reflects the decline in the importance of the lineage and the rise in that of the village and the teams, organizations created by the CCP-led state. The almost complete lack of name cards, ubiquitous in the cities, reflected that Fengjia residents felt little need to extend their networks beyond their kin and fellow villagers who knew them well.

In Fengjia, collectivization began relatively early, with the village brigade (*dadui*) being organized by 1955. In 1958 the brigade became part of the Sunzhen People's Commune (*renmin gongshe*). As elsewhere, communization in conjunction with other Great Leap Forward policies led to economic disaster. During the "Three Difficult Years" Fengjia residents were reduced to eating leaves. More than thirty people died, and fertility rates were one fifth their previous level.[2] Yan (1993) describes how those who starved in a Heilongjiang village during the aftermath of the Great Leap Forward were those whose *guanxi* networks were the weakest. Though I heard little about those who died in Fengjia, one man described how gifts of sweet potatoes from affinal relations reduced hunger in his family. In 1961 the Sunzhen People's Commune was disbanded. Fengjia then remained a collectivized brigade until 1978, when a process of decollectivization, much more gradual than that in most of the country, began.

As elsewhere, the collectivization process entailed the development of a work point (*gongfen*) system to distribute the proceeds of the harvest. Workers received points for all tasks done for the collective. Work points, according to the size and value of a given year's harvest, minus the state-levied grain taxes, could be exchanged for grain and cash. Work in this collective system was assigned by team leaders; individual families had little to say about the arrangement of tasks and approached their work more like factory workers than farmers. A fifty-year-old farmer said, "During that time you didn't have to worry about a thing, you just listened to orders from above."

The nature of work on the collectives had several implications for strategies of *guanxi* formation. Most significantly, the importance of extrahousehold *guanxi* for women increased greatly. Older residents said women in the pre-communist period could be described as *neiren* —literally "inside people"—who rarely left the confines of their households. Women cooked; made, washed, and mended clothes; and cared for children, the sick, and the elderly. Labor and transactions outside the household, including trips to the market to buy food, were handled by men. Women's labor did not require extensive *guanxi,* and younger women were often prevented from leaving the household by their parents or mothers-in-law. When the communists reorganized rural labor on the collective farms, they insisted on women's right to work, and rural households soon became dependent on the work points women could earn working in the fields.[3] This labor not only gave women the opportunity to spend time with extrahousehold women, but also increased their need for extrahousehold *guanxi*. By exchanging child care with neighbors or helping each other out when sick family members placed exceptional demands on their time, women could more effectively juggle the numerous roles they needed to fill.

Jean Oi (1989) argues that collectivized agriculture motivated the formation of relatively stable, vertical, patron–client ties within villages. As work assignments, private plots, and opportunities for private sidelines were often matters for the team leader's discretion, and as team leaders themselves needed popular support in the face of continual political campaigns and directives to impose unpopular policies, collectivized agriculture in the People's Republic became a fertile field for the growth of clientelist politics. Oi further argues that unlike the clientelism of a previous era — in which peasants cultivated distant relations with a wide variety of local officials, rice merchants, middlemen, and peddlers — clientelism under collectivized agriculture locked villagers into intensely close relations with a single authority figure. I did not delve into the factional politics of the collectivized era in Fengjia, but Oi's analysis makes it clear that collectivization ushered in an era in which access to party-designated power played an increasing role in strategies of *guanxi* formation. For most of the 1960s, 1970s, and 1980s, this power in Fengjia was concentrated in the hands of Party Secretary Feng Yongxi.

In 1955, at the age of twenty-four, Feng Yongxi was appointed head of the village's "people's militia" (*minbing*). After the formation of the Sunzhen's People's Commune in 1958, he became the commune's assistant leader in charge of sideline production. In 1961, after the breaking up of the commune, he was appointed Assistant Secretary of the Fengjia village brigade. In 1964, when the old Party Secretary died, he became the Party Secretary of the village, a post he still held when I last left Fengjia. During the 1970s and 1980s he gained political power at still higher levels.

Secretary Feng's political success was rooted in part in the economic development achieved under his rule. During the early 1970s, an agricultural technician, remembered only as "Mr. Wu," (*Wu Xiansheng*) came to Fengjia. Party Secretary Feng followed Mr. Wu's advice to the letter, instructing those in charge of the brigade's agriculture to plant, fertilize, and harvest exactly as Mr. Wu directed (figure 15). The result was an astounding success. During the period villagers call "the three

Figure 15   Preparing to harvest wheat with a tractor.

years with three big steps" (*sannian sandabu*), wheat production increased fivefold. In 1971 the wheat harvest had been 181 *jin/mu;*[4] in 1972 it was 326 *jin/mu;* in 1973 it was 612 *jin/mu;* and in 1974 it approached 900 *jin/mu,* a level that has been maintained or gradually improved upon every year since. In all, the collective's income from wheat almost tripled within three years. A small part of this income was passed on to Fengjia workers by giving them more grain and cash per work point. However, most of it was retained and reinvested by the collective.[5] In 1975 the brigade began building brick houses at subsidized prices for everyone in the village (houses previously had been made of mud and straw). By 1982, every family was living in a brick house. During the 1980s the collective continued to invest heavily in the village's infrastructure. Factories were built and dirt lanes were paved. In 1991, wells were installed in every house. Some households bought electric water pumps and therefore had running water. Since the "three years with three big steps," Fengjia has been considered by its neighboring villages to be relatively prosperous, though it is not as wealthy as the more industrialized villages in the southeastern part of the county.

As Friedman, Pickowicz, and Selden (1991) point out, attempting to gain access to state "largess" by aggressively adhering to the policy preferences of patrons higher up in the state bureaucracy is common throughout the Chinese Communist system. Party Secretary Feng seemed a master at this. His aggressive adherence to the agricultural policies of Mr. Wu, and the success that it brought, started his own rise in the party bureaucracy. In 1976, Feng Yongxi received his first extravillage appointment as a member of the Zouping County Standing Committee. From 1978 to 1987, he was a representative to the National People's Congress. From 1980 until I left Fengjia, he was on the standing committee of the Shandong Province People's Congress. He was the only "peasant" member of this latter committee in the entire province. In 1991, he was named a national-level model worker (*quanguo laodong mofan*). At times Secretary Feng asked Fengjia residents to make sacrifices to state demands. For example, during the late 1970s, in the form of "patriotic grain" (*aiguo liang*), Fengjia paid more taxes than its neighbors. However, these sacrifices brought clear rewards. Secretary Feng parlayed his village's successes and "ideal" behavior into political positions that he used mainly for the village's benefit. For example, in the 1980s, though supplies of chemical fertilizer and diesel fuel were short both nationally and locally, and farmers from other villages had to fend for themselves by scrounging in the shortage-stricken markets, Secretary Feng was able to secure enough of these products (often at wholesale prices) to sell an adequate supply to the entire village at just above cost. Secretary Feng also had the village's wheat evaluated as "seed grade," enabling it to fetch almost twice the price of regular wheat. By 1995, Fengjia was being hailed an agricultural model, and not without reason (see Diamond 1983). Its wheat production had reached 1,200 *jin/mu,* tops in the entire province. County, provincial, and even national-level agricultural experts came to inspect the crop and hear about Fengjia's farming methods. The village was also labeled a birth control model and by 1995 had become a county center for family planning classes.

Because of Fengjia's economic success as a collective village, as well as his own commitment to "prosper collectively," Feng Yongxi purposely slowed the pace of decollectivization in Fengjia. Not until 1986 was land allocated to individual households on a per capita basis. Though later than most villages, the timing of Fengjia's decollectivization was comparable to that of many other successful collectives (Judd 1994:24–25). Even after 1986, Fengjia organized the purchase of seed, fertilizer, diesel fuel, and insecticide; plowing; and some of the planting, irrigation, and harvesting on a collective basis. As the following case illustrates, while I was in Fengjia, tension over the village's relatively incomplete decollectivization remained.

After the winter slack season, the first major task of the agricultural year was to irrigate the cotton fields. In Fengjia this irrigation was organized collectively, and was dependent upon water diverted by the Water Bureau from the Yellow River into the local system of irrigation canals. Villagers used large diesel-engine-driven water pumps to pump the water from the canals into ditches that flowed into their fields. In the late 1980s, as Fengjia became richer, several groups of households pooled resources and bought their own water pumps. They did so both to facilitate irrigation on the occasions that it was not organized collectively[6] (other households could borrow collectively owned pumps for a fee) and because they saw that the village-owned water pumps were breaking down more and more and feared that the village would soon abandon its commitment to collective irrigation.

In late February of 1989, the "Lantern Festival" holiday had not yet passed and most Fengjia residents were still occupied with the rounds of visits connected with the spring festival season. The weather had been warm, and the Yellow River rose earlier than usual. The Water Bureau had no option but to divert water while the Yellow River had it, and the local canals were soon full. Some households in neighboring villages (where irrigation was not collectively organized) began to irrigate their fields. Fearing that irrigation would become more difficult as action in neighboring villages slowly drained the canals, one family in Fengjia began to irrigate its own fields with its own water pump without waiting for the brigade to organize. The next day two more families did the same. That night Secretary Feng called a village meeting. In a tone much more conciliatory than I had heard at previous meetings, Secretary Feng explained how individual irrigation would disrupt the collective irrigation process. Because of the lay of the land (the slope of the fields and placement of irrigation ditches), Fengjia's fields were broken down into sections (*dipian*). Irrigation was most efficient when sections were irrigated separately, beginning with the highest fields in a given section. If people irrigated individually, in random order, this efficiency would be lost. Moreover, if some households did not participate in the collective irrigation process, then the cost of irrigation for other families with land in the same sections would go up. Fees for collectively organized irrigation were calculated by section. The price of fuel and labor for irrigating one section was divided on a per *mu* basis by the households who held land in that section (in 1988 costing slightly more than ¥1 per *mu*). Finally, he said, arguments over the use of collectively owned irrigation ditches would arise, with the less aggressive families being left behind.

After finishing his speech, Secretary Feng instructed the villagers to break up into groups according to land sections, and to discuss the mat-

Figure 16   Village meeting in front of party headquarters.

ter as sections (figure 16). Most people sat around looking sheepish and did not discuss much of anything. Other village leaders went around from group to group to see if anyone still objected to collective irrigation. In the end, no one objected, and they decided to start collective irrigation the next day. The next morning Secretary Feng held a meeting with the families that had irrigated individually. In contrast to the previous evening, his tone was fierce. After much shouting on Secretary Feng's part, the families in question "agreed" to pay the fees for the irrigation that would have been done on their land.

Disputed as it was, many Fengjia residents defended the 1989 organization of agricultural production as both efficient and egalitarian. Some emphasized that by doing the major tasks collectively, the brigade could continue to make use of the large machinery it had acquired in the 1960s and 1970s. By plowing, planting, etc. at the same time, the brigade could run large tractors over entire fields. Because they did not own tractors and farmed plots too small to use tractors, households would have had to use draught animals and hand plows if they had plowed, planted, and reaped individually. With the major tasks done mechanically and collectively, even families without much labor power could grow a decent crop. In the case of irrigation, some insisted that neighboring villages had better access to irrigation canals and thus could irrigate without too much dependence on ditches or the collective organization that an orchestrated use of ditches required. Village leaders emphasized the combined benefits of individual incentive and centralized planning that their version of the responsibility system entailed. Because households reaped only the benefits from their own land, there was considerable incentive to do a good job at toilsome jobs like weeding, spraying insecticide, and picking bugs off plants. Because major tasks were organized collectively, no one could stray too far from the "scientific" agricultural strategies devised by the village expert, Assistant Secretary Zhang Lin. Secretary Feng also emphasized the importance of prospering collectively. He felt that if individual households were allowed to completely control their own farming, some, because of labor shortages or poor planning, would surely get into trouble.

Because of Fengjia's collective organization of arduous agricultural tasks, one healthy adult (often a married woman) could handle the farming responsibilities for a household of five or six. Consequently, most households had more labor power (*laodongli*) than could be absorbed in straightforward farming. During the 1980s, several options existed for additional employment within the village. Many households found positions for their extra labor on the village payroll. The village managed two relatively large factories on a collective basis: a cornstarch factory with 70 employees and the textile mill with 50 employees. In addition, the village paid salaries to members of the village committee, the doctors in the village clinic, the guest house employees, and a few equipment managers and repairmen. In all, there were about 150 salaried positions in 1989, with pay for full-time work ranging from ¥100 to ¥150 per month. Some of the larger families pooled the efforts of their individual households to bid on the village's sidelines. Under Fengjia's system of contract production (*toubiao chengbao*), households or groups of households could bid to manage the village's collectively owned steamed bread factory, general store, three vegetable gardens, and two orchards for three-year periods. Whoever bid the highest contract fee received the right to manage the property in question for a three-year period. The farmland that was put aside in anticipation of future population growth was contracted out on this basis too. Finally, some households put their efforts into small-scale agricultural sidelines, like raising vegetables and pigs. Unlike some areas of the Chinese countryside, which have witnessed a mass out-migration of labor-seeking ex-peasants, most families in Fengjia were able to arrange employment for all adult members within the village. One sixty-year-old man said there was always some work to be found. If worse came to worse, one could bicycle from village to village buying and selling vegetables. Fortunately, he added, in recent years no one in Fengjia has had to do that.

Since the implementation of the post-1978 reforms, the village's economic growth has been rapid. As the collective's capital increased, Fengjia's leaders have diversified from agricultural to light industrial production. Before 1982, all of the village's "sideline" activities were agricultural. In the spring of 1982 Fengjia built its first factory: the popsicle plant, first contracted out in 1985 and closed in 1989. In the fall of 1982 came the flour mill, contracted out in 1985 and bankrupt in 1987. In 1983 they built the cornstarch and steamed bread factories. The steamed bread factory was contracted out from the beginning, while the cornstarch plant has been run continuously by the collective. In 1986 they built an oil press that was subsumed by the cornstarch factory in 1987, and in 1989 they replaced the popsicle factory with the collectively run textile plant. In 1982, 90 percent of the collective's income was derived from agriculture, while in 1986 over half was derived from industry (Gold 1986:4). The following chart, derived from the village accountant's ledger, shows the recent dramatic increase in per capita and collective annual income.

Year	Per Capita	Collective
1970	¥113	¥154,000
1975	152	431,000
1980	500	1,130,000
1988	1,167	4,540,000

Though I found Fengjia's industrial growth impressive, county leaders complained that Secretary Feng was too conservative. They said that because he was unwilling to borrow the money needed to start really large factories, Fengjia's growth had lagged behind that of the most successful villages. These men viewed Fengjia as primarily an agricultural village.

What has this rather paternalistic but successful implementation of the responsibility system meant for the production of *guanxi* in Fengjia? To begin, the village's newfound wealth has had numerous implications for the networking strategies of its residents. For the first time ever, gift giving and banqueting on the scale described in earlier chapters became practical for the majority of residents. Previously, foodstuffs had been the primary media of exchanging *ganqing.* Oi (1989:112) suggests that grain was the primary currency of "pulling" *guanxi* in the poorer areas of the collectivized countryside. In Fengjia, where people knew starvation both before 1948 and during the aftermath of the Great Leap Forward, even middle-aged residents happily remember the transformation from eating "coarse grains" (like sorghum, corn, and sweet potato) to eating three daily meals of steamed bread. During the "three difficult years," gifts of sweet potatoes meant the difference between life and death. During the 1960s, gifts of steamed bread held real significance; by the 1980s, they were mere tokens. Cook Feng argued that spring festival was no longer a truly significant event, because "now we eat like spring festival every day." The symbolic significance of sharing food lost its life-and-death implications.

Others have linked the monetization of gift giving in rural China to an emerging crassness and instrumentalism in rural personal relations (Siu 1989b, 1993; World Journal 1994a, 1994b; and Yan 1993). In these portrayals young people's ignorance of the symbolic richness of Chinese tradition and the newfound wealth of entrepreneurial households have transformed rural ritual into little more than an occasion for building instrumental networks and the ostentatious display of wealth. In Fengjia, I saw nothing as extreme as the above portrayals would suggest. Indeed, the political economy of 1989 Fengjia was not conducive to such crassness: an egalitarian ethos still dominated; average villagers were insulated from market demands by the strength of Secretary Feng's collective farming; and few purely entrepreneurial households existed. However, though I would not dispute that the emergence of cash gift giving was linked to a rising instrumentalism elsewhere, I believe the case of Fengjia demonstrates that the monetization of gift giving can occur without crass instrumentalism. As argued in chapter 3, the dislike of cash gifts reflects Western gift-giving sensibilities more than elucidating those in Fengjia.

Many scholars have commented on the effects of decollectivization on the family-building and networking strategies of rural people (Croll 1987, 1994; Davis and Harrell 1993; Philip Huang 1990; Oi 1989; Wang, Yang, and Li 1990). During the collectivized decades, villagers approached their work like factory workers. Household strategies were limited to maximizing "work points" earned in tasks assigned from above. After decollectivization, rural households were forced to take responsibility for securing their own supplies, organizing their own labor, and marketing their surplus. These activities forced rural families to build a wider network of extravillage *guanxi*. For households that established their own small businesses, the need for extravillage *guanxi* was greater still. Even in Fengjia, the responsibility system greatly increased the range of production decisions and responsibilities of individual households. Though partially sheltered from the responsibilities of complete decollectivization, Fengjia residents were still exposed to more extravillage market relations than before. Those households with sidelines and small businesses sought *guanxi* as producers, while all households, with their newfound wealth, participated in the local markets as consumers.

Judd (1994) suggests that the "feminization of farming" that has followed rural decollectivization has tended to isolate women, because most feminized farming chores do not require interhousehold cooperation. In Fengjia too, decollectivized farming chores were most often done individually, by women. Though this division of labor had many exceptions and was not reinforced with an articulated ideology of gender roles (cf. Beaver, Hou, and Wang 1995), it did seem to reflect an emergent pattern in the late 1980s.

In contrast to the decollectivization of farm chores, infrastructure improvements facilitated the integration of everyone into wider social networks. Fengjia's first paved road was completed during the 1980s, while the county hoped to pave at least one road to every village by 1996. In 1992, Fengjia installed its first direct-dial telephone in the village office. Perhaps most importantly, the county was in the process of building enough schools to make junior high school mandatory for all children and expand the number of students who attended high school. As all post-elementary education took place outside of the village, expansion of secondary education directly increased the proportion of people that had an extravillage network of friends and classmates.

Kelliher (1992:190–196) describes how the responsibility system led to increased demands for loans for agricultural inputs and business start-ups by rural households. Since the agricultural banks were not able to provide this credit, local governments were forced to tolerate private loans, often at high rates. Though Fengjia residents were not hard-pressed for agricultural inputs, several described how they had relied on *guanxi* to borrow money for small business ventures or to finance a new house for their son's marriage. Others said they wanted to build good networks so that they would have access to loans in the future.

Transformations of the social organization of production in Fengjia have led to numerous changes in the types, gender, and uses of the *guanxi* residents have formed. The influences of class differences in forming *guanxi,* the value of intravillage versus extra-village *guanxi,* the comparative needs and opportunities for men and women to form *guanxi,* and the place of *guanxi* in entrepreneurial activity waxed and waned with residents' adaptations to CCP policies. A rising standard of living bolstered residents' ability to give gifts and banquets and otherwise finance *guanxi* formation. Infrastructural improvements made extravillage contacts more convenient. However, economic transformations were not the only CCP policies to influence Fengjia *guanxi* production. Changing regulations on marriages, births, and other family matters did too. Since kinship socially and conceptually grounded village social relations, these changes directly altered *guanxi* production in Fengjia.

Family Strategies

The Marriage Law of 1950 was one of the first legislative acts of the CCP (C. K. Yang 1959:31). By setting minimum ages for marriage, requiring brides and grooms to personally register, and allowing marriage without parental permission between consenting adults, the CCP hoped to end the betrothing of child brides, the "buying and selling of women," and parental control of marriage in general. In Fengjia before 1948, though weddings were often arranged before children reached the age of ten, most brides and grooms did not meet until their weddings. In most marriages the bride was older than the groom; often the man was fifteen while the woman was seventeen. Older residents said that the woman needed to be more mature because she had to adapt to a new family and thus needed to understand the ways of the world (*dongshi*). The man would merely continue to live as a minor in the family in which he had been raised. The implementation of the marriage law brought two major changes to Fengjia marriage practices. First, though engagements continued to be arranged by parents, teenagers were given a chance to meet before the engagement was finalized. Furthermore, by inventing a custom of engagement visits, young couples were encouraged to meet at least four times a year between engagement and marriage (Huang Shu-min 1993). Thus, after 1948 many young couples knew each other fairly well by their wedding day. Secondly, minimum marriage ages not only raised the average marriage age, but also reversed the age differences between brides and grooms. In the 1980s, because the minimum marriage age was twenty for women and twenty-two for men, most grooms were older than their brides.[7]

Most older residents, echoing the language of CCP propaganda, said that the law ended arranged (*baoban*) marriages, and described what took place in the 1980s as "free love" (*ziyou lianai*). However, some younger people dismissed this claim. They were well aware that urban young people often initiated their own marriages in a process considerably more "free" than their own. Likewise echoing the language of various CCP campaigns, these youth blamed the continued existence of *baoban* marriages on "feudal" attitudes or the influence of Confucius. Engagement plans usually were well worked out by the time young people were given a chance to meet, and considerable pressure was brought upon the young couple to accept the marriage. No one I spoke with could remember an instance where young people had rejected such a marriage. However, though many young people would perhaps have wanted to find their own spouses, they were still grateful to their parents for arranging a marriage, since it would be almost impossible to find a spouse on one's own.

Tani Barlow (1989a) describes how the CCP more or less abandoned struggles for the liberation of "youth" and "women" as groups of individuals in favor of "class" struggles for the consolidation of state power by a party that identified itself with (male) "workers and peasants." In the process, the CCP co-opted rather than obliterated filial relationships. In Fengjia there was little opportunity for young people to look for a spouse without the supervision of elders. Area schools likewise seemed to have successfully stifled most romances. Thus both during and after their education, Fengjia youth had little opportunity to find their own spouses. Though outwardly wanting to empower youth in the area of marriage choice, the CCP's utilization of local power structures to control the education, job choice, and geographic mobility of youth all reinforced the elders' control of marriage.

Though in 1989 60 percent of the household heads in Fengjia had the surname Feng, the land reform and Cultural Revolution seemed to have destroyed all forms of lineage relations. Before 1948 the Feng lineage had an ancestral shrine, corporate trust lands, burial grounds, and a genealogy that incorporated several groups of "late comer" (*wailai*) Fengs with the "local" (*zaidi*) Fengs into four branches of single lineage. Some of the other families also had their own burial grounds, though none had ancestral halls or trust land. With the dispersal of Feng lineage land during the land reform and the Cultural Revolution destruction of the Feng ancestral temple and four of five copies of the family genealogy, the lineage ceased to be a significant unit in Fengjia. When I was in

Fengjia, though people still mentioned the four "branches" of the Feng family, there were no practices that produced or reproduced lineage-level organizations. The remaining copy of the Feng genealogy, kept in secret during the Cultural Revolution, seemed to have little influence. Some older Fengs complained that most younger residents barely knew how they were related to each other.

The responsibility system has further engendered changes in practices of family reproduction. Older residents said that before 1978 it was unheard of to partition one's family (*fenjia*) before a daughter-in-law had her first child.[8] As a result of increasing demands made by brides' families in marriage negotiations (described in chapter 5), during the 1980s most young couples would *fenjia* within six months of marriage. People gave two reasons for this change in practice. Some said that since economic conditions have improved, more often than not brides' families demanded the building of a separate residence for the young couple before they would consent to an engagement. By so doing they guaranteed the physical availability of a separate room to "split" into. Others, echoing CCP propaganda about why the division of village property under the responsibility system spurs production, said that giving young couples control of their own land and property "gives play to their enthusiasm [for work]" (*fahui tamende jijixing*).

Reactions to the birth control policy have led to the most radical changes in practices of the production of family units. Since the early 1980s, national policy has limited couples to a maximum of one son. If the first child was a daughter, the parents could petition to have a second child five or six years later. The exact timing of permission for the second child depended on the age of the parents and on how the village as a whole was meeting its population growth rate targets (set by county birth control officials). No one was allowed to have more than two children.[9] Before marriage, young couples were instructed in birth control methods by family planning officials. In Fengjia, birth control pills, condoms, and IUDs were all available. Most women used IUDs. Every three months the county family planning inspector came to the village. All married women who had not reached menopause had to come to the village clinic for a pregnancy test. If a woman was pregnant and her situation was not one in which it was permissible to have a child, she would be scheduled for an abortion.

Ikels (1993) argues that patrilocal kinship in rural China has implied an intergenerational contract in which sons and daughters-in-law have primary responsibility for their aged parents and, consequently, in which sons receive greater parental investment than daughters. Though there is a general tendency toward these patterns in Fengjia, I have tried to show that kinship obligations were always being contested and that parents invested in and made *ganqing* claims on daughters as well as sons. In terms of caring for elderly parents, though sons tended to give more financial support, daughters often gave more physical and emotional care than either sons or daughters-in-law. Parental ideals of family composition reflected these patterns. In 1988–90 Fengjia, as in Greenhalgh's (1993) studies of the Shaanxi countryside during the 1980s, most parents felt that the ideal family included one son and one daughter, but preferred one son and no daughters to two daughters and no sons. In anticipation of sonless families, local officials emphasized that the law equally obligated daughters and sons to care for their aged parents. Since the first generation of parents to be affected by this policy were still young, no one knew exactly how daughters would share this responsibility. However, by 1989 Fengjia residents had at least partially adjusted their expectations. Because brotherless women were legally obligated to their natal parents, they were considered less desirable spouses than women with brothers.

Before the implementation of the birth control policy, families that did not have sons were usually able to adopt them. There were many forms of adoption, and through the late 1970s the majority of Fengjia families were involved in either the giving or receiving of children; by the late 1980s, there were hardly any adoptions and no legal ones. Previously, adoption was considered beneficial to all parties involved. Sonless parents could adopt male children who would look after them in their old age. Parents with many sons could place one of their sons in another family where he would be the sole inheritor and reserve their own property for their remaining offspring.

The most common form of adoption was called "passing the succession" (*guoji*). In it, a family with multiple sons would give one to a related family that had no sons. The following example of two brothers' swap of children is illustrative.

> Older brother A's wife had three daughters between 1968 and 1972. Younger brother B's wife had one son in 1977 and a second in 1978. After the 1978 birth, B traded his first son for A's youngest daughter. Unfortunately, in 1982 B's remaining son died, and the birth control policy had in the meantime been

implemented. As a family with only one daughter, B pleaded his case with the village family planning committee. Eventually he was allowed to have another child and it was a boy.

The adoption of a child from a family one doesn't know was called *fuyang* or *baoyang*.[10] Though less common than *guoji*, it still occurred often before 1978. In some of these cases the family that gave up the child did not have the economic resources to raise it. Usually a small amount of money was given to the natural mother. This money was not considered a price for the child, but rather a gift to the mother to help her buy the "supplements" (*bupin*) she would need to recover from childbirth. In the 1980s, this practice still existed, but the prices for baby boys (and they were then considered prices) were astronomical (I heard estimates of ¥10,000). Moreover, to avoid creating a market for children secretly born in remote regions, the Birth Control Bureau had made such adoptions illegal. The few illegally adopted children in Fengjia were not registered in the *hukou* lists. Consequently, their families were not given the extra land that was usually allocated for new family members in the triannual, responsibility-system land reallocations. However, to avoid personally punishing the adopted children, the village committee decided to give the additional land to these children's families when they reached eight years of age, and to allow them to attend the village school.

Before the implementation of the birth control policy, there were also a few cases of matrilocal marriage in Fengjia. Families with many sons were sometimes willing to allow one of them to move in with their daughter-in-law's family. Parents with daughters but no sons were usually amenable to this idea. In the 1980s, though the CCP officially promoted matrilocal (*nan dao nujia luohu*) marriages, the birth control policy's elimination of multi-son families ended the basis for this practice.

Finally, the birth control policy has limited the child care responsibilities of younger women. Not only are there fewer children to take care of, but grandparents (especially grandmothers) often relieve young mothers of this chore (cf. Judd 1994:192–199). Kim Faulk (personal communication), who did research in another Zouping county village during the 1990s, suggests that this reduction in child bearing and care responsibilities has significantly improved the status of young women, who now can spend much more of their time in income-generating activities. Insofar as young women earn income away from their homes (rather than purely from farming the household plots), this reduction in child care responsibilities might also increase the scope of their extra-household networks.

Ritual Activities

As described in part I, rituals were major occasions for *guanxi* production. However, ritual life in Fengjia was far from stable. Residents revised their rituals not only in reaction to the changes described above but also in response to direct CCP attacks on the "feudal" aspects of pre-communist ritual. Party hostility to rural ritual had many reasons: a desire to replace "superstition" with science, a hostility toward the types of *guanxi* that many rituals produced, and a frugal concern with the "wasteful" use of resources in ritual events.[11] In its efforts to reform rural rituals, the CCP directly banned some sorts of ritual actions and—by redesigning wedding vows, folk songs, spring festival couplets, and local operas—co-opted others.[12]

In Fengjia, CCP control of ritual activity waxed and waned, with the Cultural Revolution marking the period of strictest control. Between 1966 and 1968, Fengjia youth divided into two camps of Red Guards: a group that supported Secretary Feng and an "anti-countercurrent clique" (*fanniliupai*). The two groups competed to outdo each other in "smashing the four olds."[13] Not only did they raze the Feng ancestral temple and burn four of the five copies of the Feng family genealogy, but they also leveled all of the village's graves and destroyed any ritual paraphernalia that wasn't successfully hidden, including, most importantly, every family's ancestral scrolls. In 1969, the leader supported by the "anti-countercurrent" clique was offered a position in the army and left town. Secretary Feng retained his power and the most destructive struggles ended. After the 1978 reforms, restrictions on ritual activity were considerably relaxed.

Before 1948, funerals were the most elaborate ritual activity in the village. The lineages played an important role. If the deceased were old and the family wealthy, a funeral could last seven days. Friends and relatives came from near and far, bringing gifts and commemorative couplets. Even an "average" funeral could last three days. In her description of North China funerals between 1870 and 1940, Susan Naquin (1988:42) details the "completing the tablet" ritual. In Fengjia, the same ritual was completed on scrolls, a common substitute for the more expensive tablets throughout North China (M. Cohen 1990). A lineage elder who had a lot of "culture" (*wenhua*) would add a "dot" to the deceased's ancestral scroll to change the character for lord (*wang*) to the character for host (*zhu*). This finished the scroll's calligraphy and allowed the deceased's spirit to join the ancestors. The scrolls would then be hung in the Feng family temple (or stored in homes, for families other than the Fengs). The deceased's spirit could then be honored in front of his/her scroll on the appropriate occasions. After the funeral, the corpse was buried on family land.

The equalization of wealth brought about by the land reform led to an equalization of funerals. Though the richest could no longer afford grandiose funerals, even the poorest could afford a decent one. Though land had been redistributed, families who gave up land in the land reform did not give up their burial sites. The previously landless buried their dead on their new land. After collectivization, families continued to bury their dead on their former ancestral land, even though they no longer owned the plots in question. As time went on, more and more graves obstructed plowing in a seemingly random pattern on the newly collectivized fields. To mitigate this problem by consolidating future burial sites, the village constructed a "public grave" (*gongmu*) in 1964. Though leveled just two years later during the Cultural Revolution, this site continues to be used as a place of ancestral offering by those who buried their ancestors between 1964 and 1966.

The Cultural Revolution brought about huge restrictions on funerary activities. All graves were leveled and Fengjia residents were forced to cremate instead of bury their dead. Ancestral scrolls were burned. In most cases, people were forbidden to attend the funerals of friends and neighbors. If the deceased had a poor-peasant class label, close relatives who were also poor peasants were allowed to visit and *ketou* in front of the deceased's cinerary casket. Weeping, gift giving, and interclass attendance and *ketou*ing were forbidden at funerals. The night after cremation the family of the deceased would usually sneak out and bury the cinerary casket in an unmarked grave on ancestral land.

After the post-1978 reforms, most restrictions on funerals were eased. Though cremation was still mandatory, residents legally buried their cinerary caskets on their former ancestral land. Though under the responsibility system, one's family's pre-liberation ancestral land was most likely allocated to another family, the family that was currently farming the land allowed the family of the deceased to bury their dead. The cinerary casket was buried deeper than before (so that it would not interfere with plowing), and the temporarily constructed grave was plowed under when the time came to prepare for the next crop. Funerals, though fairly elaborate, became one-day affairs. Lineages were no longer important, and there were no new ancestral scrolls. Though there were no gifts or couplets given at funerals, friends and family from a wide area attended. In the late 1980s, *waisheng* (the children of one's sister or daughter) began bringing flower wreaths (*huaquan*) to funerals. This practice was an adaptation from urban funerals seen on TV, and was stimulated by the introduction of these wreaths to local markets. Banqueting, weeping, and performing *ketou* at the appropriate moments again became important.

Weddings, though the largest ritual event in the 1980s, previously had been secondary to funerals. Before 1948, weddings in Fengjia usually took three days, with the bride going back to her natal home for the "third day return" (*santian huifang*). Chinese astrology (*shuxiang*) and fortune-telling (*suanming*) were often referred to during the selection of spouses, and were crucial to the selection of the wedding day. Considerable symbolic weight was given to the procession from the bride's natal home to her marital home in which the bride, accompanied by relatives of the groom and musicians, rode a sedan chair (*huajiao*). Legitimacy was also embodied in the use of "engagement papers" (*dinghunshu*) (issued by the local government) in the marriage ceremony. The ceremony itself involved the bride and groom performing *ketou* to heaven and earth, the ancestors, the family, and each other. Brides and grooms were forced to *ketou*.

After 1948, several changes took place. The CCP banned astrology and fortune-telling, labeling them forms of superstition. The Marriage Law of 1950 made registration with the local marriage bureau the legal determinant of marriage. The CCP wanted this registration to be the sole criterion of legitimacy. Toward this end, they banned the use of sedan chairs. Grooms began picking up their brides in horsecarts with tents constructed on top. The engagement papers became a superfluous document.

During the Cultural Revolution, marriage ceremonies were further constrained. Individual, private ceremonies were replaced by collective weddings (*jiti jiehun*). All the couples who were to marry in the same year convened in the center of the village on a designated day. After each bride and groom made a short speech promising to "endlessly support the revolution" or "spur on production," everyone simultaneously bowed from the waist. Though some couples had small private parties at home afterwards, there were no large banquets, few guests, and no drinking was allowed. Class criteria were important in both the selection of spouses and the attendance of private ceremonies.

During the 1980s, private ceremonies with large banquets and much drinking became the norm. However, post-Mao weddings were not mere copies of pre-1948 ones. Though the older version of the wedding vows was revived, forced *ketou* was not. As described in chapter 5, brides and grooms often did not even bow during the ceremony. Secondly, sedan chairs were no longer used. Brides were brought from their natal homes via bicycles, tractors, cars, and trucks. Thirdly, in the late 1980s, weddings were compressed into one day. Better roads had reduced travel time between the villages, so that the trips between the bride's and groom's homes that previously took three days could be accomplished in one long day. What had been the first day's main banquet took place at breakfast, the second day's at lunch, and the third day's at dinner. Finally, in the 1980s the number and size of wedding gifts and the splendor of wedding banquets far exceeded those of earlier periods.

The communist decades have seen many other ritual changes. Ancestral offerings continued to be carried out five times a year. However, before the Cultural Revolution these offerings were organized by the lineages and, for the Fengs, took place inside their ancestral temple. During the 1980s, they were matters for individual families. Elders say that the lineage-organized offerings were considerably more "ceremonious" (*longzhong*) than those of the 1980s. During the Cultural Revolution ancestral offering was done stealthily, if at all. Spring festival visits and *ketou* were also banned during the Cultural Revolution, though they too were occasionally done on the sly.

Wedding and spring festival couplets, hung on inner and outer doorways on the appropriate occasions, underwent a major transformation after 1948. The CCP co-opted these message-bearing decorations as propaganda tools. From the late 1940s until 1986 it was illegal to use couplets other than the official ones published annually in local newspapers. Though in the late 1980s it was technically legal to think up one's own couplets, most Fengjia residents conservatively stuck to the official ones.

In general, the expanding wealth of the 1980s has allowed an enriched ritual life. Several occasions that previously were minor family get-togethers (such as birthday parties for one-year-olds) became major gift-giving and banqueting opportunities. Others, like the engagement visits described by Huang Shu-min (1993), were invented from scratch.

Finally, it seems that the CCP was fairly successful in stamping out what it considered "superstition." In the local markets I saw no fortune-tellers, and those I spoke with said that superstition no longer played a role in practical affairs like farming and finding spouses. Except for a few families who used Chinese astrology to select a wedding day "for the fun of it" or those who pasted couplets invoking the protection of the spirits on the beams of new houses, I saw no evidence of "superstitious" activity.

At all times from 1948 through 1990 there were ways of conceiving and manipulating *guanxi* and reasons for having them. Yet, *guanxi* production in Fengjia was anything but static. Since *guanxi* touch on every aspect of life in Fengjia, CCP policies of all sorts have influenced the whos, hows, and whys of their production. Though these changes fail to form any single pattern, they dispel structural-functional conceptions of a constant place of *guanxi* in village life. Some of the major changes may be summarized as follows:

1. State restrictions on migration have produced extreme levels of residential stability, which have allowed *guanxi* production to proceed under assumptions of life-long relationships.

2. Many CCP policies have influenced the gendered organization of household labor and thus the needs and abilities of various household members and types of households to form *guanxi* for economic production. The land reform eliminated tenancy. Collectivization removed from individual households much of the responsibility for production and introduced women to agricultural work. Fengjia-style decollectivization returned limited responsibility to households and diversified the range of household strategies. Birth control reduced the burdens of child care.

3. The destruction of lineage organizations and the birth control policies radically altered the structure and meaning of the kinship bases of *guanxi* production.

4. The building of schools and introduction of compulsory junior high school education for men and women have expanded the range of extravillage contacts for all Fengjia youth.

Viewed historically, the practices described in part I took place in a new and contingent social context that reflected the historical convergence of several CCP policies and socioeconomic trends. The household registration, land reform, collectivization, and conservative decollectivization policies created a geographically stable and relatively egalitarian community. The land reform and Cultural Revolution dismantled the lineages. The birth control policy ended the possibility of multi-son families. Increases in wealth provided more capital for buying gifts, banqueting, and ritual life in general. The responsibility system (as implemented in Fengjia) led to shifting patterns of household labor. The post-Mao relaxations of ritual restrictions allowed for the (re)invention of much ritual. The Cultural Revolution engendered bitter factional struggles within the village, while its conclusion allowed for at least partial reconciliation. Though these developments cannot be said to have determined practices of *guanxi* production in 1988–90 Fengjia, they both provided the context within which residents acted and formed the objects of their struggles for further change. If there was a constant to *guanxi* production during this period, it was the value of maintaining good relations with one's neighbors to protect oneself from the radical reversals of state policy.

8   *Guanxi* Versions throughout China

Most of the previous chapters examine practices of *guanxi* production in Fengjia. By concentrating on *ganqing* in a relatively collectivized, egalitarian rural village, this portrayal might seem naive to those familiar with more instrumental, even corrupt, manipulations of *guanxi* in other PRC settings (e.g., Smart 1993). Not only did I concentrate on a relatively egalitarian village, but I also emphasized the sort of *intra*village *guanxi* that almost always involve long-standing, kinlike relations. Given the high visibility of the research project with which I was affiliated, I was hesitant to describe examples of Fengjia residents manipulating distant, extravillage *guanxi* in the pursuit of instrumental gains of questionable legality. However, my portrayal of intravillage *guanxi* has its own merits. Not only is such kinlike *guanxi* production widespread, but it often serves as the model imitated in more distant *guanxi* manipulations.

This chapter focuses on *guanxi* production in other Chinese settings. It compares the intravillage *guanxi* production of Fengjia with studies of *guanxi* in urban settings in the People's Republic, in Chinese business firms, and in CCP policies toward its own members and society at large.

Urban *Guanxi* in the PRC

Almost all of the *guanxi* production I described in Fengjia took place among people who were, if not relatives or close friends, at least long-term acquaintances. Urban *guanxi* networks more often involve strangers. In part this difference reflects the contrast between the urban and rural social contexts generated by CCP policy.[1] During the 1980s, urban residents were entitled to state-provided jobs and housing. Powerful officials often controlled the distribution of such necessities well beyond the range of their immediate acquaintances. In contrast, in rural areas, at least after the disbandment of the communes, central life concerns like housing and job assignments were not controlled by unknown officials. Rather, they were responsibilities shared by individual families and a village leadership who in many cases were kin to almost everyone in the village. Rural villagers had less need than urbanites to seek *guanxi* outside of their local networks.

At Nanjing University, I heard college students differentiate between two types of friendships. One was based on deep mutual *ganqing* and a willingness to sacrifice materially for one's friend. The other consisted of an affected *ganqing* and was established for the purpose of enabling mutually beneficial material exchanges. The sarcasm adopted when calling both sorts of *guanxi* "friendships" illustrates the difference between these two sorts of *guanxi*. However, here I would also emphasize the similarity. Even when two "friends" desire only a mutually beneficial exchange, they still find it necessary to affect *ganqing*. In both instances, *ganqing* and mutual indebtedness go together.

The term *la guanxi* (literally, to "pull" relationships) is closely related to this second, more venal sort of "friendship." Mayfair Yang calls this practice "the Chinese gift economy or 'the art of *guanxi*'" and provides an excellent description of its workings in an urban Chinese context during the 1980s:

> Certainly *guanxi* extends into the economic and political realms. Such tasks as obtaining and changing job assignments, buying certain foods and consumer items, getting into good hospitals and buying medicines, buying train, theater, and sports tickets, moving from one town to another, obtaining housing, and even gaining Party membership, often call for the "art of *guanxi*." Yet while in function *guanxi* may resemble bribery, in both its form and the cultural understanding of practitioners, they are distinct. Form, that repertoire of ethics and etiquettes governing the practice of the gift economy, is of the essence. In addition to the skillful and strategic giving of gifts, the gift economy also involves the cultivation of what Bourdieu has called "symbolic capital" (1977), "face," honor, relations of obligation, indebtedness and reciprocity, which are not crucial components in bribery. Instead of the impersonal relationship of bribery linked by mutual materialist utility, the gift economy integrates utility into non-state personalistic relationships of friendship and kinship, such as classmate, neighbor, native-place, co-worker, and superior-subordinate relationships. (1988:411)

For my purposes, Yang's description of the art of *guanxi* should be contextualized in three further points. First of all, Yang's comparison of the art of *guanxi* with bribery has a double source. It refers both to the negative, official discourses that dismiss official banqueting and gift giving as unprincipled, illegal, and harmful (e.g., *Village Masses* 1988, 1989d; also see note 5) and to Western understandings in which the giving of gifts to officials for the purpose of eliciting favors is equated with bribery (e.g., Rocca 1992). Whether one considers a specific act of "pulling" *guanxi* a form of bribery really depends upon one's point of view. In official CCP pronouncements, much of such "pulling" counted as bribery. Unofficially, what bribery consisted of was a matter of moral debate. Though most people drew a line between bribery and the art of *guanxi* somewhere, they did not all draw it in the same place.

Second, the "form" of ethics and etiquette that separates "pulling" *guanxi* from bribery adds *ganqing* to a relationship of "mutual materialist utility." Etiquette, the giving of gifts, or inviting someone to a banquet purposefully mimics the means of constituting *ganqing* within the family and among true friends. Which form of and how much *ganqing* must be added to one's "mutual materialist utility," however, was again a matter of ongoing ethical debate. Finally, and consequently, the line between the two types of "friendship" discussed above blurs. If the person who comes to be in charge of railroad tickets is one's close friend from college or one's sister, so much the better. Likewise, if a person on whom one relies for "mutual materialist utility," through repeated contact and exchanges of affected *ganqing*, grows to be a "true friend," so much the better.

In Nanjing I often witnessed the use of intermediaries to extend *ganqing* to unknown parties for the purpose of material exchange. To give a gift to an official one didn't recognize, one found a mutual friend and gave the gift through that person (usually also giving a small gift to the intermediary). At times these chains could become quite long, involving friends of friends of friends. The term "pulling" *guanxi* perhaps came from these occasions; one pulls a chain of *guanxi* links to reach a target official. The use of such intermediaries was a moral as well as practical matter. Most people I met, urban and rural, wouldn't give a gift directly to someone they didn't know. Without a pre-existing *ganqing* basis, such "mutual material utility" would approach bribery.

However, I also observed and met people, usually small entrepreneurs, who engaged in direct gift giving to former strangers. On a train I saw a clothing stall owner buy a ¥2 railway ticket with a ¥10 note and say, "finding change is too much trouble, keep it." The ticket taker hesitated, but finally accepted when the stall owner said, "I take this train often, soon we'll become friends." Some scholars argue that strict regulation of entrepreneurial activities forced such businessmen to give aggressively (Gold 1989, Wank 1994). However, despite the stall owner's boldness, minimal form remained important. The gift was cloaked as saving the ticket taker trouble, and the relationship described as becoming friends.

During the 1980s, most urban Chinese worked in socialist "work units" (*danwei*). More than a simple workplace, these units, depending on their size and power, distributed housing, foodstuffs, furniture, and/or other goods; ran nurseries, schools, and/or health clinics; carried out CCP social and political campaigns; and approved marriages, divorces, adoptions, passports, and visa applications (Henderson and Cohen 1984; Whyte and Parish 1984; Mayfair Yang 1989a, 1989b). Thus, work units were a major site of political and social control and the distribution of goods as well as economic production. Andrew Walder (1986:7) describes how this system of economic distribution drove people to rely on *guanxi*. Since workplace officials rather than the marketplace determined who got what, establishing *guanxi* with officials became a primary tactic of consumption. Pulling *guanxi* even facilitated finding a workplace in the first place (Bian 1994). Mayfair Yang (1989a) links the distribution of goods in work units to CCP biopolitics. Work unit distribution policies categorized and normalized workers; those who conformed with the birth control policy, married at the correct age, acted as model workers, or demonstrated loyalty to the factory received priority. By placing so much power, so many distributive decisions in the hands of petty officials acting in the name of the universalistic ethics of the state, the work unit system engendered an expansion of *guanxi*-producing practices to get around this power. Manipulations of *guanxi* to secure goods and services thus constituted both a method of consumption and an evasion of state biopower.

The art of *guanxi* invokes a moral emphasis on the relational ethics of *ganqing* exchange at the expense of the universalistic ethics of state normalization. In Nanjing I met a manager who complained that workers constantly pressured him to attend their personal banquets. If he did not attend, his workers would label him a snob and attempt to undermine him. I also met factory workers who argued that "personal loyalty" or "righteousness" (*yiqi*) was the most important personal virtue. In both of these instances workers challenged the normalizing priorities of the state with an ethics of *ganqing*.

How does this urban *guanxi* production compare to that of 1988–90 Fengjia? Whyte and Parish (1984) describe how the socialist system of lifetime employment along with the household registration policies and state control of housing led to high degrees of workplace and residential stability among urban Chinese (at least through the mid-1980s). Consequently, Chinese cities could hardly be described as centers of anonymous social relations. Ruan Danching (1993) further argues that the personal networks of Chinese urbanites contain mostly people within their own work unit. As with Whyte and Parish, Ruan thus suggests that communist social structures narrow and tighten the range of urban social relations. Nevertheless, few urban work units could be as intimate and restraining as a rural village. Unlike in Fengjia, few coworkers in urban work units would be relatives. Moreover, urbanites often had separate living and working quarters. Though some urban work units controlled their workers' housing, many did not, and their workers lived in housing units scattered throughout their cities. In Fengjia, fellow villagers lived, worked, and passed most of their lives in an area of a few square blocks. Thirdly, the size and density of urban settings made anonymous relations possible, even if they were not dominant. In Fengjia, or even within many of the marketing communities surrounding Fengjia, it was impossible to eat, buy, sell, etc. anonymously. Finally, for those urbanites whose work units commanded few resources or, increasingly during the 1990s, who didn't belong to work units at all, the constraints and opportunities of the socialist work unit distribution system would be absent altogether. In brief, though communist social structures encouraged a sort of gemeinschaft in some urban contexts, they did not lead to personal relations as close-knit and contained as those of Fengjia.

Guanxi in Business, Business in *Guanxi*

Scholarly investigations of business organizations in Taiwan, Hong Kong, and Southeast Asia have emphasized the importance of *guanxi* networks to Chinese firms. Hamilton and Kao (1990) describe how Taiwanese businesses resist the formal structures common to large Western corporations. By avoiding command hierarchies with well-defined roles and responsibilities, business owners prevent anonymous, professional managers from gaining control of their firms. Instead, power remains in the hands of a closely linked handful of owners and/or their trusted confidants. Such firms also resist public stock offerings, which would likewise erode the personal control of the firms' inner circle. This personalized control tends to limit the size of Chinese business organizations. Consequently, Taiwanese and Hong Kong business groups average less than one-third the employees of Korean groups and one-fifth the employees of Japanese ones (Hamilton and Kao 1990; Redding 1990).

Though often organized around a well defined set of people, the *guanxi*-producing practices of Chinese firms can be very flexible. Inner circles may be composed of family members or long-term friends and confidants (Hamilton and Kao 1990); external *guanxi* may be based on networks of lineage members, native place organizations, church members, classmates, or simply long-term business connections (Redding 1990).

Internal organization around an inner circle of closely related people facilitates the use of *guanxi* in business transactions. People have *guanxi;* roles in a command hierarchy do not. Since the inner circle closely identifies itself with the firm, the firm can rely on the *guanxi* of those people in external transactions. Owner/managers cultivate *guanxi* with an eye toward their firm's growth, while professional managers network to enhance their own careers. In Taiwan, interpersonal linkages form the basis for the business groups (*guanxi qiye*) that dominate the economy (Numazaki 1991). Thus, though networking may be a strategy of Western corporate managers as well, "[b]usiness networks in Taiwan form the foundation of the economy, whereas in the United States the corporation does" (Hamilton and Kao 1990:150).

Chinese firms may also emphasize *guanxi* in labor relations. Redding describes a Hong Kong executive who says "People are more loyal to people than to an organization. I like people to be loyal to me. People down below should be loyal to the superior rather than to the firm itself" (1990:166). Redding gives another example of a Chinese businessman who prepared his son for taking over the company by having him work, from the bottom up, in all of the firm's departments. The purpose of this preparation was not only to give the son "experience" but also to allow him to cultivate *guanxi* throughout the firm. Executives who desire the type of personal and hierarchical loyalty described above must first establish *guanxi* on an individual basis.

Lin Yueh Hua's (1947) depiction of two families and their business ventures in Fujian province during the Republican period usefully illustrates the place of *guanxi* in the family firms of that time. A Chinese native educated in anthropology and writing in English, Lin meant his fictional chronicle as a sociological account of the factors that affected the rise and fall of families in Republican China. He begins as follows:

Our lives, after all, can be coldly charted out. The circle of our daily associations is like a delicately-poised network of bamboo sticks tautly connected by
elastic rubber bands. Pull one bond too hard, to the snapping point, and the
whole network tumbles into ruin. Each tautly connected stick is one of the
human beings to whom our life has tied us. Pull one of them completely away,
and we tumble, too, in pain, to ruin, and all ties go temporarily slack. (1947:2)

Throughout the book, Lin describes the rise and fall of individuals, their
families, and their businesses in terms of their management of *guanxi,*
envisioned above as a delicate balancing act of bamboo poles and tautly
drawn rubber bands.

Redding (1990) points out that Chinese business firms historically
arose in legal contexts where property rights and contract law were unreliable. The *guanxi*-oriented styles of these firms were necessary for
survival. A close-knit inner circle allowed them to keep their financial
situations relatively secret in a climate where corrupt government or
tax officials might be eager to expropriate any wealth they know about.
The cultivation of long-term, reliable *guanxi* built the trust necessary
to carry out business transactions in places where contract law or the
courts were unreliable. Hamilton (1991), Kao (1991), and Redding (1990,
1991) all argue that personal trust continues to serve as the primary
basis for business transactions among Chinese firms in Taiwan, Hong
Kong, and Southeast Asia.

At least since 1978, business organizations have emerged as important institutions in the People's Republic as well. These organizations—
whether foreign-owned, joint-venture, "private" (*getihu,* or *siying*), or
local rural cooperative (*xiangzhen qiye*)—likewise have a marked tendency to create, involve, and rely on *guanxi* in their business ventures.
Wank (1994, 1995) describes how the legacy of the PRC's command
economy gave rise to an institutional environment in which capitalist entrepreneurs needed to form alliances with CCP officials. Access
to commodities and raw materials, land, financial capital, public customers, and permits of all sorts, as well as protection from bureaucratic
harassment, tax collectors, and political campaigns all required entrepreneurs to form *guanxi* with well-placed cadres. Many Xiamen entrepreneurs began establishing cadre *guanxi* through sporadic gift giving,
delivering presents whenever they needed help. However, as their firms
and resources grew, they tried to shift to more stable and reliable ties
by incorporating officials into their firms through partnerships or long-

term buildups of *ganqing* (Wank 1994). In both Xiamen and Sichuan provinces, strategic marriages became a useful strategy for consolidating reliable entrepreneurial *guanxi* (Odgaard 1992; Wank 1995).

The most common means of cultivating *ganqing* and *guanxi* by PRC businessmen resemble those described in Fengjia. Gift giving and banqueting are ubiquitous. Many urban work units, and even rural villages like Fengjia, build guest houses with banquet rooms and hire cooks and servers to take care of their networking needs. Wilson (1994) writes of a suburban Shanghai village that developed orange orchards to grow fruit for village factory gift giving and a mushroom farm to produce delicacies for factory banquets. He further describes how local officials, bankers, managers, and entrepreneurs call each other "banquet buddies" (*jiurou pengyou*) and argues that their banqueting facilitates rural industrialization. In 1995 the *Canton Evening News* reported that cadres' yearly expenditures on banqueting amounted to US $12 billion (*World Journal* 1995). In addition to gift giving and banqueting, Wank describes Xiamen entrepreneurs who visit officials at work to assess their needs and develop *ganqing*. He quotes one as saying,

> I often go and visit the bureau to talk with them. Shoot the breeze, smoke some cigarettes. Sometimes I will just sit for several hours chatting about this and that. Sometimes they will talk about their families or some problem that I can help them with. They have much experience and I can learn a lot. If you sit with somebody long enough you develop emotion (*ganqing*). (1994:18)

Business owners may also rely upon and cultivate *ganqing* among employees. In small firms in Xiamen, family members are often hired as managers (Wank 1994). Throughout China work units and factories hold New Year's banquets for employees. Employers may also demonstrate their concern for the health of their workers or otherwise act paternalistically in an attempt to develop *ganqing* (e.g., Wank 1994). Yet it would be mistaken to confuse the paternalistic *ganqing* strategies of Chinese business owners with a more humane form of capitalism. Though some village- and township-owned enterprises, like the factories in Fengjia, take local employment and development as their raison d'être, many private and/or nonlocally owned firms are quite exploitive. Ong (1993), for one, counts the labor practices of overseas Chinese businessmen, whether in the PRC or elsewhere, as among the most exploitive in the world.

Indeed, strategies of exclusion and distancing are common wherever appeals to *guanxi* are likely. Hwang (1987) describes how upper-class Chinese generally attempt to limit obligations by downplaying the importance of *ganqing*. James Watson (in Tu, Milan, and Wachman 1992:92–95) argues that lineage relations in South China were as much about excluding outsiders as internal sharing. Wank (1994) describes how Xiamen entrepreneurs applied these principles. Owners divided workers into insiders and outsiders on the basis of whether or not they were locals. Insiders got the easiest jobs with the most responsibility, while the dirty, dangerous jobs went to outsiders. Since outsiders lacked the local *guanxi* to get employers in trouble, their potential complaints went unheard. Since owners could afford to treat a limited number of insiders well, they established *ganqing* and *guanxi* with them, and trusted them with more important tasks. If they did have difficulty with an insider, they could approach him or her through local intermediaries. Outsiders could simply be fired. Chan et al. (1992:299–305) describe a similar pattern in southern Guangdong, where locals and Hong Kong entrepreneurs teamed up against outsiders to insure good jobs for locals and a docile labor force for entrepreneurs. Given the large migrating labor pool of the Dengist period, this pattern has likely been widespread.

Fried (1953) gives an earlier example of how *ganqing* can mediate hierarchical business relations. Writing of landlord/tenant, owner/ worker, and other vertical relations during the Republican period, he states:

> For the most part, *kan ch'ing* [*ganqing*][2] expresses a relationship between two individuals who are not on precisely the same social plane. It is possible to say that your *kan ch'ing* with a friend of the same social level is good, but it is not likely in [Chu county] that you would use the word in such a way. *Kan ch'ing* is the primary institutionalized technique by which class differences are reduced between non-related persons, or even, as we shall see below, between distantly related kin. (1953:103)

and later,

> *Kan ch'ing* differs from friendship in that it presumes a much more specific common interest, much less warmth and more formality of contact, and includes a recognized degree of exploitation. It is the common property of all classes. We have stressed certain manifestations of *kan ch'ing*, particularly those which are of aid in binding the landlord–tenant relationship. We have also reviewed the relationship which helps gentlemen of lower status to stabilize their position with regard to the power of the state. (1953:226–227)

Fried's description reveals an interesting shift in vocabulary from the *ganqing* described in 1988–90 Fengjia. Fried never mentions *guanxi* and translates *ganqing* as a certain type of relationship rather than human feeling. Indeed, in Fried's description *ganqing* is a relationship devoid of warmth. In 1988–90 Fengjia *ganqing* could exist between equals, among family members, and in power relationships in both directions, rather than only in certain hierarchical class relationships. However, rather like in Fengjia, the main methods of establishing *ganqing* described by Fried were gift giving and banquets. In any case Fried's description illustrates the adaptation of *ganqing* production to contexts in which class-based conflicts of interest undercut the grounding of *guanxi* in trust and warmth.

In part I, I emphasized that *guanxi* involve a conflation of material obligation and *ganqing*, and contrasted *guanxi* with Western capitalist relations that separate emotional and economic transactions. This chapter, however, reveals Chinese contexts in which the congruence of personal feeling and material obligation seems strained at best. In the end, in contexts where Chinese and Western businessmen interact, or perhaps even in some Chinese markets, the line between *guanxi* and economic exchange in the Western bourgeois sense (where *ganqing* has no acknowledged role) becomes fuzzy. As Arjun Appadurai (1986) points out, drawing too sharp of a line between gift giving and other types of exchange mystifies as much as it clarifies (see also Smart 1993). Though *guanxi* involve some sort of *ganqing* and obligation, any effort to precisely pin down the place of material obligation and *ganqing* in *guanxi* will be frustrated both by the wide variety of practices that constitute *guanxi*, and by the ongoing moral discourses and debates on the proper place of *guanxi* in social practice. There is no way to draw a single, precise line between "true" and "affected" *ganqing* or between bribery and "pulling" *guanxi*. Because the production of *guanxi* is a series of ongoing, morally contested social practices, it cannot be acontextually essentialized. At best, one may describe *guanxi* as countless variations on the theme of unity between *ganqing* and material obligation.

Guanxi in CCP Politics and Policies

Perhaps the most detailed discussion of *guanxi* in politics is Jacobs's (1979) portrayal of rural Matsu township (Taiwan) during the early 1970s. In contrast to Fried's (1953) descriptions of *ganqing*, the vocabulary described by Jacobs closely resembles usages in Fengjia. *Ganqing* refers to the feeling involved in *guanxi*. The better the *ganqing* the closer the *guanxi*. The closer the *guanxi* the more reliable or dependable (*xinyong* in Matsu township, *kekao* in Fengjia) it is for material and/or political favors. *Ganqing* is established through gift giving, eating together, and coming and going, or social interaction (*laiwang*) in general. *Ganqing* exists in both hierarchical and nonhierarchical relationships. In hierarchical relationships, from the subordinate point of view it takes the form of respect (*zunjing* in Matsu township, *jingyi* in Fengjia); from the superior point of view it becomes either love (*aihu*) in personal settings or trust in bureaucratic settings. Between equals, it exists as friendship or love. The parallels in vocabulary between Taiwanese local politicians speaking Hokkien dialect, and mainland rural villagers speaking Shandong dialect are striking.[3] In addition to *ganqing*, Jacobs emphasizes the importance of what he calls the *guanxi* "base." He argues that a base of identification—such as family, hometown, school, or place of work—enables *guanxi* to be formed and acts as the foundation for future exchanges of *ganqing*.

Whether the role of *guanxi* in CCP politics mimics that of Matsu township is open to question. However, that *guanxi* of some sort play a role in CCP politics is not. Scholarly investigations of the founding of the CCP (van de Ven 1991; Dirlik 1989) explore the role of intellectual and personal *guanxi* in party politics from the CCP's beginnings in the May Fourth movement. Jacobs discusses the role of *guanxi* in CCP politics during the pre-1949 war years.

> According to Chang Kuo-t'ao in his interviews with William Whitson, Chinese Communist soldiers were "probably motivated more by personal loyalty than by considerations of ideology to endure the bitter defeats of 1927–30." Lawrence Sullivan suggests [that] overcoming the dominant reliance on particularistic ties in the leadership of the Chinese Communist Party (CCP) in the 1920s constituted a critical task facing the Russian Returned Students in the early 1930s. Elizabeth Perry documents CCP reliance on particularistic ties for peasant organization in the Huai River Valley during the 1930s and 1940s, while Mark Selden suggests the importance of particularistic ties in the Yenan area, at least before the Rectification Movement of 1942–44. (Jacobs 1979:239)[4]

Several scholars describe the place of *guanxi* in the post-1949 party-state. Michel Oksenberg (1970) considers the role of *guanxi* in advancements through the party bureaucracy of the 1950s and 1960s, Tanner with Feder (1993) document the place of family ties in elite CCP politics, and Cheng Li (1994) demonstrates the place of university networks in the Dengist technocracy. In brief, from the 1920s to the present, *guanxi* have been an important element of CCP politics.

However, if *guanxi* bases and *ganqing* exchanges have long played a role in CCP politics, so has an awareness that "particularistic ties" alone could not form the basis of, and were even inimical to, a Leninist Party organization. The CCP hoped to construct a socialist nation, a goal that people whose heart/minds were formed in particularistic *ganqing* exchanges would have trouble pursuing. A 1972 editorial in the official party journal, *Red Flag*, nicely illustrates the problem:

> There is a proverb: "Within the scope of his power, a person makes things a little more convenient for his co-workers [*t'ung-shih*], his superiors, his subordinates, or his relatives and good friends. This normal human sentiment [*qing*] has been considered reasonable since ancient times." This kind of thought turns its back on the class and mass viewpoints of Marxism and is directly opposed to the spirit of the aims and principles with which Communists wholeheartedly serve the people . . . Of course, everyone has social relationships [*guanxi*] of friends and relatives. We have never opposed normal social interaction [*jiaowang*] between relatives and friends. But, for a revolutionary, the relationships of relatives and friends must first be relationships of revolutionary comrades. The more people are relatives, friends, co-workers, superiors or subordinates, the more they must mutually and strictly demand that they regard the interests of the party and the people as important, that they take Marxism, Leninism, and the Thought of Mao T'se-tung as the standard, and that they help each other in politics and administrate according to Party principles. (cited in Jacobs 1979:238)

During the Chinese Civil War, when many families had affiliations with both the CCP and Nationalist Party, the problem of replacing "normal human sentiment" with "the class and mass viewpoints of Marxism" reached an apex. When recruiting new members, the CCP had to be certain that potential recruits would put the policies of the Communist Party ahead of the desires of family members whose political loyalties lay elsewhere. As Mark Selden put it: "the heterodox composition of the party, government and army, whose ranks had swelled since 1937, required education and training to instill primary loyalty to the party in the face of powerful enemy forces and conflicting personal bonds" (1971:190).

What, then, did the CCP do to promote "class and mass viewpoints of Marxism" and loyalty to the party in place of the particularistic loyalties of *ganqing*? One answer lay in inventing practices and rituals of human interaction that constructed human subjects differently than the *ganqing*-dominated heart/minds produced in *guanxi* practices. The "rectification" (*zhengfeng*) campaigns of the Yenan period (1936–46) were one such ritual (Selden 1971:188–210; Whyte 1974:29–35). They involved routinized ideological study and criticism and self-criticism in public meetings in which party members ritually examined their behavior for instances of political incorrectness or disloyalty and pressured each other to reform. The public criticism in particular was meant to destroy the personalized loyalties that demanded *ganqing* sensitivity and, hence, the avoidance of face-to-face criticism.

CCP members also addressed each other with the term *tongzhi* (comrade) instead of the relational kin terms common in *guanxi*-dominated organizations. Though usually translated as comrade, *tongzhi* predates the modern period and still carries connotations of "those with the same convictions" (Cihai Bianji Weiyuanhui 1979:196). In response to my request for an explanation of *tongzhi*, a retired Fengjia teacher said, "a person with the same ideas (*sixiang*), like someone who has the same ways of raising pigs," an answer that startled me since I had always associated the term with orthodox party politics. In any case, in CCP usages the term implies that both speaker and addressee are committed to Marxism, Leninism, and the thought of Mao Zedong, and that both are loyal members of the party. In contrast to the personalized, relational subjects constructed in kin terms (described in chapter 1), the term *tongzhi* frames interlocutors as disciples of an impersonal, non-localized political doctrine.

In its post-1949 recruitment of party members, the CCP continued to emphasize alternatives to personalized *guanxi*. Andrew Walder (1986) describes how the relationships between party members and their potential recruits in large PRC factories differed from the particularized *guanxi* that constituted many other aspects of workplace relations. Supervisors and party members evaluated recruits (called activists) on the basis of their political attitudes and self-presentation (*biaoxian*). Activists avoided receiving *ganqing*-producing favors in order to enhance their displays of rectitude. In brief, activists tried to present themselves as subjects motivated by loyalty to the CCP and belief in the universal validity of Marxism, Leninism, and the thought of Mao Zedong rather than a *ganqing*-constructed heart/mind.

In addition to creating alternative methods of subject construction for its own members, the CCP attempted to reform the *guanxi*-producing habits of society at large. Hoping to destroy the pre-1949 class hierarchies that practices of *guanxi* production and exclusion helped to maintain and to motivate the "masses" toward the broad impersonal goals of "building socialism," the party viewed most relationship-producing ritual with suspicion (Parish and Whyte 1978:249). As shown in earlier chapters, the CCP often restricted *guanxi*-producing practices, like performing *ketou,* weeping at funerals, and even the use of kinship names. "Comrade" became the preferred form of address in public urban arenas for most of the Maoist and early Dengist periods. In addition, political study and rectification campaigns were carried out in work units and villages. A system of individual dossiers was set up, and superiors, coworkers, friends, neighbors, and even family members were encouraged to report each other's misdeeds for recording in their files (Vogel 1965; Mayfair Yang 1989a). Such surveillance made personal *guanxi* risky. The person to whom one gave a gift might report the fact that the gift was given. In the place of *guanxi* and *ganqing,* PRC citizens were supposed to relate to each other as comrades, anonymously loyal to the party and Marxism, Leninism, and Mao Zedong thought. Lei Feng, the mythical model soldier who without any friends, family, or *guanxi* whatsoever set out to anonymously serve the masses, became the model for public emulation.

Mayfair Yang (1994) in particular has pointed to the opposition between impersonal statist ethics and the art of *guanxi.* In addition to demonstrating the utility of *guanxi* in resisting state biopower, she traces echoes of this opposition deep in Chinese history, when Legalists denounced Confucian ethics, and describes the historically self-conscious identification of the CCP with anti-*guanxi* ethics in Mao's approval of Qin Shihuang's legalism. Yet this approach can be taken too far. Though it reveals much about the politics of manipulating, suppressing, and talking about *guanxi,* it also can mystify some of the CCP's actual workings. The party may present itself as being constructed out of something totally different from *guanxi,* but just like any other organization, the party must construct relationships of some type to build itself and mobilize the people. The line between these relationships and *guanxi* has been difficult to police and difficult to define. Just as the difference between *guanxi*-producing gift giving and bourgeois business dealing blurs in the practices of businessmen in China, so does the line between "comrades" and "friends," between impersonal, idealistic politics and heartfelt *ganqing,* blur in many CCP political actions.

Indeed, I would like to suggest that the CCP co-opted, reinvented, and versioned practices of *guanxi* production as much as eliminating them altogether. Tani Barlow (1989a) argues that the CCP revitalized an ideology of family relationships during the Yenan period to create a "class-based neo-familism." Nowhere was this more apparent than in the assignment of class labels and the mobilization of "class *ganqing*" (*jieji ganqing*) during the land reform.

In his famous 1926 essay, Mao Zedong argued that the CCP could distinguish its "friends" from its "enemies" on the basis of class. In the countryside, class was measured in land ownership, and the Red Army, following Maoist strategy, searched for allies among land-poor villagers. To win the support of these poor peasants, the CCP carried out land re-forms in the areas it governed even before it consolidated control of the country as a whole. However, most accounts of the land reform sug-gest that poor peasants were reluctant to trust outside CCP cadres over landlords and rich peasants who in many cases were relatives (Chan et al. 1992:19–20; Crook and Crook 1959; Hinton 1966). In other words, at least initially, poor peasants put family *guanxi* ahead of class *ganqing*. Consequently, the CCP had to devise techniques and rituals to rally class sentiment.

Perhaps the most basic of these techniques was the "three togethers": living, eating, and working with the poor peasants (Madsen 1984:85–88). When a CCP work team arrived in a village, its members sought out poor families to live with. If possible, they slept in the same house, at times even sharing beds with poor peasants of the same sex. They ate whatever the members of these families prepared, paying for what they consumed. In the afternoons, or whenever their political work allowed, they helped their hosts with agricultural tasks or household chores. These actions created "class *ganqing*" in two senses. First, by spending time with, eating with, and making economic contributions to specific poor peasant households, the work team created personal *guanxi* with a particular group of poor peasants. Second, by doing manual labor and sharing the harsh material conditions of poor peasant life, work team members demonstrated their political rectitude, sharing the "superior" moral attitudes supposedly characteristic of the working classes.

Denouncing the crimes of the land rich was the next step in the land reform. After spending time with the poorest households of the village, work team members attempted to recruit them into the poor peasants' associations and convince them to speak out against the richest land-owners in the village. Often they were successful. Not only had the work teams established *guanxi* with these households, but the poorest house-holds were also the ones with the most to gain from the land reform.

Once they had enough speakers, work teams held large public meetings. Poor peasants would tell stories of their suffering under the landlords: how they were forced to sell their children or let their aged mother starve to death, how they were beaten or cheated out of money. Often both speakers and audience cried (e.g., Hinton 1966:116). As emotions rose, the former landlords would be brought onstage and attacked. Potter and Potter give the following descriptions of land reform struggles in southern Guangdong.

> [T]he leaders of the peasants' associations were the first to speak out, setting the example, so the peasants began to tell how they had been beaten and robbed by the landlords, overcharged in rent and interest, and had seen their families destroyed by the landlords' rapaciousness. With tears streaming down their faces, they angrily shouted accusations at the landlords and came up to the stage to beat them. Nephew spoke out against uncle, and members of the same lineage branch spoke out against their close kinsmen. (1990:48)

In such "speak bitterness" struggle sessions, "class *ganqing*" was made into a powerful collective emotion that was simultaneously personalized, in that the speakers and audience all were closely related, yet congruent with an impersonal, generalized Marxist theory.

In later campaigns, work teams in both rural and urban China would try to mobilize these techniques. The "three togethers" became standard procedure. "Recall bitterness" sessions were held to whip up "class hatred" and to paint a rosy comparison with the "sweetness" of post-1949 conditions. Siu and Stern describe how in urban areas

> [d]uring the Socialist Education Campaign of 1963–1966, the schools held "recall bitterness" sessions in which peasants recounted to the students their bitter experiences before the Communist liberation. Such sessions were supported to reinforce the correct class feelings of the children of workers and peasants and help the children of the former ruling classes dissociate themselves ideologically from their parents. (1983:xix)

The manipulation of class *ganqing* may even have been extended to American POWs. On a train ride a Chinese veteran of the Korean War described to me how his squad shared food with American POWs, giving them the best portions. "We knew that American soldiers were members of the working class," he said, "and we were told to develop *ganqing* with them. Some of them even cried when they left."

Of course, as indicated in Mao's original essay, the designation of some people as friends meant classifying others as enemies. Consequently the development of class *ganqing* for some always implied the exclusion of others from the field of *ganqing*. If work team members were friendly toward poor peasants, they were likewise icy toward those with bad class labels. During the Cultural Revolution, taking a class stand, denying any sort of relationship with those having bad class labels, went so far as children disowning their parents. At least in Fengjia, much *guanxi*-producing activity, from attending funerals and banquets to even addressing fellow villagers with kin terms, was prohibited across class lines. Indeed, for the thirty years in which class labels were inheritable through patrilines, it seemed that class *ganqing* meant the permanent exclusion of some families from all normal social interaction. Here was the ugly underside of Barlow's "class-based neo-familism." Finally, as Philip Huang (1990:295) points out, Maoist interpretations of class *ganqing* glorified manual labor, allowing the exclusion of intellectuals, who by definition did not work with their hands, from full socialist citizenship.

Perhaps because they combined personalized *ganqing* with Marxist theory and, at least during the land reform, with real material benefits, CCP deployments of class *ganqing* were initially quite successful. Class designations rapidly reshaped the social landscape, replacing other criteria of social hierarchy. During "speak bitterness" rituals, class *ganqing* created powerful "magnetic fields of human feeling" that motivated many to tears and violence. Finally, class *ganqing* created a *guanxi*-based coalition that could be imagined to extend across the entire country, or even the entire world. When traveling Red Guards or distant work team members sought out poor peasants or factory workers, class acted, in Jacobs's terms, as a *guanxi* base for *ganqing* exchanges. A widely extended "imagined community" (B. Anderson 1991) could at least be conceived. However, despite their initial success, thirty years of overuse and abuse eroded the effectiveness of the techniques of class *ganqing* (Chan et al. 1992; Madsen 1984). In 1979 Deng Xiaoping eliminated them altogether.

Yet if Deng ended CCP manipulations of class *ganqing*, he did not stop party concern with and manipulation of *guanxi* production. During the more limited campaigns of the 1980s and early 1990s, officials still relied on rectification. Lei Feng–type models, who ignored personal and family *guanxi* in order to devote themselves to impersonal careers or to selflessly (perhaps *guanxi*-lessly) "serve the masses," continued to make regular appearances in the official press. In the most widely read newspaper in Fengjia, articles regularly criticized gift giving as a feudal remnant and a form of corruption.[5] In Beijing, charges of high-level corruption fueled the 1989 protests and led to much party infighting over how to curb nepotism (Tanner with Feder 1993).

In addition to the continued attempts at repressing *guanxi*-building activities among its own members and the public at large, the official press of the Dengist era appeared to find some more positive means of manipulating *ganqing*. During the Yangzi River flood relief efforts of the summer of 1991, I constantly heard the slogan "Flood waters are without sentiment, only the CCP has *[gan]qing*" (*hongshui wu qing, zhi you gongchandang you qing*). In TV interviews, flood victims who had received material aid would describe their deep *ganqing* for the party. TV shows further suggested that the prevalence of small framed portraits of Mao Zedong and Zhou Enlai in Wuhan and Anhui was an expression of this *ganqing*.[6] As in the land reform, CCP pronouncements linked the dissemination of concrete material benefits to a generalized *ganqing* for the party. TV news shows also devoted much time to descriptions of CCP leaders hosting, visiting, exchanging gifts with, banqueting, and otherwise constructing *guanxi* with foreign dignitaries. Apparently, like Fengjia residents who see hosting banquets as part of the job of their party secretary, viewers are to gain a positive impression of CCP leaders from their *guanxi*-constructing diligence. Indeed, since the *mianzi* involved in playing host points in two directions (see chapter 2), such news clips allowed the party to give their own leaders *mianzi*, and display their own internal hierarchies.

This section has concentrated on official CCP portrayals and manipulations of practices of *guanxi* production. In conclusion I would emphasize that this examination should be taken as neither a denial of the unofficial role of *guanxi* in cliques and promotions in the CCP itself nor a description of the art of *guanxi* in society at large. Official portrayals always mask unofficial actions, while official manipulations always face popular subversion. Indeed several scholars argue that the extremes of rectification, surveillance, and economic retrenchment of the Cultural Revolution actually spurred private manipulations of *guanxi* to new heights (Gold 1985; Walder 1986; Mayfair Yang 1989a). Nevertheless, even if they did not always have the intended effects, official reconceptions of *guanxi* and *ganqing* remain important. They both diversify the picture of what *guanxi* and *ganqing* can mean and have produced social realities that continue to influence popular and official discourse.

9 *Guanxi* and Peasant Subculture

Economically the contradiction between town and country is an extremely antago-
nistic one both in capitalist society, where under the rule of the bourgeoisie the
towns ruthlessly plunder the countryside, and in the Kuomingtang areas in China,
where under the rule of foreign imperialism and the Chinese big compradore
bourgeoisie the towns most rapaciously plunder the countryside. But in a socialist
country and in our own revolutionary base areas, this antagonistic contradiction
has changed into one that is non-antagonistic; and when communist society is
reached it will be abolished.
Mao 1967[1937]:345

In the previous chapter I suggested that the manipulation of class *gan-*
qing constituted a new and effective practice of *guanxi* production and,
hence, subjectification. It combined personalistic exchanges of work,
sentiment, and etiquette with the politically expansive, imagined community of class. In itself, this sort of combination might not be terribly
new. As Prasenjit Duara (1993a, b) argues, the "imagined communities"
that Benedict Anderson (1991) linked to print capitalism and modernity
often have premodern antecedents. Here, the native place associations
(*tongxiang hui*) of Ch'ing dynasty urban areas (see Skinner 1977: part 3)
could be seen as such an antecedent. They imagined broad-based communities into existence to serve as the basis for personalistic *ganqing*
exchanges among otherwise unconnected people. What was new, or at
least distinctive, about class *ganqing* was the type of imagined community it created. Not only was the scope of the community huge (the
"working classes" could be imagined as including more than half the
world's population), but the community itself was defined by a particular experiential background and moral outlook. One gained class *gan-*
qing not just by forming particularistic ties with members of the lower
classes, but by the experience of class oppression and the cultivation of a
CCP-defined moral rectitude. The subjects constructed in class *ganqing*

were simultaneously personalistic ones as well as impersonal replicas of an official ideal.

In this chapter I argue that some Fengjia residents developed another version of class *ganqing* that outlasted the official, Maoist rendition. I call it "peasant subculture."[1] To explain how residents of Fengjia came to imagine themselves as "peasants" and to define a "peasant" moral outlook, I review the CCP policies that delineated "peasants" and "nonpeasants," examine the rhetoric in which party officials and intellectuals defined the moral characteristics of these groups, and discuss how Fengjia residents accepted, contested, and redefined their own identities within and against these official demarcations and representations. I conclude, unfortunately, that communist political imaginings sharpened rather than erased the rural/urban antagonism described by Mao in the quote above.

The *Hukou* Policy: Peasants and Nonpeasants in the PRC

Central to the continued demarcation of "peasants" during the 1980s were the household registration (*hukou*) laws. Implemented in the late 1950s, these policies make a binary distinction between "peasants" (*nongmin*) and "nonpeasants" (*feinongmin*), labeling most village dwellers (approximately 80 percent of the nation's population) "peasants" and almost all town and city dwellers "nonpeasants." The distinction is not strictly a matter of occupation. In Fengjia, for example, the household registers labeled even those people who worked full-time in the cornstarch factory as peasants. The distinction organizes the distribution of state resources. During the 1980s, peasant households were allocated land on which to grow grain for food and grain taxes; they were not provided jobs by state agencies and were not eligible for the same sorts of retirement and welfare benefits as urban workers. Nonpeasants did not receive land but were assigned to work units (described in chapter 8); they were eligible to buy grain from the state at subsidized prices. In both Fengjia and the Canton delta village described by Potter and Potter (1990:298), peasants characterized nonpeasants as "eaters of public grain" (*chi gongliangde*). Especially during the Maoist decades, urbanites were considerably better off than peasants (see Hinton 1983; Oi 1993; Unger 1984). Though urban advantages declined during the 1980s, in 1989 many Fengjia residents still considered nonpeasant status and the right to buy public grain as privileges.[2]

One inherited one's household registration designation from one's parents. In the case of intermarriage between people of different designations, children received the peasant designation. Consequently, marriages between people of different designations were extremely limited. Several of the village's matchmakers told me that the first thing they considered in arranging matches was the potential mates' household registration, that they always matched a peasant registration with a peasant registration and a nonpeasant with a nonpeasant. A college student in Nanjing told me that he couldn't find a girlfriend because his name was too peasant sounding.

Though children receive the same *hukou* as their parents, post-Mao peasant students theoretically can gain a nonpeasant *hukou* through success at school. During the 1980s, 90 percent of Fengjia's children attended junior high school. After junior high, about 25 percent of Fengjia's children were able to test into a high school, the best going to the academic high school in the county seat or to one of numerous nationally run technical high schools (*zhongzhuan*). Of those who made it to the academic high school, about 60 percent went to college. If one made it to college or a nationally run technical high school, one was assigned a job in a city after graduation and given a nonpeasant *hukou*. Of the approximately 160 students who graduated from the Fengjia elementary school between 1975 and 1983, 13 made it to the academic high school, 8 to college, and between 10 and 15 to a nationally run technical high school. In all, 10 to 15 percent succeeded in becoming nonpeasants.

Objectifications of Peasants in Rhetoric

Myron Cohen (1993) points out how the term peasant (*nongmin*) itself came to China carrying the weight of decades of Marxist theorization about peasants, society, and revolution. These theories were hotly debated among Chinese Marxists after the birth of the CCP and have influenced CCP policies and propaganda from the 1920s to the present (Kelliher 1994). They all assume a teleology in which human societies follow a historical trajectory from feudalism to capitalism to socialism to communism. Since the CCP's mission was to lead China to the future heaven of communism, any theorization that linked peasants to feudalism or capitalism implied they were backward-looking and bad, while those that linked them to socialism or communism implied the opposite.

The CCP has used the terms "feudal" and "capitalist" to denounce practices they deemed inappropriate as well as to objectify (Dominguez 1989) classes of people. In general, during the 1980s, rural resistance to

CCP policy was called feudal, while urban resistance was called capitalist.[3] When I was in China, "excesses" of banqueting, gift giving, ritual, and filiality, and a desire for many (or male) children were described as "feudal remnants," while "selfishness," demands for consumer goods, and intellectual and stylistic freedom were called "bourgeois liberalization."

Though the teleology of CCP ideology has remained fairly consistent, specific descriptions of rural and urban people have changed radically. The post–Cultural Revolution abolition of class statuses was matched by shifts in the characterizations of "peasants," "workers," and "intellectuals" in both official party propaganda and popular and intellectual writing. The majority of propaganda before 1978, which for my purposes can be called Maoism, described peasants as the "backbone" of the 1949 socialist revolution, and as the revolutionary class that was continuing to drive the nation forward toward communism.[4] One saying went: "Peasants are the eldest brother, while workers are the second eldest" (*Nongmin shi dage, gongren shi erge*). The continued material deprivation of rural people after 1949 only added to their revolutionary potential. Their poverty augmented their "class *ganqing*." Official rhetoric urged the "slow" or "foot-dragging" classes of privileged, intellectual urbanites to go down to the countryside and learn from the peasants.[5] Authors were criticized for not writing for the peasants, and folk art was encouraged at the expense of the literati tradition of Chinese painting. Though Mao's writings on peasants were contradicted and complex (see, for example, Meisner 1985), the majority of public propaganda associated with Mao presented peasants as a "forward moving" or "advanced" class whose cultural production should be emulated.

Mao himself embodied the redness of the peasant/worker revolutionary spirit. For "poor peasants," Mao worship was in a sense self-worship. The glorification of Chairman Mao reflected their own revolutionary dignity. In Fengjia village the evidence of such an identification with Mao was extant in the continued presence of prominently displayed Mao portraits in some households in 1989.[6]

After 1978, the CCP reversed its objectifications of the peasantry. It ended the glorification of poor peasant revolutionary spirit and resurrected an orthodox, pre-Maoist Marxism that conceived of peasants as backward (*luohou*). Plans to supersede the peasants replaced exhortations to learn from them. As Zhao Ziyang put it in his speech at the Thirteenth Party Congress, the primary stage of socialism is the stage for gradually casting off poverty and backwardness; it is the stage of gradually replacing a country where farming based on manual labor forms the basis and peasants constitute the majority, with a modern industrial nation where nonpeasant workers constitute the majority. (Zhao 1987:10–11)

From this point of view, peasants should get rich, thus eliminating that part of their identity (being poor) that was valued positively under Maoism. More importantly, peasants as a class should work for their own transformation into a proletariat, eliminating the farming part of their identity. Ironically, it was the efforts of "peasant workers" that were responsible for much of China's economic growth during the 1980s. In any case, post-Mao rhetoric has emphasized the inherited "backwardness" that results from peasants' former participation in "feudal" modes of production rather than the progressiveness that results from their former oppression. I call this ideology orthodox Marxism.

In local arenas, party officials can use class objectifications to play off the demands of rural and urban populations on one another. When I was at Nanjing University school officials commonly justified policies restricting student behavior by citing the supposed opinions of peasants. According to university officials, student dating, wasting food in the cafeteria, and many books and movies popular among urban intellectuals were all "offensive to the peasants." In this objectification, "peasant feudal backwardness" shows its relatively benign face (from the party's point of view) of parental severity and a demand for filial obedience. Indeed, here peasants play the role of what Vera Schwarcz describes as "the 'unspoiled, the real Chinaman' [that] has been the ideal with which nationalist leaders, whether of the Communist or Guomindang (KMT) persuasion, tried to whip cosmopolitan intellectuals into line" (1991:92).

Since the household registration policy made peasants a distinct group of people whose interests sometimes diverge from those of non-peasants, and since CCP officials use objectifications of the peasantry to justify policies that circumscribe urban people, it is perhaps not surprising that post-Mao urban intellectuals have developed their own, often derogatory objectifications of rural people. Liu Kwang-Ching (1981), for example, gives an excellent summary of Chinese historiography on the contributions and limitations of "peasant rebellions." According to Liu, Maoist historiography credited peasant rebels with a fairly sophisticated ideological stance that included economic "equalitarianism" and sexual equality.[7] Against this view, other historians have constructed peasant rebellions as futile. Such rebellions might replace one group of leaders with another, but the society they constructed was essentially the same as the one they destroyed. Not surprisingly, during the Cultural Revolution Maoist historiography reigned. During this period, as Liu puts it, "To the peasant was ascribed a revolutionary consciousness equal to, if not stronger than, that of the proletariat" (1981:297). After the Cultural Revolution, more press was given to divergent views. Some intellectuals accused peasant rebels of being "feudal," patriarchal, and of overemphasizing loyalty. "Peasant equalitarianism" was dismissed as utopian. A few even accused modern peasant cadres of sharing these faults with the peasant rebels of old, and linked problems of the Cultural Revolution with the negative side of "peasant consciousness." Linking Mao himself to such objectifications of the peasantry was a comment made to me by a professor of Chinese literature: "We [i.e., Chinese intellectuals] think that Mao Zedong was not a true communist, but merely a little peasant economist (*xiao nongmin jingjizhe*), who bore the weight of China's long feudal history."

The infamous TV series *Deathsong of the River* (*Heshang*) likewise used objectification of peasants as feudal and backward to attack conservative (Maoist) elements within the CCP. The series was televised in China twice in June and August of 1988 and may have been viewed by several hundred million people. After the Tiananmen Massacre, the authorities accused the filmmakers of purposefully fanning student dissent. One of the principal authors was arrested, while the other fled to the United States (Bodman and Wan 1991:64–66). Drawing heavily on Western scholarship, the series insists that China stagnated in the feudal stage of history for thousands of years and that all of the peasant rebellions during this period (by insinuation including the 1949 CCP victory) lacked "revolutionary significance." One paragraph sums up its portrait of the peasantry:

> In the vast backwards rural areas, there are common problems in the peasant makeup such as a weak spirit of enterprise, a very low ability to accept risk, a deep psychology of dependency and a strong sense of passive acceptance of fate. No wonder that some scholars sigh with regret: faced with the [psychological] makeup of people such as this, not to mention the many limitations of government policy, even if a great economist like Keynes were to come back to life, what could he do about it? It's not the lack of resources, nor the level of

GNP, nor the speed [of development], but rather this deficiency in the human makeup that is the essence of this so-called notion of "backwardness." And the decline of the makeup of the general population is caused precisely by the rapid increases in its numbers. This truly is an agricultural civilization caught in a vicious cycle. Do we still have any reason to praise or to be infatuated with it? (cited in Bodman and Wan 1991:169–170)

Objectifications of the peasantry have been at the heart of Chinese politics for the past forty years. The end of the Cultural Revolution marked a major turning point in both the relationships among intellectuals, peasants, and the party, and in the objectifications of peasants. As the party established academic think tanks and provided intellectuals with a greater role in guiding policy (Barlow 1991), official objectifications of peasants portrayed them as nonessential, and even detrimental, to the project of modernization. The guiding principles of modernization and scientization have themselves gone unquestioned.

Peasant Subculture in Fengjia

Perhaps the majority of Fengjia residents were not as concerned with the politics of speaking for the nation as the intellectuals and CCP cadres described above. However, Fengjia residents could avoid neither the structure of opportunities that the household registration and education policies created nor the local versions of national rhetoric that village party members and intellectuals reproduced. Since they and their ancestors and children had been labeled peasants by the household registration policy and the rhetoric of local cadres and intellectuals had attempted to define the contents of their peasants' consciousness, many Fengjia residents concerned themselves with what it meant to be a peasant.

Though the pressures arising from the policies and rhetoric described above were national in scope, several particularities of Fengjia village may have made peasant subculture especially prominent there. Fengjia's rate of educational success was double the provincial average (State Statistical Bureau 1990), and outstanding in comparison with that of rural areas reported elsewhere (P. Huang 1990:292; Potter and Potter 1990:309). This success, in combination with a prosperous agricultural economy and a strong conservative party secretary committed to collective agriculture, created a situation in which a number of conflicting ideals and lifestyles were visible. The strength of party organization allowed the official voice of the CCP to speak loudly; the educational presence gave voice to local intellectuals; the agricultural prosperity supported a peasant subculture. The cultural contrasts among these groups made each of them more distinctive.

THE CHRONOTOPE OF PEASANT SUBCULTURE

Mikhail Bakhtin suggests that distinctive genres of social discourse have particular methods of constructing space and time, which he calls chronotopes (Bakhtin 1981, 1986:60–102; Todorov 1984:80–85). Nowhere is this more apparent than in peasant subculture. Its proponents viewed historical time differently than either the orthodox Marxist teleology that objectified peasants as feudal and backward or the Maoist teleology that objectified peasants as advanced. Both orthodox Marxism and Maoism are oriented toward a future condition, communism, that is different and better than the present. Both construct teleologies that view "backward looking" or historically previous practices and worldviews in a negative light. Maoism and orthodox Marxism differ only over whether peasants as a group are future-oriented and thus good or past-oriented and thus bad. In contrast, advocates of the peasant subculture emergent in 1988–90 Fengjia claimed to be past-oriented, and evaluated this orientation positively. Instead of constructing the future as something new that necessitated the rejection of the past, they constructed the future as something to be purposefully filled with the re-creations of past practices. In the village, those who rejected peasant subculture tried to be advanced (*jinbu*) and saw peasant characteristics as backward; those who valued peasantness saw their subculture as a tradition (*chuantong*) that should be passed on to the future (*chuanxialai*) in order to respect (*xiaojing*) one's ancestors.

Recall that in Zhao Ziyang's "primary stage of socialism" peasants themselves are part of the "past" that needs to be replaced to form a new future. In Fengjia, as elsewhere, the (re)invention of calendrical and life-cycle rituals coincided with the negative objectification of peasants in the "primary stage of socialism" propaganda that emerged after 1978. Local nonpeasants took up the post-Mao official rhetoric by scorning much of the (re)invented ritual of Fengjia peasants as backward and feudal (*fengjian*). In contrast, residents who were "peasant and proud" contested this objectification by flaunting their new ritual. These people made constant efforts to explain to me (a nonpeasant outsider) the importance of etiquette and ritual (*lijie*) in village life and were delighted when I tried to observe various conventions of local etiquette. They taught me how to hold my cup when I received tea, where and how to sit when I visited friends, and how to eat and drink at their banquets. They filled their houses with square wooden tables and straight-backed chairs even though they could afford the more "modern" sofas and coffee tables available in the local furniture stores. In their weddings they used symbolic displays from past eras even when they couldn't remember what they meant. Like so many other "subcultures," peasantness delighted in precisely those elements that outsiders scorned (Hebdige 1979).

FUNERALS, FILIALITY, TRADITION, AND SUBCULTURE

Peasant subculture and negative objectifications of peasants both posit an intimate relation between peasants and "tradition." Negative objectifications portray peasants as mired in feudal tradition and backward. Peasant subculture emphasized passing on past practices both because these practices were seen as having inherent value and because the practice of "passing on" in itself had value. Respecting past practices by passing them on was a way of respecting one's elders. Both outlooks exaggerated the extent to which 1989 practices were, in fact, replicas of past practices.[8]

The word usually translated as tradition, *chuantong,* is itself illuminating. Consisting of the characters *chuan* and *tong,* the compound is a return graphic loan from Japanese (L. Liu 1995:340). Though the word has ancient Chinese roots, the modern form derives from Japanese translations of Western social science. Nevertheless, perhaps because of its prevalence in official propaganda, the word has found a place in the everyday speech of Fengjia residents. Moreover, they use it in a manner consistent with other, more homegrown phrases that include the verb *chuan. Chuan* typically means to pass on, hand down, impart, or teach. Child raising and ritual practices, for example, were often described as *chuanxialaide* or "passed down." Even more revealing is the saying *"Yibei chuan yibei,"* which might be translated "Each generation passes on to (and is replaced by) the next." It encompasses an entire ideology of filiality. Not only should one have children to continue patrilines, but one should impart to them skills, knowledge, and practices that constitute genuine generational continuity. Parents have a responsibility to teach, and children have the responsibility of accepting the teachings of their parents, and of becoming responsible parents themselves. Seen in this light, *chuantong* has more active connotations than the English tradition. It is something that is purposefully conveyed rather than unconsciously inherited.

The conflation of filiality with peasantness was particularly important in funerals and ancestral offerings. Even those who usually presented themselves as advanced emphasized tradition in these contexts. One woman explained that though her family avoided performing *ketou* in weddings and over the Chinese New Year, they could not eliminate *ketou* from funerals. She said that if they did, people would say that they weren't filial (*buxiao*). I once asked Teacher Feng if he had ever been a master of ceremonies in a funeral. He replied that because he was a teacher who had for all his life "espoused science instead of superstition" (*jiang kexue bujiang mixin*), he would never be asked to be a master of ceremonies. In funerals, villagers asked someone who was seen as traditional to organize the ritual. In a similar vein, several residents told me that it was inappropriate for a party member to be a master of ceremonies. Party members were supposed to be oriented forward, toward communism, and thus were unreliable bearers of tradition. Most party members themselves asked more traditional members of their extended families to organize their funerary rituals.

In funerals one wishes to embody respect and filial piety for the deceased. Filiality implies continuing past practices and, hence, tradition. Indeed, tradition itself is a form of remembrance. To adopt an advanced posture at a funeral would imply "forgetting" one's ancestors. The same may be said of ancestral offerings. When asked why he performed ancestral offerings if he no longer believed in ancestor spirits, one man said, "Ancestral offering is a tradition. It shows that we will never forget our ancestors" (*wangbuliao zuxian*).

Utterances of Peasant Subculture and Its Opposition

I heard and saw a great variety of evocations of and comments on peasantness while I was in Fengjia. Though delimited by the chronotopes of tradition and backwardness, these utterances still covered a huge expanse of stylistic and rhetorical territory. The range of practices or characteristics that could be associated with peasants seemed unlimited.

Ketou and bows were one of the major components of peasant subculture. Residents who wished to construct themselves as nonpeasants tried to avoid situations that required bows and *ketou*. If they could not avoid the situation entirely, they would perform the gesture in the most superficial manner possible. One man told me that his son, who had graduated from college and now lived in a city, would not perform *ketou* when he came home to visit each year during the spring festival. Another middle-aged Fengjia man, who identified himself as a nonpeasant (though technically he was a peasant), not only refused to participate in the spring festival intravillage *ketou* but also eliminated from his sons' weddings the parts of the ceremony where *ketou* or bows would occur.

Assertions of the positive aspects of peasant traditionalism took other forms as well. Many emphasized how hospitable (*haoke*) local residents were. They took pride in the *ganqing* created through local etiquette and village reciprocity. One man elaborated on this point. He told me that carrying on traditional etiquette was a matter of respect and *ganqing* for one's elders. He went on to explain that *ganqing* for one's elders led one to treat everyone well, because old people were interested in the welfare of children and in continuing the prosperity of the village. Then he added that in large cities people did not know their neighbors and, thus, did not have to worry about *ganqing* and carrying on tradition. He concluded that peasants had more *ganqing* than city people and were more likely to help out their neighbors. In addition to emphasizing the relation between tradition and *ganqing*, other villagers delighted in how ceremonious (*longzhong*) local rituals were.

Mueggler (1991) similarly links village reciprocity to an anti-statist local identity in a Naxi (Chinese minority) village. He points out that labor and gift exchange in combination with religious practices, temples, and images of local mountains all form a local, ethnic identity that the state has continually attempted to at least neutralize and at times obliterate. Though this Yunnan village and Fengjia are distant in space and perhaps custom, they share a concern with a state that has in one period or another tried to control almost every detail of village life.

Doing research in the rural areas of the lower Yangzi valley, Philip Huang (1990:295) reports that by "Chinese standards of beauty the contrast between the 15-year-old girl, still in school, and her elder sister who has worked in the fields for a number of years is striking." He argues that the dark, sunburnt skin characteristic of women who worked in the fields was another reason for youth to flee the countryside for urban jobs. In Fengjia too, parents who wanted their daughters to become nonpeasants protected them from work in the fields in the hopes of preserving their "nonpeasant beauty." However, it would be a mistake to see peasant appearance as simply a negativity, an inability to conform to urban standards. Rather, it is a purposeful construction that implicitly critiques urban tastes. When I dressed according to their standards of simplicity, proud peasants complimented me as being "*pusu*," meaning plain, simple, or, given the Maoist legacy of the term's use, perhaps "proletarian." Proletarian styles for women included straight (not curled in a permanent), collar-length hair; little makeup; pants of a single, usually dark, color, light-colored shirts during the summer; darker padded pants and jackets during the colder months; plastic sandals during the summer and plain, dark, handmade cotton shoes during the winter. Proletarian styles for men were similar except that their hair was even shorter. Many men shaved their heads completely in the heat of summer. Proletarian styles announced that frugality and comfort were more important than vanity or beauty. Proletarian clothes concealed dirt and were inexpensive and long-wearing. A husband and wife who had raised their daughters working in the field told me that peasants preferred a wife (or daughter-in-law) who was hard-working to one who was beautiful. They suggested that anyone who saw beauty as more important than contributions to family prosperity through labor had twisted standards.

As discussed above, filiality and attempts to secure family continuity through sons could be seen as assertions of peasantness. Especially in the context of patrilocality and the one-child policy, such assertions could be quite sexist. I heard desire for many and male children and the segregation of sexes at banquets and in local etiquette both defended as tradition and criticized as feudal. When a former resident returned from Beijing and held a banquet in which men and women sat at the same table, two men commented on how advanced this seating arrangement was.

In Fengjia, critiques of peasant traditionalism were grounded in the visions of two alternative perspectives—those of intellectuals and those of the CCP. Critiques of the latter sort emphasized party rhetoric and policy as the origin of the new practices that people should use to replace tradition. In this view peasants and intellectuals were both classes of people who should follow the party's guidance on the road to communism. The thirty-plus party members in the village were expected to be, and for the most part were, proponents of this view. As peasants headed by a party secretary strongly committed to agriculture, many also exuded an earthy peasantness whenever they could. However, their role in upholding party policy compromised any truly subcultural commitment.

During my stay in Fengjia, vocal support of the birth control policy demonstrated party members' loyalty. Once every three months the county birth control inspector came to Fengjia to give pregnancy tests to every married woman who had not reached menopause. The village's own doctor, also a party member, had the responsibility of ensuring that these women showed up at the village clinic at the proper time. I stumbled upon an inspection when I noticed a long line of women outside the clinic door. I entered the clinic and found the village doctor sheepishly seated behind a desk in the front room. The door to the back room burst open and a man (the county official) walked out, glared at the doctor, and growled that two women were missing. Upon seeing me (a fellow nonpeasant), he loudly commented: "Peasants, so backward, so feudal, they are such a waste of time." One of his female assistants came out and added, "They can't be trusted, too backward." The village doctor had no choice but to go along. "Some people are too feudal," he meekly added as he told one of the women waiting in line to find the missing people. Usually a confident and earthy man, the doctor's party affiliation necessitated his adoption of an anti-peasant, advanced position.

In the intellectual critique, "science" and knowledge gained in formal education in general were constructed as the proper roots for the new practices that should replace tradition. Intellectuals were seen as a group of people who rightly had more influence than peasants. Retired teachers, intellectuals sent to Fengjia during the Cultural Revolution, and families who hoped their children would become nonpeasants through educational success often took this view. Such residents often explained to me how certain present (and many past) agricultural, child rearing, and social practices were "superstition." In emphasizing the superiority of science over feudal superstition, they echoed rhetoric that has been a mainstay of CCP propaganda since the May Fourth movement.

Junior high and especially high school students often seemed conflicted in their attitudes toward peasant subculture. They hesitated in the performance of ritual actions like the *ketou* and could be careless about the conventions of local etiquette. I suspect their status as students was more important to this indifference than their age. Recall that students still had a chance of testing into a nonpeasant *hukou* classification. Even if a particular student's chances were not too high, I speculate that the high schools and perhaps even the junior highs were dominated by an ethos other than that of peasant subculture. For one, these institutions were boarding schools located in the towns and cities. Secondly, the students themselves could escape peasanthood through educational achievement. Moreover, since the schools as a whole and teachers individually were evaluated on the testing successes and failures of their students, the school's teachers and administrators (all nonpeasants) had institutional interests in fueling this ambition. In short, the schools were thoroughly nonpeasant institutions.

Indeed, young people who were not students seemed more positive about peasant subculture. For example, though in most of the wedding ceremonies I saw the bridegrooms hesitated to bow deeply, the two who bowed the deepest had both left school after junior high, and thus had both been peasants for at least four years. In contrast, the two who seemed most averse to bowing at their wedding ceremony had both gone to the academic high school, and had only six months previously given up on testing into college and thus on becoming a nonpeasant. For these young men, marriage, permanent residency in the village, and designation as peasants had come all at once.

I do not want to oversimplify. Going to high school did not simply or directly cause a refusal to bow. However, an emergent peasant subculture did create contradictions for would-be nonpeasant youth and their parents. Being designated as a peasant and accepting (even asserting) one's peasant identity avoided these contradictions. This reconstitution took time, and young residents hesitated to show their peasantness while the memory of their dreams of becoming nonpeasants still mattered. In other words, these youths' subjectification as peasants was not merely a matter of institutional classification, but the creation of a subject within and against that classification. Only after accepting their classification and creating something positive within it, could they act properly as subjects of a certain identity.

Party Secretary Feng himself was a "youth" who chose to *ketou*. As described in chapter 7, Secretary Feng was by far the most powerful person in the village. However, because his generational name was a young one, and because his father was still alive, in 1989 he was by traditional reckoning a rather junior member of the village. At spring festival he dutifully paid his respects to his "elders" in his family and throughout his village. What did it mean for such a powerful man to acknowledge his youth in a seemingly unimportant hierarchy? The significance of Secretary Feng's *ketou*, as with those of other youth whose heart/minds (*xin*) were constituted firmly as both peasants and villagers, lay in its affirmation of his peasant subculture and his reconstitution as a resident of Fengjia.[9]

Elders could both invoke subcultural notions of filiality to assert their authority and use their authority to enforce the standards of peasant subculture. One peasant and proud man described how much he objected to village youth dressing in urban styles. He said that he always lectured his nephews on their hairstyles and that if his nieces wore high-heeled shoes, he would cut off the heels with an axe. On June 3, 1989, the day before the crackdown in Tiananmen Square, this man prophetically suggested that the protesting students should be mowed down with a machine gun. I believe that the image of protesting college students was doubly offensive to him. The youth of the protestors suggested a rejection of filial obedience while their status as college students suggested an assertion of the power of intellectuals. To this man, unfilial youth and intellectual power were two of the greatest threats to a positive peasantness.[10] Peasant subculture in 1988–90 Fengjia was not necessarily sexist, domineering of youth, or anti-intellectual. Indeed, many residents tempered proud assertions of peasantness and local tradition with considerable tolerance. However, as a form of traditionalism that was attacked by intellectuals and that existed in an androcentric context, there was considerable potential for steering peasant subculture in these directions.

The couplets posted on doors and doorways at weddings and over spring festival, and the framed couplets permanently displayed in the main rooms of many Fengjia homes were sometimes used to evoke or reject peasantness. Every year local newspapers published a list of suggested sayings for copying in wedding and spring festival couplets. A local official proudly pointed out that the couplets at his son's wedding were not copied from the newspapers but chosen by a regionally famed calligrapher. He further explained that peasants, as the lowest class of people, had to "follow the orders of the party" (*ting dangde hua*) and copy official couplets and that the more "artistic" couplets he posted demonstrated his superior status. Indeed, most did copy the official couplets. When I asked why, some said that they did not have enough "education" (*wenhua*) to think up their own, while others said it was illegal, or until very recently had been illegal, to do so. In any case, from the point of view of outside officials, there was something quite peasant about using any of the official couplets.

Even among the official couplets there was a fair selection. For example, there were twenty-two couplets published in *Village Masses* before the 1989 spring festival. Those that I saw displayed in the village included some that emphasized the power of science and others that were more traditional. The most intellectually oriented couplet I saw was "Science (offers) universal knowledge and a vast future / Knowledge broadens all steps, paths, and roads" (*Kexue tongtian qiancheng yuan / Zhishi wei jiedaolu kuan*). A more traditional couplet went "The jade dragon flies departing the old year / The golden snake dances wildly welcoming the new spring" (*Yulong tengfei ci jiusui / Jinshe kuangwu ying xinchun*).[11] Even the official couplets, then, clearly offered a medium for announcing attitudes about science and tradition.

Couplets hung permanently in Fengjia homes were not copied from official slogans and thus offered an opportunity for more subtle expression. However, because they had not been prefiltered by the sieve of party censorship, the selection of permanent couplets undoubtedly required some political caution. I saw no strongly worded subcultural couplets. However, in a retired teacher's house I saw the couplet "Books become the endeavor of all heros under heaven / Virtue is the root of wealth among people" (*Shu wei tianxia yingxiong ye / De shi renjian fugui gen*). In the house of a more traditional man I saw "When brambles and trees have flowers, brothers are happy / When inkstones and fields are without taxes, descendants plow" (*Jingshu youhua xiongdi le / Yantian wushui zisun geng*).[12] These couplets are complex and poetic, and their political implications are (perhaps purposefully) muted. However, the emphasis on education in the one, and reference to a filial line of descendants in the other are significant. Though requiring political caution, the permanent couplets hung in houses also provided a medium for utterances about education and filiality.

Conclusions

This description of utterances of peasant subculture and its opposition could go on, but I believe the point has been made. Though remarkably diverse — ranging from gestures like bows and *ketou*, to hair and dress styles, to banquet seating and written couplets — these utterances were organized by the chronotopes of tradition and backwardness and made sense within evolving, oppositional genres. Though some of them may have had ancient roots, the oppositional chronotopes that organized them could be no older than the CCP's twentieth-century project of socialist "modernization." Far from eliminating the "contradiction between town and country," as Mao asserted in the passage quoted at the beginning of this chapter, socialist modernization in China has provided the framework within which the oppositions between town and country could be expressed through allochronic slurs (Fabian 1983) and the assertion of filiality.

Ironically, unlike many of the specific ritual actions invented in post-1978 Fengjia, filiality itself appeared to be unchanging and, thus, traditional. However, its very continuity modified its significance. During the Ch'ing dynasty and earlier, filiality was the essence of statist ideology, the linkage between family ritual and the naturalization of imperial rule (Zito 1987). Since 1949, however, state ideology has been firmly forward-looking, and filiality seems subversive. The more filiality persisted, the less traditional it became.

Returning to the assertion made at the beginning of the chapter, consider again the similarities between peasant subculture and class *ganqing*. Note first that most practices of peasant subculture were also practices of *guanxi* production. Fengjia residents used bows and *ketou*, certain styles of gift giving and banqueting, and various ritual elements of weddings and funerals to assert or comment on peasantness *and* to construct *guanxi*. Even written couplets, which were pasted on doors at weddings and hung over the chairs for receiving guests in north rooms, could be seen as media used in the production of *guanxi*, as well as peasant subculture. Thus, like class *ganqing*, peasant subculture had its particularistic aspect. In addition, both peasant subculture and class *ganqing* had a transcendent moral and political dimension. In the place of class *ganqing*'s experience of class oppression and Marxist moral rectitude, peasant subculture featured the experience of PRC peasanthood and a moral outlook organized around filiality. As a consequence of this simultaneously particularistic and transcendent character, the practices of peasant subculture and class *ganqing* subjectified residents in a dual sense—in specific "magnetic fields of human feeling" and in imagined, morally defined communities of class or peasanthood. Finally, like class *ganqing*, peasant subculture subjectified its members in opposition to, and exclusion of, those with the wrong "class" (peasant/nonpeasant) designation.

Class *ganqing* officially disappeared in 1978. However, the style of subjectification and *guanxi* formation it engendered continued to inform popular memory through the 1980s at least. In Fengjia and most likely elsewhere the emergence of peasant subculture blended transcendent and personalistic practices in a manner as effective as the class *ganqing* of old.

Epilogue

In August of 1992, Secretary Feng's commitment to "prospering collectively" seemed to be weakening. Nationally, a major propaganda push eulogizing "Deng Xiaoping's Tour of the South" emphasized the importance of individual entrepreneurship. County officials told me: "The most profitable firms are all run by individual entrepreneurs (*getihu*); then come the ones run by groups of entrepreneurs, then come the village enterprises, then the township ones; state-run enterprises are the worst of all." They further suggested that Fengjia's factories were not making much money: "a village like Fengjia is happy if it can provide employment for its residents; they don't worry about profit." Though Secretary Feng told me that he had started to encourage residents to establish private businesses, the county officials didn't think he was doing enough.

In the village I learned of three new businesses owned and run by individual households: a store, a restaurant, and a chicken factory. I decided to interview the owners about the role of *guanxi* in their enterprises. Their answers were diverse, but I was particularly taken aback by the replies of the middle-aged woman who owned and managed the Benefit the People Store (*Li Min Shangdian*).

She built the store into the part of her house that was adjacent to the street and ran it entirely by herself, explaining that her husband didn't have enough education (*wenhua*) to help and that women were naturally more careful with money than men anyway. She opened it each day for three periods: early in the morning, during the noon rest period, and in the evenings. She explained that since most of her customers worked in the fields in the mid-morning and afternoon, she could close her store during these periods without losing much business. She herself often did farm work at these times. Once a week or so she bicycled to a local market town, bought supplies, and hired a three-wheeler to bring them back to her store.

Though she needed little start-up capital and was self-sufficient in the areas of securing supplies and labor, I still believed her store to be deeply imbedded in local *guanxi* networks. The village already had a much larger store that was contracted out to another family. This store was open all day, had a wider variety of goods, and at least for the sample I asked about, had exactly the same prices. The two stores were about 50 yards apart, and I suspected that *guanxi* between customers and store manager determined where individuals shopped. Since the owner of the Benefit the People Store was a member of a Feng family household in the third team, and the village store was contracted by members of the Lin family in the first team, I wondered if family or team ties played a role in shopping decisions.

My suspicions deepened when I learned of the origins of the glass-framed decorations hung on her store walls. As described in chapter 3, people classified these items as "congratulatory gifts" and often gave them to friends who were getting married. Assuming that she had a recently married son, I pointed to the decorations and asked when the wedding had been. She explained that there had been no wedding, but that she had decided to open the store on her birthday and had held a celebration to mark the occasion.[1] Many friends had come and given glass-framed decorations as gifts. As with the congratulatory gifts given at weddings, these decorations had the giver's name written on them in large characters along with messages like "Congratulations on a new business." Like the shop owner, almost all of the givers were members of the third team and the Feng family. I took the giving of such gifts by the shop owner's friends and relatives and her own prominent display of them to be archetypal *guanxi*-building activities.

I asked if these gift givers were also regular customers. She replied "yes" and I thought to pay her a compliment by saying: "Your skill at forming *guanxi* has helped speed your success" (*guanxi gao de hao shi ni chenggong de kuai*).

I was surprised when she replied, "*Guanxi* has nothing to do with it. I rely entirely on myself."

"But aren't your best customers also the friends and relatives who gave you these decorations?" I asked.

"Yes," she said, "but I charge everyone the same price, so *guanxi* has nothing to do with it."

"What about your business license?" I asked.

"Party Secretary Feng helped me get that, and he's my nephew, so that doesn't involve *guanxi* either."[2]

In brief, from this shop owner's perspective, neither customer relations that did not base price on closeness of relationship nor governmental relations that involved close relatives could be considered matters of *guanxi*.

On one level, there was nothing in this way of looking at *guanxi* that contradicted what I learned between 1988 and 1990 and presented in part I. *Guanxi* involve particularistic material exchanges; charging everyone the same price does not. The term *guanxi* often implies relationships outside of one's own family and thus could be interpreted as excluding family members (*benjiaren*). Yet her reply pushed the limit of these definitions. First of all, despite her uniform pricing policy, there was a clear history of gift exchanges between the customers and the shop owner. Moreover, the customers had another option. Why shouldn't the mere fact of purchasing items at her store, instead of the main village outpost, be considered a "particularistic material exchange?" Secondly, given that most Fengjia residents could, within reason, extend the borders of their "family" to include everyone within the village and many outside, then most of the relationships described in part I could be considered intrafamilial and thus outside of the realm of *guanxi*. The concept of intravillage *guanxi* would become an oxymoron.

The shop owner's reply shocked me into realizing the implications of my own earlier conclusions. No unchanging, single form of *guanxi* exists. This book presents urban *guanxi*, rural *guanxi*, business *guanxi*, all-female *guanxi*, owner/tenant *guanxi*, class *guanxi*, marriage *guanxi*, comrade *guanxi*, husband/wife *guanxi*, mother-in-law/daughter-in-law *guanxi*, classmate *guanxi*, and more. Each of these relationships carries its own connotations and its own social/historical specificity. The meanings of words like *guanxi* and *ganqing* cannot be fixed. As Fengjia's new entrepreneurs adapted their social tactics to emergent opportunities and risks, they worried little about consistency in their terminology. They invented new ways of creating, manipulating, and talking about *guanxi*, and perhaps even new forms of social relations.

Discussions of *guanxi* always require details. Describing who makes *guanxi* with whom, what the significance of these relations are, where, why, when, and how they are formed illustrates how sociocultural processes operate in multiple directions. Cultural essentialisms that present the production of *guanxi* or *ganqing* as the center of an unchanging Chinese or neo-Confucian cultural formation run against the diversity of social relations labeled by those words. Defining once and for all what *guanxi* and *ganqing* are or mean is a hollow exercise, useful only to those reifiers of culture who seek to bind Chinese people in a separate and exotified social realm or to exclude non-Chinese from the production of *guanxi*.

However, though it is not reducible to any fixed cultural essence, the production of *guanxi* is cultural. Presenting it as the mere pursuit of economic or political interest masks the cultural and historical background that allows social agents to communicate and to form effectively the social relationships that come to be called *guanxi*. To capture the specificity and diversity of *guanxi* in any given context requires a simultaneous focus on the historical worlds of meanings that actors draw upon and their practical concerns in the present—that is, a theory of practice.

In arguing that the elucidation of *guanxi* production requires historical and contextual specificity, however, I do not mean to imply that the significance of studying *guanxi* remains local. Indeed, the possibility of translating Fengjia's practices of *guanxi* production for a First World, English-reading audience rests upon that audience's experience of having their heart/minds swayed by *ganqing* of one form or another.

Perhaps nothing could be further from the *ganqing*-constructed heart/minds described in this book than the processes of subjectification described by Fredric Jameson (1984). He argues that contemporary, "postmodern" culture increasingly involves the construction of subjects who are "depthless," composed entirely of fragmenting surfaces without history, who feel only a generalized euphoria rather than specific emotions. In contrast, subjects constructed in magnetic fields of human feeling are pulled by the remembrance of specific, past *ganqing* exchanges. Yet, though these two types of subjectification differ sharply, I would not restrict one to Fengjia and the other to the postmodern West. Instead, I believe they exist side by side in both places. I would be surprised if Fengjia's turbulent history did not at times induce generalized euphorias and depressions marked by a rejection of historical memory. More importantly, I cannot imagine a people so postmodern, so unmarked by remembered emotional contacts with others, that their hearts and minds could not be influenced by the expressions of *ganqing* of those who were near to them. Anthropologists have documented the networking and mutual aid strategies of African American families (Stack 1974) and poor, working-class, and upper-class Americans (Rapp 1978), and described the affective ties American women forge to hold communities together (Yanagisako 1977). But even more basically, anyone who has been raised by parents, fallen in love or married, or brought up children experiences the social power of human emotion. In this sense, lessons learned from examining the production of *guanxi* and *ganqing* in Fengjia tell us something about ourselves, wherever and whoever we are.

Notes

Introduction

1   During the land reform (completed in Fengjia in 1948), the Chinese Communist Party assigned patrilineally inheritable class labels — like poor peasant, middle peasant, or landlord — to all rural families. During the Cultural Revolution the "red" or "revolutionary" classes (consisting primarily of poor peasants) were empowered at the expense of the counterrevolutionary classes (which in the countryside consisted primarily of landlords and rich peasants).

2   Like all Chinese nouns, *guanxi* and *ganqing* can be either singular or plural. Throughout the book, I allow context to determine whether these words are treated as singular or plural.

3   My approach to cultural interpretation has been shaped by Geertz's (1973, 1979) interpretive anthropology, Hans-Georg Gadamer's (1975:258–71; 1976) philosophical hermeneutics, and Quinn and Holland's (1987) work on cultural models.

4   Comaroff (1985), Farquhar (1994b), and Ortner (1984) provide useful discussions of the uses and problems of practice theory.

5   Sun is a Taiwan-born anthropologist who was educated at Stanford and writes in Chinese as well as English. As far as I know, his book *Deep Structure of Chinese Culture Zhongguo Wenhuade Shenceng Jiegou,* 1987) has never been fully translated into English, though excerpts appear in Barme and Minford (1986). All translations in this study are my own. I use Sun's (1987) terminology with some reservations. As the title of his book implies, Sun uses an essentialized, psychologized notion of Chinese culture, of which *guanxi* subject construction is the central component, to paint a negative picture of Chinese the globe over. Sun describes a series of "Chinese characteristics" — including an underdeveloped sexuality, an inability to control bodily fluids and functions in public, a sycophantic personality, a rejection of rationality, and political despotism — as entailments of a desire to construct and be constructed by *guanxi* subjects. Sun's analysis was originally written as a cultural self-critique for a Chinese-language audience, and I fear a total appropriation of his work into English would

border on racism. Thus, I wish to emphasize that I see none of the above characteristics as entailments of the *guanxi* construction of subjects.

6   Weedon, Tolson, and Mort (1980:214) make a similar criticism of certain readings of Foucault.

7   Alitto (1979) has previously written a biography of the rural reformer Liang Shuming. Liang Shuming established his Rural Reconstruction Institute in Zouping County in part because in his eyes it had a "representative variety of geographic and economic features" (Alitto 1988). Present-day Zouping County is larger than the corresponding administrative unit in Liang Shuming's day, though Fengjia village belonged within it both then and now.

8   In 1991, the county was officially opened to foreign researchers. Special travel permits are no longer needed to go to Zouping, and the range of living situations legally open to foreigners has expanded.

9   After Deng Xiaoping's rise to power in the third plenary session of the Eleventh Central Committee of 1978, the decollectivization of the country-side was effected through implementation of the responsibility system (*zerenzhi*). Under the responsibility system, a village's land (though still owned by the state) was contracted out to individual households, the acre-age calculated on a per-person basis. In return for the right to work the land, peasant families were required to provide the state with a certain amount of grain (based on the size of their land allocation) at an artificially low price. For good introductions to the state policies governing decollec-tivization, see Croll (1994), Domes (1982:253–258) and Kelliher (1992:58). See Huang Shu-min (1989) for an excellent description of how decollectiv-ization took place in another village.

10   The PRC designates a few villages throughout the nation as "model" villages, giving them federal subsidies and using them as showcases for domestic and international tourists. Though Fengjia received no official subsidies, the socialist economy offers many opportunities for unofficial favoritism to the well-connected, and Fengjia certainly received some of these (see chapter 7). Friedman, Pickowicz, and Selden (1991) describe the processes by which certain individuals, villages, or "units" gain access to socialist state "largess" by aggressively adhering to the policy preferences of powerful party patrons. "Model" conformity to state policies is thus a rather common strategy in the PRC. For more on models, see Diamond (1983).

11   During the summer of 1992, in the context of an increasing push in national propaganda toward privatizing the economy, I made a brief return trip to Fengjia. At this time more people were engaging in individual entrepre-neurial activity. However, at least according to officials in the county seat, Fengjia still "lagged behind" the southeastern villages in this regard. The bulk of my research was carried out during a period of relatively minimal nonagricultural, private-sector participation.

12   See Anagnost (1989), Judd (1994:181–187), Minchuan Yang (1994), and Yan

(1992) for discussions of how polarizations of wealth can disrupt social interaction in rural Chinese villages.

13   Because of a hesitance to install a coal-burning stove in the guest house, my winter stay in Fengjia was spent in the party committee building (see map 3). During that winter, the latter building was essentially used as a guest house. The living situation was more or less the same as in the guest house proper.

14   The *Qingming* (Great Brightness) holiday is an occasion for mourning the dead.

15   Leaving the village after the Tiananmen Square incident was a demand of my American sponsors, not my Chinese hosts. The official Chinese position was that not much had happened and that international exchanges should go on as usual.

PART I   INTRODUCTION

1   In addition to *guanxi* and *ganqing,* the term *renqing* can also be used to speak of human sentiments in social reciprocity. King (1991:74) suggests that *ganqing* refers to emotions in a personal sense, while *renqing* has more to do with social reciprocity. However, in Fengjia I found that the term *ganqing* was often used to indicate a social relation. Oi (1989) and Fried (1953) go so far as to directly translate the term *ganqing* as a type of personal relationship. More important than pinning down translations is to note that all three of the terms cross the boundaries between material obligation, social relationship, and sentimental attachment and hence invoke a world in which these domains overlap.

2   Because I invoke Bourdieu's (1977, 1990) notion of practice and because he also speaks of "economism," I should distinguish our views. My critique of economism is directed more at a crass materialism than at the asocial, ahistorical subject of formalist economic anthropology that Bourdieu justifiably attacks. I do not believe, as Bourdieu says of Kabylia gift giving, that the etiquette of gift exchange provides a "sincere *fiction* of disinterested exchange" (1977:171, emphasis mine) that serves to repress the "objective truth of economic activity" (1977:172). As I stress throughout, gift giving, like all practices of *guanxi* production, is a practical activity that must be conceived of in terms broader than the material. Human feelings are just as much of an "objective truth" as is economic exchange.

3   Which is not to say that markets for land, labor, and capital—what some would call "capitalism" (see Gates 1987)—were absent from Chinese history. Rather, the point is that Chinese market culture (as I would prefer to call it) did not involve the mystifying and constitutive ideology of Western, bourgeois capitalism—that is, the separation of economic activity from all else. See chapter 8 for a discussion of what Tu (1991:6) calls *guanxi* capitalism.

1. EVERYDAY *GUANXI* PRODUCTION

1   Following Roland Barthes (1967, 1972), I use the term "metonymic" to refer to entities that follow and replace each other in a temporal sequence rather than "stand for" something in a nontemporal logical relation of meaning (i.e., "metaphor"). I do *not* use metonymy to refer to parts that stand for a whole (as some linguists do).

2   Sinologists have long noted the relative weakness of lineage organization in North China. Sangren (1984) suggests that sinological anthropology has overemphasized the importance of jural principles of lineage kinship in general. In 1988–90 Fengjia, reference to formal lineage relationships were all but absent. In other recent North China village ethnographies, Cohen (1990) describes lineage relations as still carrying some importance in a Hebei village, while Yan (1993) describes a Heilongjiang village in which lineage relations are so weak that agnates in general are less important than affines. See chapter 7 for a history of lineages in Fengjia. See Duara (1988:86–90) and Goody (1990) for useful summaries of the relevant literature.

3   For a critique of the sinology that takes Chinese ritual in general as a mere symbolism of underlying realities, see Hevia (1994, 1995).

4   Literally, *song hezi* is the "delivery of boxes." Some said the name referred to the delivery of the dowry, which would be sent out from the bride's house on that day, while others said it had to do with the presents (mostly cash) that were given to the bride's family on this occasion. This event took place the day before a bride left her natal family.

5   For each surname there is a set of generational names. For example, in 1989 for the surname Feng, the Ru, Da, Yue, Yong, and Chang generations still had living members. Generational names come after the surname when writing or speaking a person's name. Thus a member of the Ru generation with the given name Hai would be called Feng Ru Hai. In theory, members of the Ru generation are two generations older than a person named (for example) Feng Yue Hai. However, because there are four branches of the Feng family in the village, and because this set of generational names has been in use for twenty generations, some people with the generational name Yue are older than some with the generational name Ru. These cases create some ritual awkwardness, as it is unclear who should play the role of the senior. See Kates (1976 [1952]:162–163, 235) for a discussion of generational names in North China during the 1930s. Wang and Micklin (1996) analyze the decline in use of generation names in China since the 1960s.

6   As Fei (1939) also points out, use of the same kinship term when addressing people within and outside one's family, does not necessarily imply the same closeness of *guanxi* or the same level of material obligation. *Guanxi* are re-created in many ways. The production of *guanxi* that occurs when addressing someone must be considered within the context of the history of the entire range of *guanxi* production practices extant between the interlocutors.

7   When Fengjia residents addressed someone who was younger in years but of an older generation, they often combined the addressee's *xueming* with the appropriate kinship term. For example, a man whose *xueming* was Dacheng and who by generation was one's *shushu* (father's younger brother) could be called Dachengshu. In order to clearly distinguish the addressee when many fellow villagers of similar gender and generation were present, even those younger by both years and generation might use this form of address.

8   In Shen Rong's short story "The Secret of Crown Prince Village," set in rural China during the late 1970s, "Fifth Li's wife" similarly cannot remember her name. A cadre finally digs up a list of names from the land reform, where she is referred to as "Mrs. Li, née Pan" (Shen 1987:329).

2. GUEST/HOST ETIQUETTE AND BANQUETS

1   Current scholarship places authorship of the novel (the collection of folk-tales into a single text) in the fourteenth century (Shapiro 1986:i). As teacher Feng emphasized to me, the story takes place in Shandong Province not far from Fengjia. Episodes from it have been dramatized often in the public media.

2   In North China, south-facing house orientation dates to the Shang dynasty (1500–1000 B.C.) (Fairbank and Reischauer 1989:28–30). After living in Beijing during the 1930s, George Kates noted that "there was not a house of any size, even the humblest, that was not oriented to the cardinal points of the compass" and quoted the proverb "Rich men use not east-south rooms: Summer not cool; winter not warm" (1976 [1952]:252).

3   See Kipnis (1995a), Hu (1944), and Cheng Chung-ying (1986) for discussions of the many meanings of *mianzi* and the problems of translating this word as "face."

4   In the usage referring to seats in the People's Congress, the character *xi* is combined with the character *wei* (meaning position) for the compound *xiwei.*

5   For comparisons with banquet customs in Hong Kong, see E. N. Anderson (1988) and Cooper (1986).

6   The semantic cluster around the word for fat is much more positive in Chinese than in English. One word for fat, *fei,* is used in the word for fertilizer, *feiliao; feimei* means rich and fertile. Another, *zhi,* is used in the compound *zhifen,* meaning cosmetics, and *zhigao,* meaning fruits of the people's labor or wealth of the people. Thus, in contexts that were especially meaningful to rural agriculturalists, fat took on connotations of embodied surplus or of a product to be used to bolster productive ability and beauty. At personal, ritual banquets, fatty meats in general were preferred (as a matter of taste and not of economy). In contrast, in the banquets of county seat officials, lean meats were preferred. This town/village difference in taste and cooking styles reflected distinctive genres of style that are examined in chapter 9.

7   Ann Anagnost's (1988, 1991) analyses of CCP newspaper articles illustrates the usefulness of reading such articles as tools for yielding ideological effects rather than as representations of social facts.

8   Two April 1989 *Village Masses* (1989b, 1989c) articles that exemplify this tendency were "Calculating the Bill for, and Stopping, Drinking and Eating on the Public Account" (*Suan xizhang shazhu gongkuan chihefeng*) and "The Origin of a Riddle" (*Yiju xiehouyude laili*). The "riddle" was "How do you describe a guest of Qujia village?"; the answer was "without a host to accompany them." The article claimed that in Qujia village, village officials no longer hosted guests who had to eat in the village on official business; the guests ate by themselves. The village masses were supposedly happy with their officials for saving money that would have been spent if the village officials had hosted banquets.

3. Gift Giving

1   The *xiang* in this *xiang qin* is a different character from the one in the *xiangqin* that I translated as "fellow villager." This *xiang qin* translates literally as "to examine relatives." See glossary.

2   In his analysis of a wedding ceremony in rural Jiangsu Province, Fei Xiaotong (1986:123) reports that the portion of the newlyweds' furniture given by the bride's family as dowry was marked with red ribbons. Though I observed no red ribbons in Fengjia, the spirit of ascertaining the exact value of the dowry was similar.

3   In 1989 the exchange rate was 3.71 yuan per U.S. dollar. Hereafter yuan is abbreviated ¥. In 1989, per capita income in Fengjia was approximately ¥1200 per year.

4   This month was the mother's recuperation period. An older man told me that during this month the mother neither works nor leaves the room. In practice, however, I noted considerable individual variation.

5   At this point, as a result of extensive legwork by the matchmakers, the bride and groom themselves and their families would know a fair amount about each other, would have probably seen each other from a distance, and would be generally satisfied with the match.

6   At spring festival, *Qingming* festival, after the wheat harvest, and at mid-autumn festival. See Huang Shu-min (1993) for a history of this invented tradition. Some couples supplemented these with frequent informal visits.

7   I was told that the bride's family generally gives more in the dowry than they receive in the bridewealth, and that to give less would be a loss of *mianzi*. Fei Xiaotong (1986:123) and Yan (1993:chapter 8) have also found this to be the case in other Chinese villages during the 1980s. However, as these negotiations were private matters, I would not preclude the possibility that some families tried to profit directly from their daughter's bridewealth.

8   In 1989, the village was divided into three production teams. See chapter 7.

4. "Kowtowing"

1   There are two Chinese words translated as "kowtow": *ketou* and *koutou*. I use the former because it more closely approaches Fengjia pronunciation.

2   The definition of what counts as a *ketou* in both this film and Fengjia is perhaps not the same as in imperial ritual. Though the details of court protocol are beyond the scope of this study, one older man said that a 1980s rural North China *ketou* required only one bow of the head performed while kneeling, while the Ch'ing court version required the "knocking" of one's head on the ground three times in each of three directions while kneeling.

3   Croll (1981) presents a general discussion of arranged versus free marriage in the PRC.

4   I saw or heard of ancestral offerings being done on five occasions: spring festival, *Qingming* festival, "ghost festival" (*guijie* or *qiyueshiwu*, the fifteenth day of the seventh month of the lunar calendar), the mid-autumn festival, and on the death anniversary of one's parents. Some emphasized ancestral offerings more than others.

5   Clearly the bride's *ketou* would constitute relationships to others besides the husband, but no one else would share all five groups.

6   In those cases where the daughter was already "lost"—i.e., in cases where, either through attending college or manipulating connections, the daughter had found work outside the village and thus had effectively already moved out of her home—the dowry party (*song hezi*) became a relatively cheerful event.

5. Weddings, Funerals, and Gender

1   For a general theoretical analysis of the dilemmas of postmodern feminist anthropology, see Micaela di Leonardo's (1991) introduction. See Barlow (1989b) for a critical examination of how gender has been analyzed in Chinese contexts.

2   Productive analyses of the types of policies and social conditions that empower or constrain women, however, are certainly possible. For two such analyses of North China villages during the reform era, see Beaver, Hou, and Wang (1995) and Judd (1994). Diamond (1975) provides a similar analysis for the collectivized decades.

3   Chan et al. (1992:191) describe how the advantages of keeping their daughters close led brides' families to accept intravillage marriages in Chen Village, Guangdong Province, during the late 1960s and 1970s. During the 1980s, when the building of roads and availability of motorbikes had made longer distance travel more convenient, Chen Village marriage patterns again shifted toward village exogamy, but without a reduction in contact between women and their natal families (Chan et al. 1992:296). During the late 1980s convenient motorized transportation was not yet prevalent enough to influence marriage patterns in Fengjia. However, in 1992, county officials said that building a paved road to every village in Zouping was a goal they planned to reach in the near term.

4   The double happiness (*shuangxi*) sign consists of a pair of the character that means happiness and is a decorative motif used in marriages throughout China.

5   The *dongfang* is the room the new couple lives in after they are married. If the groom's family had built a new house in anticipation of the marriage, the *dongfang* was the north room of the new house. If the new couple was initially to live with the groom's parents, the *dongfang* was a separate north room in the groom's parents' house.

6   The sedan chairs would have been carried by members of the wedding procession, and only the bride would have ridden inside.

7   For a fictional depiction of a rural North China *naofang* that almost degenerates into gang rape, see Zhu Xiaoping's short story "Amongst the Western Mountains" (*Xi Fu Shan Zhong*) (Zhu 1992:41–45).

8   James Watson (1988) has emphasized the importance of ritual specialists in Chinese funerals. Unlike the specialists Watson describes, masters of ceremony in 1988–90 Fengjia were not paid. Consequently, Fengjia funerals did not entirely follow the nine-part structure of late imperial funerals laid out by Watson. Not only did they not include paid specialists, but they also lacked music. The other seven steps, however, were present.

9   I was told there were different styles of writing the name depending on the family and on the generation and gender of the deceased. One man told me that in his family the name of a male who was a member of the oldest living generation and whose name was, for example, Feng Dajian, would have been written "Deceased Father Venerable Mister Feng Dajian Spirit Position" (*Xiankao Fenglaoxiansheng Dajian Lingwei*); the name of a female of the oldest living generation and natal surname Zhang would have been written "Deceased Mother Venerable Madame Zhang Spirit Position" (*Xianpi Zhangshi Laotaitai Lingwei*). The name of a man who was survived by relatives of an older generation would have been written "Dajian Venerable Mr. Feng Spirit Position" (*Dajian Fenglaoxiansheng Lingwei*).

10 A. Wolf (1970) describes grades of mourning dress in Taiwan during the late 1960s, while Freedman (1958) presents the official mourning grades codified in the law of the late Ch'ing (nineteenth century). Both Wolf and Freedman frame their discussions in considerations of the rights and obligations of lineage members, especially with regard to the inheritance of land from the deceased. Though mourning grades influenced the structure of funerals in 1988–90 Fengjia, their practical significance had attenuated. Land was no longer inheritable and lineage organization was nonexistent.

6. Feeling, Speech, and Nonrepresentational Ethics

1   See, for example, Campbell's *The Romantic Ethic and the Spirit of Modern Consumerism* (1987, especially 138–160) and Rosaldo (1984:146). Campbell links the rise of an ethic of emotional expression with consumption. In the

ethic he describes, expression of one's inner feelings is a moral imperative; controlling one's spontaneity is simply wrong.

2   The point here is not to deny that *ganqing* has psychological effects. Certainly, individual heart/minds are caught up in "magnetic fields of human feeling." Rather the point is that *ganqing* is not a substance that originates and exists only in individuals.

3   A further example of the suspicion that can be aroused by relationships created without appropriate intermediaries may be found in Ding Ling's story "Miss Sophia's Diary." When Sophia is seen with a man who is neither family, a classmate, or from the same native place, it is assumed that they have an illegitimate sexual relation. See Tani Barlow's translation (Barlow 1989a:64, 356 note 9).

4   These examples were given in a class on Maoist thought taught by Professor Liu Linyuan at Nanjing University. The two "whatevers" were: "Resolutely enact whatever Chairman Mao said, [and] resolutely carry out whatever Chairman Mao instructed" (*Fanshi Maozhuxidehua, douyao jianjuede zhaoban. Fanshi Maozhuxidezhishi douyao jianjuede zhixing*). For more on the historical significance of "Seek truth from facts," see Thompson (1990:30-31) and Philip Huang (1995:135-136).

5   On official language as an occasion for humor, see Farquhar (1994a). On official language as an instrument for personal gain, see Perry Link (1992), Barrett McCormick (1993), and Michael Schoenhals (1992). For detailed studies of how the political/moral language of Maoism became an instrument of personal gain in one rural village, see Chan et al. (1992) and Madsen (1984).

PART II   INTRODUCTION

1   Despite the criticism to which it has been subjected, structural-functional holism remains influential in certain quarters of sinological anthropology. Potter and Potter (1990) more or less explicitly embrace a structural-functional outlook. Even works that concentrate on historical process, like Friedman et al. (1991), tend to invoke "traditional Chinese culture" as a self-reproducing black box that explains otherwise troublesome historical continuities. For critiques of holism in anthropology, see Appadurai (1992), Thornton (1992), and Gupta and Ferguson (1992).

2   See P. Cohen (1984) for a critique of the deployment of "traditional Chinese culture and society" as theoretical construct in American sinology.

3   Though much of Foucault's work may be cited here, the most explicit formulations of "subjectification" occur in Foucault's essay "The Subject and Power" (1982) and in Rabinow's (1984:7-13) introduction to *The Foucault Reader*.

4   In examining the historical influence of state activities on social subjectivities, I follow a Foucauldian tradition of historical work that spans the globe. Cohn's (1987) description of the impact of British colonial laws and

census taking on the culture of rural India, B. Anderson's (1991) discussion of colonial census taking in Southeast Asia, and Corrigan and Sayer's work on the relevance of "state activities, forms, routines and rituals [for] the constitution and regulation of social identities, ultimately of our subjectivities" in England (1985:2) are three of the more noteworthy examples. Recent sinological work in this vein includes Duara's (1988) examination of the relations between "state strengthening" and local culture in early-twentieth-century, rural North China, and Gladney's (1991) account of "ethno-genesis" among Muslims in the People's Republic.

7. GUANXI IN FENGJIA, 1948–90

1 During the land reform, rural families were classified as landlords, rich peasants, middle peasants (of which there were three types—upper, middle, and lower), poor peasants, and tenants. Landlords lived entirely off of rents; rich peasants worked their own land and had some excess which had to be worked by hired labor; middle peasants had enough land to be self-sufficient; poor peasants had some land, but not enough to support their families and had to hire out their labor part of the time; tenants had no land and earned their living as hired laborers. Mao Zedong originally devised this system in his famous 1926 analysis of classes in China (1967[1926]).

2 In the periods before and after the "Three Difficult Years," approximately thirty-five children a year were born in the village. From 1960 to 1962 the numbers ranged from five to seven a year (based on village immunization records); also see Odend'hal (1989).

3 This is not to say that women had the same opportunities as men did. Women were rarely allowed to earn as many work points as men. Still, the amount they could earn was significant. See Chan et al. (1992) and C. K. Yang (1959) for discussion of this issue.

4 These numbers, along with all those on village income, are taken from the ledger book of the village accountant. One *jin* equals 0.5 kilograms (1.1 pounds). One *mu* equals 0.0667 hectares.

5 In 1970 the collective's income was ¥154,000; in 1975 it was ¥431,000. In 1970 per capita income was ¥113; in 1975 it was about ¥150.

6 In general, if a given irrigation project depended upon the state-organized canals, it was organized collectively. Irrigation work that depended on well water was done individually.

7 These marriage ages are the results of the 1981 Marriage Law, which also embodies the logic of reducing fertility rates by postponing marriage (see *China Daily* 1988). Marriage ages in the 1950 version were twenty for men and eighteen for women. Selden (1993:161) notes a similar reversal of marriage ages in Hebei Province.

8 M. Cohen (1976), Fei (1939:65–69), Huang Shu-min (1989:158–162, 1992), Judd (1994:174–181), Potter and Potter (1990:219–220), and Yan (1993:207–213) all give good descriptions of the tensions around *fenjia* in other vil-

lages. Here a brief introduction to practices in 1988–90 Fengjia will have to suffice. After a son married, he and his wife could ask to split off from their parents' family (i.e., *fenjia*). This splitting did not necessarily require moving out of the parents' house. Rather it involved a division of property (that is, a sort of early inheritance), a separation of household economies, and, therefore, a separation of cooking and eating. If there were many brothers in a family when the first brother "split," decisions were made about what part of the family's property would eventually belong to each offspring. Decisions were also made about which siblings would have how much responsibility for looking after the parents in their old age. A common practice in Fengjia was for the youngest brother to continue to live with the parents until they die. His household would have a greater role in supporting the parents in their old age and would inherit the parents' house. Often an older relative of the father was brought in to mediate the negotiations. Since the responsibility system made the household the unit responsible for land and taxes, all *fenjia* had to be registered with the village committee, and were recorded in the *hukou* when it was updated.

9   Birth control policy in China has a long and tortuous history. It was first advocated in 1950 but opposed by Mao. Propaganda encouraging birth control was alternately suppressed and disseminated until 1974 when birth control advocates gained the upper hand. From 1974 to 1978 propaganda was stepped up, but no firm policies were enacted. In 1979 the provinces were told to design and enforce a policy of one child per family. In Shandong Province the policy was designed in 1980 and implemented in 1981. In 1984, an experimental policy to allow peasants whose first child was a girl to petition to have a second child was implemented in Zouping County. In 1986, the policy was extended to the entire province. See Croll (1994:185–197) for a general introduction to birth control policy and Greenhalgh (1990) for a discussion of its evolution in Shaanxi Province.

10   The distinction between *guoji* and adoption from outside the family had a basis in imperial Chinese law. During the Ch'ing dynasty, only *guoji* foster children had inheritance rights. The legal distinction ended under the Nationalist government. See Meijer (1978:462–463) and Chikusa (1978).

11   On scientism and the "anti-superstition" arguments of CCP intellectuals, see Kwok (1965) and Barlow (1991). On CCP problems with the personal loyalties that pre-1948 rituals produced, see chapter 8. On official attitudes toward "wasteful" consumption in pre-1948 rituals, see Parish and Whyte (1978:250). During the 1980s, the official press continued to criticize this "waste" (e.g., *Nanjing Daily* 1989).

12   The Maoist principle behind this co-optation is "the mass line" — that is, "From the masses, to the masses." For a discussion of this process during the Yenan period, see Selden (1971:268–275). For Mao's own call for this sort of work, see Mao (1967[1944]).

13   The "four olds" were old thought, old culture, old customs, and old habits (*jiu sixiang, jiu wenhua, jiu fengsu, jiu xiguan*). Destroying the four olds

(*po sijiu*) was a guiding slogan of the Red Guards. It was coined by Lin Biao at the beginning of the Cultural Revolution (Gao and Yan 1986:51).

8. GUANXI VERSIONS THROUGHOUT CHINA

1   Being an urbanite was not simply a matter of where one was living but rather was designated in the household registration records. During the late 1980s, these records defined every citizen of the PRC as either a "peasant" or "nonpeasant," resident in a specific city, town, or village of differentiated sizes. See chapter 9.

2   Fried uses the Wade-Giles system of romanizing Chinese characters, while I use the pinyin. In the Wade-Giles system *ganqing* is written as *kan ch'ing*, *guanxi* as *kuan hsi.*

3   In both Taiwan and Shandong the sound spoken would not be the same as the standard pinyin I have given here. However, the same written character would be used.

4   Jacobs cites the following sources: Whitson with Huang (1973:50), Sullivan (1976), Perry (1976:18–20), and Selden (1971:183, 197–198, 241). Also see Perry (1993) for a discussion of *guanxi* politics in the Shanghai labor movement of that period.

5   Two such articles were "The Knock of Gifts Doesn't Open the Door to the Agricultural Bank" (*Liwu qiao bukai nonghangde men*) and "Gifts Become Life Insurance Fee" (*Lipin biancheng renshenbaoxianjin*) (*Village Masses* 1988 and 1989d, respectively). Both articles describe "good" officials who find ways of not accepting gifts. In the first, the cadre simply turns in the gift giver to his higher-ups, dismissing the gift as a bribe. In the latter, a village secretary uses the money gotten from returning New Year's gifts to the local store to pay the mandatory life insurance fees of the neighbors who gave the gifts. The second article further characterizes the neighbors' gifts as "traditional" ones that the secretary used to accept before his appointment to an official post. To save "face" for his neighbors, he could not simply refuse the gifts. Rather, he had to accept them and later return them to the store himself.

6   From friends and acquaintances in Beijing I heard more subversive interpretations of these portraits — that they reflected a working-class protest against the inflation and corruption prevalent under Dengist economic policies.

9. GUANXI AND PEASANT SUBCULTURE

1   I take the concept of subculture from Hebdige (1979), who uses the term to describe symbolic practices that undermine the assumptions of hegemonic ideologies. In a later self-critique (1988:212), he abandoned the concept because of the historical closure and negativity he then felt the term implied. I rescue the term on the following grounds. First, I don't think one needs to assume that the term culture (and by extension subculture) implies closure either in the historical sense or in the sense of evenly belonging to a

single group of people. Cultures and subcultures always exist in overlapping and contradictory relations to various groups of people. In addition, to build on the biological metaphor (i.e., a bacterial "culture"), one can assume that cultures are always developing, dying, or mutating—somehow changing over time. If one allows the term culture this flexibility, then Hebdige's second misgiving is more easily handled. As Hebdige so powerfully described in 1979, during certain historical moments some cultural practices derive their power from their ability to undermine more hegemonic understandings. To point at this critical, destructive power with the word *sub*culture is not to deny these practices either their productive aspects, nor their potential to develop into something positively or even hegemonically "cultural."

2   Many cases have been reported of peasants buying grain at the market (i.e., not state-subsidized) price to pay their grain taxes and feed their families. However, I did not hear of this happening in Fengjia village. As some nonpeasants (particularly rural teachers) continue to live in villages and some peasants move into the cities with friends and relatives, the peasant/nonpeasant split is not strictly a village/town one. In Zouping County in 1990 only about 7 percent of the population had nonpeasant household registration designations. See Chan (1994) on the problems of defining the rural and urban populace in China. For more on the household registration policy, see Cheng and Selden (1994), Gongan Zhengcefalu Yanrongshi (1981), Philip Huang (1990:288–301), Judd (1994:168–174), Kipnis (1995b), Potter and Potter (1990:296–312), Whyte and Parish (1984:9–26), and Wang Fuchu (1985:235–253).

3   Before and during the Cultural Revolution, official rhetoric would sometimes describe as "capitalist" the desires of rural people to market their produce or to enlarge their private plots. Indeed, one of the rationales for collectivization was to place the peasantry into the same sort of work environment as a proletariat, thereby simultaneously destroying the context that might engender petite bourgeoisie consciousness (family ownership of small private plots) while creating the environment that would supposedly engender a radical proletarian outlook (see Zweig 1989:192 on this point). However, by the 1980s this conception of the peasantry had seemingly disappeared from the popular imagination. Popular books like *Poverty within Wealth* (*Furao de Pinkun*) (Wang and Bai 1986) suggested that the poorer rural areas were "underdeveloped" because the "feudal" consciousness of their people prevented proper market mechanisms from working (see Bodman and Wan 1991 for further commentary).

4   In CCP usage, socialist societies were those in which people were paid according to their work. Such societies were defined to be advancements over capitalist societies in which bourgeois classes were paid in excess of their labor while working classes were not paid the full value of their labor. Communist societies were defined as those in which people would receive according to their needs (rather than according to their work).

5   Being "slow" or "foot-dragging" implied lacking a desire for speed on the historical trajectory toward communism.

6   In contrast, Davis (1989) writes that in the mid-1980s Shanghai residents had purged their homes of all vestiges of party images. Though it did not seem to be the case in Fengjia, there may be Chinese contexts in which the presence or absence of party imagery is a marker of a peasant "subculture" as discussed below. Laing (1989) describes general differences between rural and urban house decoration. Mayfair Yang (1994:247–276) discusses the type of subject construction that resulted from Mao worship.

7   Chinese historians distinguish between *pingdengzhuyi* (egalitarianism), which refers to the notion of formal political/legal equality (developed in Western political thought), and *pingjunzhuyi* ("equalitarianism"), which refers to substantive economic equality.

8   These exaggerations were somewhat problematic for me as an ethnographer. Residents, whether "peasant and proud" or critical of "backward and feudal practices," often answered cursory questions about the origins of present practices by describing them as "passed down from previous generations" (*chuanxialaide*). However, the same people would respond to detailed questioning about the same practices with histories of significant change. Though many revealed keen historical memories, the everyday conversations of residents of divergent political outlooks all tended to construct "peasant" practices as timeless. My insistence on the recent (re)invention of much ritual practice is thus counter to (though at the same time based on) the predominant constructions of Fengjia residents.

9   In general, though I have been emphasizing the subcultural implications of filiality, I do not wish to imply that filiality is undertaken merely as a form of protest. It is also positively valued in and of itself. Thus, Secretary Feng's *ketou* also assert that his job and actions have been a form of filial service to his seniors for the benefit of their families and village.

10 Ironically (since Mao instructed youth to rebel and destroy the old), this man also considered himself a "Maoist" who thought that the policies of the Cultural Revolution were more favorable to "peasants" than post-Mao policies. Arguably, his "Maoism" resonated with the anti-intellectualism and the more favorable rhetoric about "peasants' characteristics" that prevailed during the Cultural Revolution. Friedman et al. (1991) argue that anti-intellectualism in the CCP was reinforced by the party's pre-1949 recruitment of lower-class, rural, illiterate male leaders.

11 According to the Chinese lunar calendar, 1988 was the year of the dragon, 1989 the year of the snake.

12 Imperial literati sometimes compared their inkstones to fields, implying that both were necessary tools of work and sources of productive output.

EPILOGUE

1   Though I had heard of and attended birthday parties for one-year-olds and the elderly, I had never heard of such an event being held for a middle-

aged woman. Thus, the store opening was probably the primary reason for this celebration.

2   Party Secretary Feng is older than this store owner, but has a younger generation name.

Glossary of Selected Chinese Characters

Pinyin	Character	English
anding tuanjie	安定团结	stability and unity
bai	拜	to bow or kowtow, to embody respect for
bainian	拜年	bow on New Year's day
baoban	包办	arranged (marriage)
baoyang	抱养	form of adoption
beifang	北房	north room
benjiaren	本家人	family members
biaotai	表态	public declaration (wedding)
biaoxian	表现	self-presentation
buhaoyisi	不好意思	embarrassed
bulaoshi	不老实	dishonest
chuantong	传统	tradition
chubin	出殡	funerary procession
chunjie	春节	spring festival
dadui	大队	brigade
danwei	单位	work unit
dipian	地片	section of land
dongfang	洞房	bridal chamber
feinongmin	非农民	nonpeasant
Fengjia	冯家	Fengjia village
fengjian	封建	feudal
fenjia	分家	splitting house (family)
fuyang	扶养	form of adoption
ganqing	感情	feeling
gongfen	工分	work points
gongmu	公墓	public grave
guanxi	关系	relationship
gugu	姑姑	aunt (father's sister)
guike	贵客	honored guests
guoji	过继	pass succession (adoption)
haoke	好客	hospitable

he xijiu	喝喜酒	drink wine of happiness
hexili	贺喜礼	congratulatory gift
huajiao	花较	sedan chair (used for wedding)
huaquan	花圈	flower wreath
hukou	户口	household registration
jianmianli	见面礼	meeting gift
jiao hun	叫魂	call the spirits (at a funeral)
jieji ganqing	阶级感情	class feeling
jijixing	积极 性	enthusiasm and initiative
jinbu	进步	advanced
jingyi	敬意	respect
jingzi	镜子	glass framed artwork (gift)
jiurou pengyou	酒肉朋友	banquet buddies
jiujiu	舅舅	uncle (mother's brother)
jugong	鞠躬	bow
kaoyi	靠椅	chair with back
kekao	可靠	dependable; reliable
ketou	磕头	kowtow
kusang bang	哭丧棒	mourning sticks
la guanxi	拉关系	pull relationships
laiwang	来往	coming and going
laodongli	劳动力	labor power
laohuoshao	烙火烧	jujube cookie
laolao	姥姥	grandmother (maternal)
laoshi	老实	honest
laoshi	老师	professor, teacher
li	礼	ritual
lijie	礼节	ritual and etiquette
limao	礼貌	etiquette
liwu	礼物	gift
longzhong	隆重	ceremonious
luohou	落后	backwards
meiren	媒人	matchmaker
mianhua	面花	twisted fried dough sticks
mianzi	面子	face
mixin	迷信	superstition
nainai	奶奶	grandmother (paternal)
naofang	闹房	stir up the bridal chamber
niangjia	娘家	natal home
nizi	妮子	girl, lass (derogatory)
nongmin	农民	peasant
peike	陪客	accompany guests (banquet)
pengyou	朋友	friends
pojia	婆家	mother-in-law's home
qinggan	情感	emotions, feelings

qingxu	情绪	emotions, mood
qinqi	亲戚	relatives
ren qin	认亲	acknowledge relatives
renmin gongshe	人民公社	people's commune
renqing	人情	human feeling
renqingde cilichang	人情的磁力场	magnetic field of human feeling
renshiqian	人事钱	person-event-money (gift)
ruzi	褥子	thin mattress; bedding
shangyi	上椅	upper (guest) chair
shi	氏	née
shipin	食品	foodstuff
shishiqiushi	实事求是	seek truth from facts
shushu	叔叔	father's younger brother
song hezi	送盒子	dowry party
waisheng	外甥	daughter/sister's children
wenhua	文化	culture (education)
xiang qin	相亲	engagement banquet
xiangqin	乡亲	fellow villagers
xiao	孝	filiality
xiaoming	小名	baby name
xiaozhe	孝者	patrilineal descendants
xiayi	下椅	lower (host) chair
xieke	谢客	thank guests (funeral)
xin	心	heart/mind
xishi	喜事	happy event
xueming	学名	school name
yanxi	筵席	banqueting
yijian	意见	opinions
yisi	意思	meaning/feeling
yiyi	姨姨	aunt (mother's sister)
zerenzhi	责任制	responsibility system
zhengfeng	整风	rectification
zhilu	指路	show the road (funeral)
zhongzhuan	中专	technical high school
ziyou lianai	自由恋爱	free love
Zouping	邹平	Zouping County
zuoke	作客	guesting
zuozhu	作主	hosting

References

Ahern, Emily Martin. 1981. *Chinese Ritual and Politics.* New York: Cambridge University Press.

Alitto, Guy. 1979. *The Last Confucian: Liang Shu-ming and the Chinese Dilemma of Modernity.* Berkeley: University of California Press.

———. 1988. Zouping County: An Overview of Its Recent History. Unpublished manuscript, University of Chicago.

Anagnost, Ann. 1988. Family Violence and Magical Violence: The 'Woman-as-Victim' in China's One-Child Family Policy. *Women and Language* 1:16–22.

———. 1989. Prosperity and Counter-Prosperity: The Moral Discourse on Wealth in Post-Mao China. In *Marxism and the Chinese Experience: Issues of Socialism in a Third World Society,* ed. Arif Dirlik and Maurice Meisner, 210–234. Armonk, N.Y.: M. E. Sharpe.

———. 1991. The Politicized Body. *Stanford Humanities Review* 2:86–102.

Anderson, Benedict. 1991. *Imagined Communities.* Rev. ed. London: Verso.

Anderson, E. N. 1988. *The Food of China.* New Haven, Conn.: Yale University Press.

Appadurai, Arjun. 1986. Introduction: Commodities and the Politics of Value. In *The Social Life of Things,* ed. Arjun Appadurai, 3–63. Cambridge: Cambridge University Press.

———. 1992. Putting Hierarchy in Its Place. In *ReReading Cultural Anthropology,* ed. George Marcus, 34–47. Durham, N.C.: Duke University Press.

Bakhtin, Mikhail. 1981. *The Dialogic Imagination.* Trans. Michael Holquist and Caryl Emerson. Austin: University of Texas Press.

———. 1986. *Speech Genres and Other Late Essays.* Trans. V. M. McGee. Austin: University of Texas Press.

Barlow, Tani. 1989a. Introduction. In *I Myself Am a Woman: Selected Writings of Dingling,* ed. Tani Barlow, 1–45. Boston: Beacon.

———. 1989b. Beyond Dichotomies: Response, Asian Perspectives. *Gender and History* 1(3):318–329.

———. 1991. *Zhishifenzi* (Chinese Intellectuals) and Power. *Dialectical Anthropology* 16(3–4):209–233.

Barme, Geremie, and Jon Minford, eds. 1986. *Seeds of Fire: Chinese Voices of Conscience.* Hong Kong: Far Eastern Economic Review Press.

Barthes, Roland. 1967. *Elements of Semiology.* Trans. Annette Lavers and Colin Smith. New York: Hill and Wang.

———. 1972. *Mythologies.* Trans. Annette Lavers. New York: Hill and Wang.

Beaver, Patricia D., Hou Lihui, and Wang Xue. 1995. Rural Chinese Women: Two Faces of Economic Reform. *Modern China* 21(2):205–232.

Bi Jifang. 1990. *Zhixie He Daoqian* (Thanking and Apologizing). *Xue Hanyu* (November 1990):18–19.

Bian Yanjie. 1994. Guanxi and the Allocation of Urban Jobs in China. *China Quarterly* 140:971–999.

Blake, Fred. 1978. Death and Abuse in Marriage Laments: The Curse of Chinese Brides. *Asian Folklore Studies* 37:13–33.

Bloch, Maurice. 1989. The Symbolism of Money in Imerina. In *Money and the Morality of Exchange,* ed. J. Parry and M. Bloch, 165–190. New York: Cambridge University Press.

Bodman, Richard W., and Pin P. Wan, trans. 1991. *Deathsong of a River: A Reader's Guide to the Chinese TV Series* Heshang *by Su Xiaokang and Wang Luxiang.* Ithaca, N.Y.: Cornell University Press.

Bourdieu, Pierre. 1977. *Outline of a Theory of Practice.* Trans. Richard Nice. New York: Columbia University Press.

———. 1990. *The Logic of Practice.* Trans. Richard Nice. Stanford, Calif.: Stanford University Press.

Brownell, Susan. 1995. *Training the Body for China: Sports in the Moral Order of the People's Republic.* Chicago: University of Chicago Press.

Campbell, Colin. 1987. *The Romantic Ethic and the Spirit of Modern Consumerism.* New York: Basil Blackwell.

Chan, Anita, Richard Madsen, and Jonathon Unger. 1992. *Chen Village under Mao and Deng.* Berkeley: University of California Press.

Chan Kam Wing. 1994. Urbanization and Rural–Urban Migration in China since 1982. *Modern China* 20(3):243–281.

Cheng, Chung-Ying. 1986. The Chinese Face and Its Confucian Roots. *Journal of Chinese Philosophy* 13(3):329–348.

Cheng Li. 1994. University Networks and the Rise of Qinghua Graduates in China's Leadership. *Australian Journal of Chinese Affairs* 32:1–32.

Cheng Tiejun, and Mark Selden. 1994. The Origins and Social Consequences of China's *Hukou* System. *China Quarterly* 139:644–668.

Chikusa, Tatsuo. 1978. Succession to Ancestral Sacrifices and Adoption of Heirs to the Sacrifices: As Seen from an Inquiry into Customary Institutions in Manchuria. In *Chinese Family Law and Social Change in Historical and Comparative Perspective,* ed. David Buxbaum, 151–175. Seattle: University of Washington Press.

China Daily. 1988. Marriage Rites Set in Sight of the Law. December 24.

China News Digest. 1995. News Briefs (item no. 6). April 28, 7.

Chun, Allen. 1985. Land Is to Live: A Study of the Concept of *Tsu* in a Hakka

Chinese Village, New Territories, Hong Kong. Ph.D. dissertation, Anthropology Department, University of Chicago.

———. 1991. La Terra Trema: The Crisis of Kinship and Community in the New Territories of Hong Kong before and after "The Great Transformation." *Dialectical Anthropology* 16(3–4):309–332.

Cihai Bianji Weiyuanhui (Sea of Words Editorial Committee). 1979. *Cihai, Suoyinben.* Shanghai: Shanghai Cishu Chuban She.

Clifford, James. 1988. *The Predicament of Culture: Twentieth-Century Ethnography, Literature, and Art.* Cambridge: Harvard University Press.

Cohen, Myron L. 1976. *House United, House Divided: The Chinese Family in Taiwan.* New York: Columbia University Press.

———. 1990. Lineage Organization in North China. *Journal of Asian Studies* 49(3):509–534.

———. 1993. Cultural and Political Inventions in Modern China: The Case of the Chinese Peasant. *Daedalus* 122:151–170.

Cohen, Paul A. 1984. *Discovering History in China: American Historical Writing in the Recent Past.* New York: Columbia University Press.

Cohn, Bernard S. 1987. *An Anthropologist among the Historians and Other Essays.* New York: Oxford University Press.

Collier, J. F., and Sylvia Yanagisako. 1987. Toward a Unified Analysis of Gender and Kinship. In *Gender and Kinship: Essays towards a Unified Analysis,* ed. Collier and Yanagisako, 14–50. Stanford, Calif.: Stanford University Press.

Comaroff, Jean. 1985. *Body of Power, Spirit of Resistance.* Chicago: University of Chicago Press.

Cooper, Eugene. 1986. Chinese Table Manners: You Are How You Eat. *Human Organization* 45(2):179–184.

Corrigan, Philip, and Derek Sayer. 1985. *The Great Arch: English State Formation as Cultural Revolution.* New York: Blackwell.

Croll, Elisabeth. 1981. *The Politics of Marriage in Contemporary China.* Cambridge: Cambridge University Press.

———. 1987. New Peasant Family Forms in Rural China. *Journal of Peasant Studies* 14:469–499.

———. 1994. *From Heaven to Earth: Images and Experiences of Development in China.* New York: Routledge.

Crook, David, and Isabel Crook. 1959. *Revolution in a Chinese Village: Ten Mile Inn.* London: Routledge and Kegan Paul.

Davis, Deborah. 1989. My Mother's House. In *Unofficial China: Popular Culture and Thought in the People's Republic,* ed. Perry Link, Richard Madsen, and Paul Pickowicz, 88–100. San Francisco: Westview.

Davis, Deborah, and Stevan Harrell, eds. 1993. *Chinese Families in the Post-Mao Era.* Berkeley: University of California Press.

de Certeau, Michel. 1984. *The Practice of Everyday Life.* Trans. Steven F. Rendall. Berkeley: University of California Press.

DeWoskin, Kenneth J. 1991. Rhetorical Authority and Coercion in Chinese

Statecraft. In *Rackham Report: Emerging Concepts of Democracy,* 30–51. Ann Arbor: School of Graduate Studies, University of Michigan.

di Leonardo, Micaela. 1991. Introduction: Gender, Culture and Political Economy: Feminist Anthropology in Historical Perspective. In *Gender at the Crossroads of Knowledge: Feminist Anthropology in the Post-Modern Era,* ed. Micaela di Leonardo, 1–48. Berkeley: University of California Press.

Diamond, Norma. 1975. Collectivization, Kinship and the Status of Women in Rural China. In *Toward an Anthropology of Women,* ed. Rayna R. Reiter, 372–395. New York: Monthly Review Press.

———. 1983. Model Villages and Village Realities. *Modern China* 9(2):163–181.

Dirlik, Arif. 1989. *The Origins of Chinese Communism.* New York: Oxford University Press.

Domes, Jurgen. 1982. New Policies in the Communes: Notes on Rural Societal Studies in China 1976–1981. *Journal of Asian Studies* 41:253–267.

Dominguez, Virginia R. 1989. *People as Subject, People as Object.* Madison: University of Wisconsin Press.

Duara, Prasenjit. 1988. *Culture, Power and the State: Rural North China 1900–1942.* Stanford, Calif.: Stanford University Press.

———. 1993a. De-Constructing the Chinese Nation. *Australian Journal of Chinese Affairs* 30:1–26.

———. 1993b. Bifurcating Linear History: Nation and Histories in China and India. *positions: east asia cultures critique* 1(3):779–804.

Edwards, Louise. 1992. Broadening Horizons: Representation of Women in Asia. *Bulletin of Concerned Asian Scholars* 24(1):59–66.

Evans, Kristi S. 1992. The Argument of Images: Historical Representation in Solidarity Underground Postage, 1981–87. *American Ethnologist* 19(4):749–767.

Fabian, Johannes. 1983. *Time and the Other: How Anthropology Makes Its Object.* New York: Columbia University Press.

Fairbank, John K., and Edwin O. Reischauer. 1989. *China: Tradition and Transformation.* Rev. ed. New York: Houghton Mifflin.

Fang Lizhi. 1990. *Breaking Down the Great Wall: Writings on Science, Culture and Democracy in China.* New York: Alfred Knopf.

Fang Xiaojun, Shan Man, Li Wanpeng, Jiang Wenhua, Ye Tao, and Wang Dianji. 1988. *Shandong Minsu* (Customs of Shandong). Jinan, PRC: Shandong Youyi She.

Farquhar, Judith. 1994a. Eating Chinese Medicine. *Cultural Anthropology* 9(4):471–497.

———. 1994b. *Knowing Practice: The Clinical Encounter of Chinese Medicine.* San Francisco: Westview.

Fei, Xiaotong. 1939. *Peasant Life in China.* London: Routledge and Kegan Paul.

———. 1986. *Shehuixue Tansuo* (Explorations in Sociology). Tianjin, PRC: Tianjin Renmin Chuban She.

Foucault, Michel. 1973. *The Order of Things: An Archaeology of the Human Sciences.* Trans. Alan Sheridan. New York: Vintage.

———. 1975. *The Birth of the Clinic.* Trans. Alan Sheridan. New York: Vintage.

———. 1978. *The History of Sexuality, Volume I: An Introduction.* Trans. Robert Hurley. New York: Random House.

———. 1979. *Discipline and Punish: The Birth of the Prison.* Trans. Alan Sheridan. New York: Vintage.

———. 1980. *Power/Knowledge.* Trans. Colin Gordon. New York: Pantheon.

———. 1982. The Subject and Power. In *Michel Foucault: Beyond Structuralism and Hermeneutics,* ed. Herbert Dreyfus and Paul Rabinow, 208–226. Chicago: University of Chicago Press.

Freedman, Maurice. 1958. *Lineage Organization in Southeastern China.* London: Athlone.

———. 1966. *Chinese Lineage and Society: Fukien and Kuangtung.* London: Athlone.

Fried, Morton H. 1953. *Fabric of Chinese Society: A Study of Social Life of a Chinese County Seat.* New York: Praeger.

Friedman, Edward, Paul G. Pickowicz, and Mark Selden. 1991. *Chinese Village, Socialist State.* New Haven, Conn.: Yale University Press.

Gadamer, Hans Georg. 1975. *Truth and Method.* New York: Seabury.

———. 1976. *Philosophical Hermeneutics.* Trans. David E. Linge. Berkeley: University of California Press.

Gallin, Bernard. 1966. *Hsin Hsing, Taiwan: A Chinese Village in Change.* Berkeley: University of California Press.

Gao Mu, and Yan Jiaqi. 1986. *Wenhuadageming Shinian Shi 1966–1976* (A Ten-Year History of the Cultural Revolution 1966–1976). Tianjin, PRC: Tianjin Renmin Chuban She.

Gates, Hill. 1987. Money for the Gods. *Modern China* 13(3):259–277.

Geertz, Clifford. 1973. *The Interpretation of Cultures.* New York: Basic.

———. 1979. From the Native's Point of View. In *Interpretive Social Science,* ed. Paul Rabinow and William Sullivan, 221–241. Berkeley: University of California Press.

Gladney, Dru C. 1991. *Muslim Chinese: Ethnic Nationalism in the People's Republic.* Harvard East Asian Monographs No. 149. Cambridge, Mass.: Council on East Asian Studies.

Gold, Thomas G. 1985. After Comradeship: Personal Relations in China since the Cultural Revolution. *China Quarterly* 104:657–675.

———. 1986. Fengjiacun: An Overview. Unpublished manuscript, University of California, Berkeley.

———. 1989. Guerilla Interviews among the *Getihu.* In *Popular Culture and Thought in the People's Republic,* ed. Perry Link, Richard Madsen, and Paul Pickowicz, 175–192. San Francisco: Westview.

Gonganbu Zhengcefalu Yanrongshi, comp. 1981. *Gongan Fagui Huibian 1950–1979* (Compilation of Public Security Laws and Regulation, 1950–1979). Beijing: Qunzhong Chuban She.

Goody, Jack. 1990. *The Oriental, the Ancient and the Primitive.* Cambridge: Cambridge University Press.

Greenhalgh, Susan. 1990. The Evolution of the One-Child Policy in Shaanxi. *China Quarterly* 122:191–229.

———. 1993. The Peasantization of the One-Child Policy in Shaanxi. In Davis and Harrell, 219–250.

Gumperz, John. 1982. *Discourse Strategies.* New York: Cambridge University Press.

Gupta, Akhil, and James Ferguson. 1992. Beyond "Culture": Space, Identity and the Politics of Difference. *Cultural Anthropology* 7:6–24.

Hall, David L., and Roger T. Ames. 1987. *Thinking through Confucius.* New York: State University of New York Press.

Hamilton, Gary G. 1991. The Organizational Foundations of Western and Chinese Commerce: A Historical and Comparative Analysis. In *Business Networks and Economic Development in East Asia,* ed. G. Hamilton, 48–65. Hong Kong: University of Hong Kong Centre of Asian Studies.

Hamilton, Gary G., and Kao Cheng-shu. 1990. The Institutional Foundations of Chinese Business: The Family Firm in Taiwan. *Comparative Social Research* 12:95–112.

Han Min, and Jerry Eades. 1992. Responsibility System and Marriage: Economic Change and Changing Patterns of Marriage in Rural Anhui Province. In *Proceedings of the Department of Humanities, College of Arts and Sciences, University of Tokyo,* Vol. 156, Series of Cultural Anthropology, 67–121.

Havel, Vaclav. 1988. *The Power of the Powerless: Citizens against the State in Central-Eastern Europe.* London: Hutchinson.

Hebdige, Dick. 1979. *Subculture: The Meaning of Style.* New York: Methuen.

———. 1987. *Cut 'n' Mix: Culture, Identity and Caribbean Music.* New York: Methuen.

———. 1988. *Hiding in the Light: On Images and Things.* New York: Routledge.

Henderson, Gail E., and Myron S. Cohen. 1984. *The Chinese Hospital: A Socialist Work Unit.* New Haven, Conn.: Yale University Press.

Henriques, Julian, Wendy Holloway, Chathi Urwin, Couze Venn, and Valerie Walkerdine, eds. 1984. *Changing the Subject: Psychology, Social Regulation, and Subjectivity.* New York: Methuen.

Hevia, James. 1994. Sovereignty and Subject: Constituting Relations of Power in Qing Guest Ritual. In *Body, Subject and Power in China,* ed. Tani Barlow and Angela Zito, 181–200. Chicago: University of Chicago Press.

———. 1995. *Cherishing Men from Afar: Qing Guest Ritual and the Macartney Embassy of 1793.* Durham, N.C.: Duke University Press.

Hinton, William. 1966. *Fanshen: A Documentary of Revolution in a Chinese Village.* New York: Vintage.

———. 1983. *Shenfan.* New York: Random House.

Holland, Dorothy, and Andrew Kipnis. 1994. Metaphors for Embarrassment and Stories of Exposure: The Not-So-Egocentric Self in American Culture. *Ethos* 22(3):316–342.

Holloway, Wendy. 1984. Gender Difference and the Production of Subjectivity. In Henriques et al., 227–63.

Honig, Emily. 1985. Socialist Revolution and Women's Liberation in China—A Review Article. *Journal of Asian Studies* 44(2):329–336.

Hu, Hsien Chin. 1944. The Chinese Concepts of Face. *American Anthropologist* 46:45–64.

Huang, Philip C. C. 1985. *The Peasant Economy and Social Change in North China.* Stanford, Calif.: Stanford University Press.

———. 1990. *The Peasant Family and Rural Development in the Yangzi Delta 1350–1988.* Stanford, Calif.: Stanford University Press.

———. 1995. Rural Class Struggle in the Chinese Revolution. *Modern China* 21(1):105–143.

Huang, Shu-min. 1989. *The Spiral Road: Change in a Chinese Village through the Eyes of a Communist Party Leader.* Boulder, Colo.: Westview.

———. 1992. Re-Examining the Extended Family in Chinese Peasant Society: Findings from a Fujian Village. *Australian Journal of Chinese Affairs* 27:25–38.

———. 1993. The State-Society Relationship As Seen in Changing Marital Strategies. Paper presented at the 45th annual meeting of the Association for Asian Studies, Los Angeles.

Hwang, Kwang-kuo. 1987. Face and Favor: The Chinese Power Game. *American Journal of Sociology* 92(4):944–974.

Ikels, Charlotte. 1993. Settling Accounts: The Intergenerational Contract in an Age of Reform. In Davis and Harrell, 307–333.

Jacobs, Bruce J. 1979. A Preliminary Model of Particularistic Ties in Chinese Political Alliances: Kan-ch'ing and Kuan-hsi in a Rural Taiwanese Township. *China Quarterly* 78:237–273.

Jameson, Fredric. 1984. Postmodernism, Or, The Cultural Logic of Late Capitalism. *New Left Review* 146:59–92.

Jankowiak, William R. 1993. *Sex, Death and Hierarchy in a Chinese City: An Anthropological Account.* New York: Columbia University Press.

Jia Ping Ao. 1992. *Hei Shi* (Madam Hei). Beijing: Zuojia Chuban She.

Jiang Zilong. 1991. *Yin-Yang Jiaojie* (Yin-Yang Succession). Beijing: Huayi Chuban She.

Johnson, Kay Ann. 1983. *Women, the Family and Peasant Revolution in China.* Chicago: University of Chicago Press.

Judd, Ellen R. 1989. Chinese Women and Their Natal Families. *Journal of Asian Studies* 48:525–544.

———. 1992. Land Divided, Land United. *China Quarterly* 130:338–356.

———. 1994. *Gender and Power in Rural North China.* Stanford, Calif.: Stanford University Press.

Kao Cheng-shu. 1991. Personal Trust in the Large Businesses in Taiwan: A Traditional Foundation for Contemporary Economic Activities. In *Business Networks and Economic Development in East Asia,* ed. G. Hamilton, 66–76. Hong Kong: University of Hong Kong Centre of Asian Studies.

Kates, George N. 1976 [1952]. *The Years That Were Fat: The Last of Old China.* Cambridge: MIT Press.

Kelliher, Daniel. 1992. *Peasant Power in China: The Era of Rural Reform.* New Haven, Conn.: Yale University Press.

———. 1994. Chinese Communist Political Theory and the Rediscovery of the Peasantry. *Modern China* 20(4):387–415.

King, Ambrose Yeo-chi. 1991. *Kuan-hsi* and Network Building: A Sociological Interpretation. *Daedalus* 120(2):63–84.

Kipnis, Andrew. 1994. (Re)inventing *Li: Koutou* and Subjectification in Rural Shandong. In *Body, Subject and Power in China,* ed. Tani Barlow and Angela Zito, 201–223. Chicago: University of Chicago Press.

———. 1995a. "Face": An Adaptable Discourse of Social Surfaces. *positions: east asia cultures critique* 3(1):119–148.

———. 1995b. Within and Against Peasantness: Backwardness and Filiality in Rural China. *Comparative Studies in Society and History* 37(1):110–135.

———. 1996. The Language of Gifts: Managing *Guanxi* in a North China Village. *Modern China* 22(3):285–314.

Kleinman, Arthur, and Joan Kleinman. 1991. Suffering and Its Professional Transformation: Toward an Ethnography of Interpersonal Experience. *Culture, Medicine and Psychiatry* 15(3):275–301.

Kondo, Dorinne K. 1990. *Crafting Selves: Power, Gender and Discourses of Identity in a Japanese Workplace.* Chicago: University of Chicago Press.

Kwok, D. W. Y. 1965. *Scientism in Chinese Thought.* New Haven, Conn.: Yale University Press.

Laing, Ellen Johnston. 1989. The Persistence of Propriety in the 1980s. In *Unofficial China: Popular Culture and Thought in the People's Republic,* ed. Perry Link, Richard Madsen, and Paul Pickowicz, 156–171. San Francisco: Westview.

Lee, Leo Ou-fan. 1973. *The Romantic Generation of Modern Chinese Writers.* Cambridge: Harvard University Press.

Lévi-Strauss, Claude. 1969. *The Elementary Structures of Kinship.* Boston: Beacon.

Levinson, Stephen C. 1983. *Pragmatics.* New York: Cambridge University Press.

Lin Yueh Hua. 1947. *The Golden Wing.* New York: Oxford University Press.

Lin Yutang. 1977 [1936]. *My Country and My People.* Hong Kong: Heinemann Educational Books.

Link, Perry. 1992. *Evening Chats in Beijing: Probing China's Predicament.* New York: W. W. Norton.

Liu, Kwang-Ching. 1981. World View and Peasant Rebellion: Reflections on Post-Mao Historiography. *Journal of Asian Studies* 40:295–326.

Liu, Lydia H. 1995. *Translingual Practice: Literature, National Culture, and Translated Modernity—China 1900–1937.* Stanford, Calif.: Stanford University Press.

Lyon, Margot L. 1995. Missing Emotion: The Limitations of Cultural Constructionism in the Study of Emotion. *Cultural Anthropology* 10(2):244–263.

Madsen, Richard. 1984. *Morality and Power in a Chinese Village*. Berkeley: University of California Press.

Mahoney, Maureen A., and Barbara Yngvesson. 1992. The Construction of Subjectivity and the Paradox of Resistance: Reintegrating Feminist Anthropology and Psychology. *Signs* 18(1):44–73.

Mao Zedong. 1967 [1926]. Zhongguo Shehui Gejiejide Fenxi (Analysis of the Classes in Chinese Society). In *Mao Zedong Xuanji* (Selected Works of Mao Zedong), Vol. 1, 3–11. Beijing: People's Press.

———. 1967 [1937]. On Contradiction. In *Selected Works Of Mao Zedong* (English version), Vol. 1, 311–347. Beijing: People's Press.

———. 1967 [1944]. Wenhua Gongzuozhongde Tongyi Zhanxian (The United Front in Cultural Work). In *Mao Zedong Xuanji* (Selected Works of Mao Zedong), Vol. 3, 912–914. Beijing: People's Press.

Martin, Emily. 1988. Gender and Ideological Differences in Representations of Life and Death. In *Death Ritual in Late Imperial and Modern China*, ed. James L. Watson and Evelyn S. Rawski, 164–179. Berkeley: University of California Press.

Mauss, Marcel. 1967. *The Gift*. Trans. Ian Cunnison. New York: Norton.

McCormick, Barrett. 1993. If I Were Real: People's Congresses and the Power of Socialism. Paper presented at the 45th annual meeting of the Association for Asian Studies, Los Angeles.

Meijer, Marinaus J. 1978. Marriage Law and Policy in the People's Republic of China. In *Chinese Family Law and Social Change in Historical and Comparative Perspective*, ed. David C. Buxbaum, 436–483. Seattle: University of Washington Press.

Meisner, Maurice. 1985. Iconoclasm and Cultural Revolution in China and Russia. In *Bolshevik Culture*, ed. A. Gleason, P. Kenez, and R. Stites, 279–294. Bloomington: Indiana University Press.

Miao, Qing, and Lu Weiping. 1987. Nongcun Hunyin Lisude Shehui Wenhua Gongneng Jiqi Shidai Bianqian (The Sociocultural Functions of Peasant Marriage Customs and Their Recent Changes). Monograph. Beijing: Beijing Shehui Kexue Yuan.

Mitchell, Juliet, and Jacqueline Rose, trans. and eds. 1982. *Feminine Sexuality: Jacques Lacan and the école freudienne*. New York: W. W. Norton.

Mueggler, Eric. 1991. Money, the Mountain, and State Power in a Naxi Village. *Modern China* 17:188–226.

Nanjing Daily. 1989. Yindao Nongmin Ba Xiaofeizijin Zhuanwei Shengchanzijin (Entice Peasants to Transform Consumer Spending into Productive Capital). December 20.

Naquin, Susan. 1988. Funerals in North China: Uniformity and Variation. In *Death Ritual in Late Imperial and Modern China*, ed. James L. Watson and Evelyn Rawski, 37–70. Berkeley: University of California Press.

Numazaki, Ichiro. 1991. The Role of Personal Networks in the Making of Taiwan's *Guanxiqiye* (Related Enterprises). In *Business Networks and Eco-*

nomic Development in East Asia, ed. G. Hamilton, 77–93. Hong Kong: University of Hong Kong Centre of Asian Studies.

Odend'hal, Stewart. 1989. Population Changes in a Shandong Village between 1987 and 1988 in Mainland China. *Asian Profile* 17:305–309.

Odgaard, Ole. 1992. Entrepreneurs and Elite Formation in Rural China. *Australian Journal of Chinese Affairs* 28:89–108.

Oksenberg, Michel. 1970. Getting Ahead and Along in Communist China. In *Party Leadership and Revolutionary Power in China,* ed. John Wilson Lewis, 304–347. London: Cambridge University Press.

Oi, Jean. 1989. *State and Peasant in Contemporary China: The Political Economy of Village Government.* Berkeley: University of California Press.

———. 1993. Reform and Urban Bias in China. *Journal of Development Studies* 29(4):129–148.

Ong, Aihwa. 1993. On the Edge of Empires: Flexible Citizenship among Chinese in Diaspora. *positions: east asia cultures critique* 1(3):745–778.

Ortner, Sherry B. 1984. Theory in Anthropology since the Sixties. *Comparative Studies in Society and History* 26:126–166.

Parish, William L., and Martin K. Whyte. 1978. *Village and Family in Contemporary China.* Chicago: University of Chicago Press.

Parry, Jonathan. 1986. The Gift, the Indian Gift, and the "Indian Gift." *Man* (n.s.) 21:453–473.

Pasternak, Burton. 1972. *Kinship and Community in Two Chinese Villages.* Stanford, Calif.: Stanford University Press.

Perry, Elizabeth J. 1976. Worshippers and Warriors: White Lotus Influence on the Nian Rebellion. *Modern China* 2(1):4–22.

———. 1993. *Shanghai on Strike: The Politics of Chinese Labor.* Stanford, Calif.: Stanford University Press.

Polanyi, Karl. 1957. *The Great Transformation: The Political and Economic Origins of Our Time.* 2d ed. Boston: Beacon.

Potter, Sulamith Heins, and Jack Potter. 1990. *China's Peasants: The Anthropology of a Revolution.* New York: Cambridge University Press.

Pye, Lucian. 1981. *The Dynamics of Chinese Politics.* Cambridge, Mass.: Oelgeschlager, Gunn and Hain.

Quinn, Naomi, and Dorothy Holland. 1987. Culture and Cognition. In *Cultural Models in Language and Thought,* ed. Holland and Quinn, 3–40. New York: Cambridge University Press.

Rabinow, Paul. 1984. Introduction. In *The Foucault Reader,* ed. Paul Rabinow, 3–29. New York: Pantheon.

Radcliffe-Brown, A. R. 1952. *Structure and Function in Primitive Society.* New York: Free Press.

Rapp, Rayna. 1978. Family and Class in Contemporary America: Notes towards an Understanding of Ideology. *Science and Society* 42:278–300.

Rawski, Evelyn S. 1988. The Imperial Way of Death: Ming and Ch'ing Emperors and Death Ritual. In *Death Ritual in Late Imperial and Modern China,* ed. James L. Watson and Evelyn Rawski, 228–253. Berkeley: University of California Press.

Redding, S. Gordon. 1990. *The Spirit of Chinese Capitalism.* Berlin: de Grupter.

———. 1991. Weak Organizations and Strong Linkages: Managerial Ideology and Chinese Family Business Networks. In *Business Networks and Economic Development in East Asia,* ed. G. Hamilton, 30–47. Hong Kong: University of Hong Kong Centre of Asian Studies.

Rocca, Jean-Louis. 1992. Corruption and Its Shadow: An Anthropological View of Corruption. *China Quarterly* 130:402–416.

Rosaldo, Michelle Z. 1984. Toward an Anthropology of Self and Feeling. In *Culture Theory: Essays on Mind, Self, and Emotion,* ed. Richard A. Shweder and Robert A. Levine, 137–157. New York: Cambridge University Press.

Ruan Danching. 1993. Interpersonal Networks and Workplace Controls in Urban China. *Australian Journal of Chinese Affairs* 29:89–105.

Rubin, Gayle. 1975. The Traffic in Women: Notes on the "Political Economy" of Sex. In *Toward an Anthropology of Women,* ed. Rayna Reiter, 157–210. New York: Monthly Review Press.

Russell, James A., and Michelle S. M. Yik. 1996. Emotion Among the Chinese. In *The Handbook of Chinese Psychology,* ed. Michael Bond, 166–188. Hong Kong: Oxford University Press.

Sangren, Steven P. 1984. Traditional Chinese Corporations: Beyond Kinship. *Journal of Asian Studies* 43:391–416.

Schoenhals, Michael. 1992. *Doing Things with Words in Chinese Politics: Five Studies.* Berkeley, Calif.: Institute of East Asian Studies.

Schwarcz, Vera. 1991. No Solace from Lethe: History, Memory and Cultural Identity in Twentieth-Century China. *Daedalus* 120(2):85–111.

Selden, Mark. 1971. *The Yenan Way in Revolutionary China.* Cambridge: Harvard University Press.

———. 1993. Family Strategies and Structures in Rural North China. In Davis and Harrell, 139–164.

Shapiro, Sidney. 1986. Preface. In *Outlaws of the Marsh,* by Naian Shi and Luo Guanzhong, i–iii. Hong Kong: Commercial Press.

Shen Rong. 1987. *At Middle Age.* Beijing: Panda Books.

Shi Naian, and Luo Guanzhong. 1986. *Outlaws of the Marsh.* Trans. Sidney Shapiro. Hong Kong: Commercial Press.

Silverstein, Michael. 1979. Language Structure and Linguistic Ideology. In *The Elements: A Parasession on Linguistic Units and Levels,* ed. P. Clyne, W. Hanks, and C. Hofbauer, 193–247. Chicago: Chicago Linguistic Society.

Siu, Helen F. 1989a. *Agents and Victims in South China: Accomplices in Rural Revolution.* New Haven, Conn.: Yale University Press.

———. 1989b. Recycling Rituals: Politics and Popular Culture in Contemporary Rural China. In *Unofficial China: Essays in Popular Culture and Thought,* ed. Perry Link, Richard Madsen, and Paul Pickowicz. Boulder, Colo.: Westview.

———. 1993. Reconstituting Dowry and Brideprice in South China. In Davis and Harrell, 165–188.

Siu, Helen F., and Zelda Stern. 1983. Introduction. In *Mao's Harvest: Voices from China's New Generation,* ed. Siu and Stern, xiii–lii. New York: Oxford University Press.

Skinner, G. William. 1964–65. Marketing and Social Structure in Rural China. *Journal of Asian Studies* 24:3–44, 195–228, 363–399.

———. 1977. *The City in Late Imperial China.* Stanford, Calif.: Stanford University Press.

Smart, Alan. 1993. Gifts, Bribes and *Guanxi:* A Reconsideration of Bourdieu's Social Capital. *Cultural Anthropology* 8(3):388–408.

Smith, Arthur H. 1894. *Chinese Characteristics.* New York: Fleming H. Revell.

———. 1899. *Village Life in China.* New York: Greenwood.

Smith, Paul. 1988. *Discerning the Subject.* Minneapolis: University of Minnesota Press.

Spock, Benjamin, and Michael B. Rothenberg. 1992. *Dr. Spock's Baby and Child Care.* 6th ed. New York: Pocket Books.

Stack, Carol B. 1974. *All Our Kin: Strategies for Survival in a Black Community.* New York: Harper and Row.

State Statistical Bureau (Guojia Tongji Ju). 1990. *Statistical Yearbook of Shandong 1990.* Beijing: China Statistical Press.

———. 1991. *10% Sampling Tabulation on the 1990 Population Census of the People's Republic of China.* Beijing: China Statistical Press.

Stockard, Janice E. 1989. *Daughters of the Canton Delta.* Stanford, Calif.: Stanford University Press.

Sullivan, Lawrence. 1976. "Cultural Revolution" and the Quest for a New Leadership Style in the Chinese Communist Party, 1921–34. Paper presented to Columbia University Modern China Seminar, April 8.

Sun, Lung-kee. 1987. *Zhongguo Wenhuade Shenceng Jiegou* (The Deep Structure of Chinese Culture). 2d ed. Hong Kong: Ji Xian She.

———. 1991. Contemporary Chinese Culture: Structure and Emotionality. *Australian Journal of Chinese Affairs* 26:1–41.

Sweetser, Eve E. 1987. The Definition of Lie: An Examination of the Folk Models Underlying a Semantic Prototype. In *Cultural Models in Thought and Language,* ed. Dorothy Holland and Naomi Quinn, 43–66. New York: Cambridge University Press.

Tanner, Murray Scot, with Michael J. Feder. 1993. Family Politics, Elite Recruitment, and Succession in Post-Mao China. *Australian Journal of Chinese Affairs* 30:89–119.

Thireau, Isabelle. 1988. Recent Changes in a Guangdong Village. *Australian Journal of Chinese Affairs* 19/20:289–311.

Thompson, Roger R., trans. 1990. *Mao Zedong's Report from Xunwu.* Stanford, Calif.: Stanford University Press.

Thornton, Robert J. 1992. The Rhetoric of Ethnographic Holism. In *ReRead-*

ing Cultural Anthropology, ed. George Marcus, 15–33. Durham, N.C.: Duke University Press.

Todorov, Tzvetan. 1984. *Mikhail Bakhtin: The Dialogic Principle.* Trans. Wlad Godzich. Minneapolis: University of Minnesota Press.

Tu Wei-ming. 1991. Cultural China: The Periphery as the Center. *Daedalus* 120(2):1–32.

Tu Wei-ming, Milan Hejtmanek, and Alan Wachman, eds. 1992. *The Confucian World Observed: A Contemporary Discussion of Confucian Humanism in East Asia.* Honolulu: East-West Center.

Unger, Jonathon. 1984. The Class System in Rural China: A Case Study. In *Class and Social Stratification in Post-Revolutionary China,* ed. James L. Watson, 121–141. New York: Cambridge University Press.

van de Ven, Hans J. 1991. *From Friend to Comrade: The Founding of the Chinese Communist Party, 1920–1927.* Berkeley: University of California Press.

Verdery, Katherine. 1991. Theorizing Socialism: A Prologue to the Transition. *American Ethnologist* 18(3):419–439.

Village Masses (Nongcun Dazhong). 1988. Liwuqiao Bukai Nonghangde Men (The Knock of Gifts Doesn't Open the Door to the Agricultural Bank). December 10.

———. 1989a. Jiuliang, Danliang, Gongzuoliang (Drinking Capacity, Courage, Work Capacity). April 18.

———. 1989b. Suan Xizhang Shazhu Gongkuan Chihefeng (Calculating the Bill for and Stopping Drinking and Eating on the Public Account). April 22.

———. 1989c. Yiju Xiehouyude Laili (The Origin of a Riddle). April 22.

———. 1989d. Lipin Biancheng Renshenbaoxianjin (Gifts Become Life Insurance Fee). April 22.

Vogel, Ezra F. 1965. From Friendship to Comradeship: The Change in Personal Relations in Communist China. *China Quarterly* 21:46–60.

Wakeman, Frederic. 1988. Mao's Remains. In *Death Ritual in Late Imperial and Modern China,* ed. James L. Watson and Evelyn Rawski, 254–288. Berkeley: University of California Press.

Walder, Andrew G. 1986. *Communist Neo-Traditionalism: Work and Authority in Chinese Industry.* Berkeley: University of California Press.

Wang, Fuchu, ed. 1985. *Jiating Yingyong Falu Zixun* (Family Legal Advisor). Shanghai: Shanghai Wenhua Chuban She.

Wang Fusan, Yang Xia, and Li Hengju. 1990. *Zhongguo Nongcun Shengchan Shehuihua Qushi* (Trends in China's Rural Villages' Societization of Production). Jinan, PRC: Shandong Daxue Chuban She.

Wang, Xiaoqiang, and Bai Nanfeng. 1986. *Furao de Pinkun: Zhongguo Luohou Diqu de Jingji Kaocha* (Poverty within Wealth: An Economic Investigation of China's Backward Areas). Chengdu, PRC: Sichuan Renmin Chuban She.

Wang Zhigang, and Michael Micklin. 1996. The Transformation of Naming Practices in Chinese Families: Some Linguistic Clues to Social Change. *International Sociology* 11(2):187–212.

Wank, David L. 1994. The Institutional Culture of Capitalism: Particularistic Relations and Private Enterprise in a Chinese City. Paper presented at the 46th annual meeting of the Association for Asian Studies, Boston.

———. 1995. Bureaucratic Patronage and Private Business: Changing Networks of Power in Urban China. In *The Waning of the Communist State: Economic Origins of Political Decline in China and Hungary*, ed. Andrew G. Walder, 153–183. Berkeley: University of California Press.

Watson, James L. 1988. The Structure of Chinese Funerary Rites: Elementary Forms, Ritual Sequence, and the Primacy of Performance. In *Death Ritual in Late Imperial and Modern China*, ed. James L. Watson and Evelyn Rawski, 3–19. Berkeley: University of California Press.

Watson, Rubie S. 1981. Class Difference and Affinal Relations in South China. *Man* (n.s.) 16(4):593–615.

———. 1985. *Inequality among Brothers: Class and Kinship in South China*. New York: Cambridge University Press.

———. 1986. The Named and the Nameless: Gender and Person in Chinese Society. *American Ethnologist* 13(4):619–631.

Weeden, Chris, Andrew Tolson, and Frank Mort. 1980. Theories of Language and Subjectivity. In *Culture, Media, Language: Working Papers in Cultural Studies 1972–9*, ed. Stuart Hall et al. 195–216. London: Hutchinson.

Weiner, Annette B. 1976. *Women of Value, Men of Renown*. Austin: University of Texas Press.

———. 1994. Cultural Difference and the Density of Objects. *American Ethnologist* 21(1):391–403.

Weiner, Annette B., and Jane Schneider. 1989. *Cloth and Human Experience*. Washington, D.C.: Smithsonian Institute Press.

Weller, Robert P. 1984. Social Contradiction and Symbolic Resolution: Practical and Idealized Affines in Taiwan. *Ethnology* 23:249–260.

Whitson, William W., with Chen-hsia Huang. 1973. *The Chinese High Command: A History of Communist Military Politics, 1927–1971*. New York: Praeger.

Whyte, Martin K. 1974. *Small Groups and Political Rituals in China*. Berkeley: University of California Press.

Whyte, Martin K., and William L. Parish. 1984. *Urban Life in Contemporary China*. Chicago: University of Chicago Press.

Wilson, Scott. 1994. About Face: Social Networks and Prestige Politics in Contemporary Shanghai Villages. Ph.D. dissertation, Department of Government, Cornell University.

Wolf, Arthur. 1970. Chinese Kinship and Mourning Dress. In *Family and Kinship in Chinese Society*, ed. Maurice Freedman, 189–208. Stanford, Calif.: Stanford University Press.

———. 1985. Introduction: The Study of Chinese Society on Taiwan. In *The Chinese Family and Its Ritual Behavior*, Monograph Series B, No. 15, ed. Hsieh Jin-Chang and Chang Ying-chang, 2–25. Taibei, Taiwan: Institute of Ethnology Academia Sinica.

Wolf, Arthur, and Chieh-Shan Huang. 1980. *Marriage and Adoption in China 1845-1945.* Stanford, Calif.: Stanford University Press.

Wolf, Margery. 1968. *The House of Lim: A Study of a Chinese Farm Family.* Englewood Cliffs, N.J.: Prentice-Hall.

———. 1970. Child Training and the Chinese Family. In *Family and Kinship in Chinese Society,* ed. Maurice Freedman, 37-62. Stanford, Calif.: Stanford University Press.

———. 1972. *Women and the Family in Rural Taiwan.* Stanford, Calif.: Stanford University Press.

———. 1985. *Revolution Postponed.* Stanford, Calif.: Stanford University Press.

World Journal (Shijie Ribao). 1994a. Urban and Rural Youth's Marriage Expenses Leap Ahead. January 19, A-11.

———. 1994b. The Trend towards Social Climbing Evident in Funeral and Marriage Expenses. February 16, A-11.

———. 1995. Officials' Meaningless Banquets Waste ¥100 Billion a Year. March 11, A-11.

Xinnong Lejia Baike (New Peasant Encyclopedia of Family Happiness). 1985. 3d ed. Tianjin, PRC: Tianjin Chuban She.

Xu Jiangmin. 1992. Lun Chi He Zai Xiangzhen Qiye Fazhanzhong De Zuoyong (On the Uses of Eating and Drinking in the Development of Rural Enterprises). *SheHui* 7:23-25.

Yan, Yun-xiang. 1992. The Impact of Rural Reforms on Economic and Social Stratification in a Chinese Village. *Australian Journal of Chinese Affairs* 27:1-23.

———. 1993. The Flow of Gifts: Reciprocity and Social Networks in a Chinese Village. Ph.D. dissertation, Department of Anthropology, Harvard University.

Yanagisako, Sylvia Junko. 1977. Women-centered Kin Networks in Urban Bilateral Kinship. *American Ethnologist* 4:207-226.

Yang, C. K. 1959. *Chinese Communist Society: The Family and the Village.* Cambridge: MIT Press.

Yang, Martin. 1945. *A Chinese Village: Taitou, Shantung Province.* New York: Columbia University Press.

Yang, Mayfair Mei-hui. 1988. The Modernity of Power in the Chinese Socialist Order. *Cultural Anthropology* 3:408-427.

———. 1989a. The Gift Economy and State Power in China. *Comparative Studies in Society and History* 31:25-54.

———. 1989b. Between State and Society: The Construction of Corporateness in a Chinese Socialist Factory. *Australian Journal of Chinese Affairs* 22:31-62.

———. 1994. *Gifts, Banquets and the Art of Social Relationships in China.* Ithaca, N.Y.: Cornell University Press.

Yang, Minchuan. 1994. Reshaping Peasant Culture and Community: Rural Industrialization in a Chinese Village. *Modern China* 20(2):157-179.

Zhao Ziyang. 1987. *Zhongguo Gongchandang Dishisanci Quanguo Daibiaodahui*

Wenjian Huibian (Edited Documents from the Thirteenth Party Congress of the Chinese Communist Party). Beijing: Renmin Chuban She.

Zhu Xiaoping. 1992. *Shi Nu: Zhu Xiaoping Xiaoshuoji* (Stone Women: A Zhu Xiaoping Anthology). Haima Wenxue Congshu (Seahorse Literature Series). Beijing: Zhongguo Shehui Kexue Chuban She.

Zito, Angela. 1987. City Gods, Filiality and Hegemony in Late Imperial China. *Modern China* 13(3):333–371.

———. 1994. Silk and Skin: Significant Boundaries. In *Body, Subject and Power in China*, ed. Tani Barlow and Angela Zito, 103–130. Chicago: University of Chicago Press.

Zweig, David. 1989. *Agrarian Radicalism in China 1968–1981*. Cambridge: Harvard University Press.

Index

Andrew Kipnis is Assistant Professor of Anthropology
at Northern Kentucky University.

Library of Congress Cataloging-in-Publication Data

Kipnis, Andrew B.
Producing Guanxi : sentiment, self, and subculture in a North China village /
Andrew B. Kipnis.
p. cm.
Includes bibliographical reference and index.
ISBN 0-8223-1883-0 (alk. paper). — ISBN 0-8223-1873-3 (pbk. : alk. paper)
1. Ethnology—China—Fengjia.
2. Fengjia (China)—Social life and customs.   I. Title.
GN635.C5K565   1997
306'.0951'14—dc21   96-36851
                                                                        CIP